The Making of History

The Making of History

A STUDY OF THE LITERARY FORGERIES
OF JAMES MACPHERSON
AND THOMAS CHATTERTON
IN RELATION TO EIGHTEENTH-CENTURY
IDEAS OF HISTORY AND FICTION

Ian Haywood

RUTHERFORD • MADISON • TEANECK
FAIRLEIGH DICKINSON UNIVERSITY PRESS
LONDON AND TORONTO: ASSOCIATED UNIVERSITY PRESSES

Associated University Presses
440 Forsgate Drive
Cranbury, NJ 08512

Associated University Presses
25 Sicilian Avenue
London WC1A 2QH, England

Associated University Presses
2133 Royal Windsor Drive
Unit 1
Mississauga, Ontario
Canada L5J 1K5

The paper used in this publication meets the
requirements of the American National Standard for
Permanence of Paper for Printed Library Materials Z39.48-1984.

Library of Congress Cataloging-in-Publication Data

Haywood, Ian.
  The making of history.

  Bibliography: p.
  Includes index.
  1. English poetry—18th century—History and
criticism.   2. Historical poetry, English.
3. Macpherson, James, 1736–1796—Criticism and interpretation.   4. Chatterton, Thomas, 1752–1770—Criticism
and interpretation.   5. Literature and history.
6. Great Britain in literature.   7. Literary forgeries
and mystifications.   8. Great Britain—Historiography.
I. Title.
PR575.H5H39   1986   821'.6'09   85-45753
ISBN 0-8386-3261-0 (alk. paper)

To my parents

Contents

Acknowledgments

All quotations from Donald S. Taylor, *The Complete Works of Thomas Chatterton*, © Oxford University Press, 1971, appear by permission of Oxford University Press. I am grateful for Oxford University Press's permission to reprint my article "Chatterton's Plans for the Publication of the Forgery," which first appeared in *Review of English Studies* 141 (1985), 58–68.

Introduction

The forgeries of James Macpherson and Thomas Chatterton have re-mained for many years almost wholly neglected by literary critics and cultural historians. With the exception of Donald Taylor's *Thomas Chatter-ton's Art* (1978), critical writing on the forgeries has been restricted to a trickle of articles appearing each year, most of them in foreign lan-guages. Of the ones in English, hardly any attempt a serious reappraisal of either Macpherson or Chatterton, and even fewer attempt to relate the forgeries to each other. Literary fashions change, of course, and once sensational works fall out of favor. The days are long since gone when Ossian[1] accompanied Napoleon on military expeditions, and Words-worth sang of the "marvellous boy." Indeed, the aim of this book is not to restore Macpherson and Chatterton to a central position in literary history. The aim is rather to give the forgeries a higher profile by placing them in what I believe to be the most relevant intellectual context: the eighteenth-century debate about the relationship between history and fiction. The forgeries are complex and unique forms of historical fiction. Their appearance as ancient literature cannot be dismissed as mere Gothic tomfoolery. I intend to show that the methods and techniques employed by Macpherson and Chatterton have a secure basis in legiti-mate historiographical theory of the time. Ancient literature was af-forded a greater historical value than were modern reconstructions of the past. The whole concept of historical fiction was in its infancy. Hence Macpherson and Chatterton transplanted their visions of the past into the past and made history from the inside. In doing so, they gave a boost to the very genre they were disguising. In exploring contemporary ideas about history and fiction and the authenticity of historical records, it will be seen how thin a line separates the forgers from literary practi-tioners who were regarded as acceptable and legitimate. Ultimately, we can conclude that the forgers participated in the intellectual debate by

11

offering bold imaginative solutions to many of the problems. The forgeries look toward Walter Scott and the historical novel.

Eric Rothstein's recent evaluation of Chatterton is indicative of the
lapsed state of the forgeries:

> Using a collection of old words chosen from glossaries and diction-
> aries, a few medieval customs, and a great many antique and pseudo-
> antique spellings, Chatterton simply made up "old" poems which he
> assigned to fictitious medieval authors. . . . though Chatterton may
> well have been a "marvellous boy," in Coleridge's phrase, he was no
> marvel as a forger. The crust of age he glued to his poems made some
> silliness and banality less visible, and allowed some very nice effects
> in sound and metre.[2]

The misattribution of the most famous phrase about Chatterton shows
up the superficiality of this reading of the forgery. I want to reverse the
idea that the forgeries were "simply made up." Donald Taylor has begun
this rectification in *Thomas Chatterton's Art*. The book is particularly
valuable for meticulously tracking down Chatterton's sources, especially
earlier historians such as Camden. However, Taylor's neglect of Ossian
and contemporary historiography make his book of only marginal use. I
do not want to refute Chatterton's greatest modern ally, but rather to
offer a different perspective.

Dr. Johnson defined forgery as both a falsification and an act of
making. This book will have succeeded if it shows Macpherson and
Chatterton as makers, not falsifiers.

The
Making
of History

1

The Influence of Historiography

The forgeries of Macpherson and Chatterton were intimately related to eighteenth-century British historiography. That term refers to both the practice and theory of history writing, which proliferated in an unprecedented manner in that century. The precise way in which the forgeries evolved from this climate can only be fully appreciated in later chapters. In this chapter, I wish to chart the relevant historiographical territory. In order to give a comprehensive survey, I cite some works and statements that appeared after the forgeries were written. In the main, however, I restrict myself to material written prior to and including the 1760s.

It is worth pointing out at the outset how popular historiography became in the eighteenth century. Hume asserted "I believe this to be the historical age and this the historical nation,"[1] echoed by Gibbon's "History is the most popular species of writing."[2] The success of Gibbon's *Decline and Fall of the Roman Empire* was summed up by himself: "My book was on every table, and almost on every toilette."[3] As early as 1694, we find Edmund Gibson writing to a friend "There's hardly a bookseller in London that is not trumping up a new history of England."[4] Though the Society of Antiquaries was founded in 1718, no professional historians existed as such, and it is notable how many writers now famous in other branches of literature turned their hand to history writing: Swift, Hume, Goldsmith, Smollett. Swift wished to be Historiographer Royal (as Dryden had been), and in 1768 Thomas Gray became Regius Professor of Modern History at Cambridge. New attention was given to historical theory. Herbert Weisinger is broadly correct when he notes that in the eighteenth century there emerged

a more sound scholarship in history and more sophisticated methodologies than had been available to historians up to this time. Actually, the process was an interdependent one: as more facts were uncovered, better methods were developed, more facts could and were established. Most important, however, was the increased awareness of the importance of theory in understanding an accumulation of facts.[5]

Affairs did not run quite so smoothly. As Weisinger notes, much of the new theory was designed to test facts, that is, to establish their factuality. But the hold on what constituted a fact or a historical truth became very tenuous indeed. It was literature, and particularly poetry, that consistently frustrated the efforts of theorists and practitioners of history writing to uncover history's bedrock of irrefutable fact.

The seventeenth-century confidence in humanist principles of history writing—the belief that renowned history books of the past were all that were needed as sources—is perhaps one reason why few speculative treatises on historiography appeared in that century. In the next century, however, a proliferation occurred. I have made use of almost twenty such works. This abundance is evidence of a major revaluation of history. Three aspects of this revaluation are relevant: the attempt to make history writing truly authentic or accountable; the need to define the historical shape of national societies and in particular to describe their origins; the establishment of a new field of historiography which we now term social and cultural history. These areas of inquiry bore directly on the forgeries. Before moving on to them, however, I want to sketch the broader network of interactions between historiography and literature, which the rest of the chapter will pare down into a workable shape.

Relevant statements by modern critics are desultory and unsubstantiated. Lawrence Lipking in *The Ordering of the Arts in Eighteenth Century England* (1970) states that

> much of the poetry of the 1750's and 1760's is interesting primarily for its attempt to salvage remnants of the past. It would not be inaccurate to say that the antiquarianism of Walpole's time survives as a subdivision or dependency of poetry; a less sympathetic reader might maintain that poetry of the mid century is a footnote to antiquarianism.[6]

No authors are mentioned. It is a mistake, I believe, to try to subordinate either antiquarianism or poetry to the other. There is also an unintentional irony in Lipking's metaphor. The footnote was a major tool of authentication in historiography and historical poetry and fiction, achieving an apotheosis in the forgeries and later in Scott's novels. John Butt's views, in the *Mid Eighteenth Century* volume of the Oxford History of English Literature, are also superficial:

no student of eighteenth-century literature should fail to observe the peculiar character of the 1760's. Though the decade is notable for the revival of satire in Churchill's meteorically bright and short career, it is more particularly marked by the unusual range of scholarly study of earlier literature, and the reflection of this in the imaginative literature of the day.[7]

The relation between the forgeries and contemporary ideas of literary history was important. Once again, however, it is a mistake to see the imaginative literature of the 1760s as only a "reflection" of the intellectual climate. The relationship was much more intimate.

There were many obvious fusions of literature and historiography. The writing of history was regarded as an art. Johnson's *Dictionary* defined history as "A narration of facts and events delivered *with dignity*" (my italics). Gibbon's *Memoirs* record his painstaking labors to form his famous style—as he termed it: "the middle tone between the dull chronicle and a rhetorical declamation."[8] The label "history as literature" could be applied here. In *Spectator* 420, Addison enthused:

> It is the most agreeable Talent of an Historian, to be able to draw up his Armies and fight his Battels in proper Expressions, to set before our Eyes the Divisions, Cabals, and Jealousies of Great Men, and to lead us Step by Step into the several Actions and Events of his History.[9]

So history told an exciting story. But Addison added an immediate disclaimer: "I confess this shews more the Art than the Veracity of the Historian, but I am only to speak of him as he is qualified to please the Imagination." So "Art" was now opposed to "Veracity." Steele put the point rather more strongly in *Spectator* 136: "Dear Sir, why should this be lying?"[10] Any identification of historiography with literature had to confront this objection: that it was fiction. The various forms in which the objection appeared, and the terminology used to make it, are very revealing. The "dignity" that literary qualities could lend to history writing were precarious when scrutinized. James Moor's *An Essay on Historical Composition* (1759) sought to prove that history writing could follow the rules of the epic. But Moor was forced to add the Aristotelian dictum that the poet should only describe what might happen, the historian what did happen.[11] Samuel Johnson did not see the historian William Robertson's powers of period "painting" as an asset:

> You must consider how that penetration and that painting are employed. It is not history, it is imagination. . . . You must look upon Robertson's work as romance, and try it by that standard. History it is not.[12]

The terms of Gilbert Stuart's comments on Robertson made an illuminating contrast to Johnson's remarks. In *Critical Observations concerning the Scottish Historians Hume, Stuart, and Robertson* (1782) he praised Robertson's account of Mary Queen of Scots:

> The various fortunes of this illustrious princess, the ever-changing scene of her life, and the tragical catastrophe which put a period to her woes, soften the detail of public affairs with the feelings of private life, and add to History all the charms and interest of Romance.[13]

But, later in the essay, Stuart made clear that this patriotic episode was an exception to the rule. Robertson's "painting" was normally defective:

> He selects those portions of the Scottish History which he can adorn, but does not place the whole before the eye. He hastens over every part of his subject, except where Mary is concerned, and by this means gives his work the appearance of a historical novel.[14]

So "romance" was applied by Stuart as a compliment, but "historical novel" as an insult. Confusion and inconsistency were apparent.[15] Stuart's words prompt us to consider the eighteenth-century novel. The label "literature as history" could be applied. Most major novels of the time posed as "History," meaning a "Life" (that is, biography or autobiography). Hugh Blair in the 1760s termed novels "Fictitious Histories."[16] Defoe in particular was concerned with historiography, and *Journal of the Plague Year*, as shall be seen in the next chapter, had many features shared by the forgeries. The connections that existed between history and literature multiply when we consider the novel as social history. Compare Clara Reeve's definition of the novel (1785) as "a picture of real life and manners, and of the times in which it is written" with the historian Gilbert Stuart's maxim (1778) that "it is in the records of history, in the scene of real life, not in the conceits and abstractions of fancy and philosophy, that human nature is to be studied."[17] Compare also Johnson's rules for genuine, not fictitious, biography writing:

> The business of the biographer is often to pass slightly over those performances and incidents which produce vulgar greatness, to lead the thoughts into domestic privacies, and display the minute details of daily life.[18]

I turn now to those aspects of contemporary historiography that were most relevant to understanding the forgeries.

The Drive for Authentication

The writers of the History of Ireland . . . have obtruded on the world a multitude of uncouth, incoherent and ridiculous Fables and Legends instead of Authentic Relations of Matters of Fact. . . .
Sir James Ware, *The Antiquities and History of Ireland* (1705)

the author of this history hath been under [a necessity] of examining every material fact in antiquity, with all the circumstances attending it, in more ways than it is easy to conceive, and with an assiduity, which nothing but the purest love of truth could inspire. . . .
Thomas Carte, *A General History of England* (1750)

The eighteenth century sought to make history writing pure, to free it from the corrupt practices so prevalent in earlier times and make it truly authentic and accountable. The methods that were devised to achieve this authentication fed into the creations of Macpherson and Chatterton. One striking feature of the following data is the recurrence of terms such as "forgery" and "imposture." A readily available means of enforcing the authenticity of your own product, of course, was to accuse your rivals of falsehood, or to stress the impurities you have avoided. But forgery was more than a rhetorical issue, as we shall see.

The MS

that universal contempt, which the world . . . has cast on all historical writers, who do not draw their materials from records. . . .
Henry Fielding, *Tom Jones* (1749)

One of the great achievements of seventeenth-century antiquarianism was the founding of great libraries and collections of MSS. Harley, Cotton, Pepys, and others provided vast repositories of MSS whose value it was the job of the eighteenth century to assess. Historical thinkers reacted promptly and positively. The MS was made the empirical unit of historical knowledge. The humanists' hallowed secondary texts of the past, though still revered, were superseded by primary sources—meaning, in an age still basically pre-archaeological, the use of extant documents. The seventeenth century had provided an abundance of these (see for example Wanley's catalogue of MSS at the end of Hickes' *Thesaurus* (1705)). The new appetite was correspondingly voracious. John Locke's plea in the *Essay Concerning Human Understanding* (1690) acted as a fanfare for the new spirit: "I think nothing more valuable than the records of antiquity; I wish we had more of them, and more uncorrupted."[19] That final addendum was important. Locke refused to see a MS *per se* as inviolable; that is, as a pure fact. He drew attention to what the MS records. The authority of that was contestable. Not all theorists were so rigorous, and Locke, as I will show later, still believed the MS to be the most elementary historical source. So it was possible for Macpherson and Chatterton in the 1760s to borrow the authority of the MS almost independently of the subject matter supposedly recorded. (The novel also exploited the authority of documentation, but in a more conventionalized way, as I will show in chapter 2.) The MS became the touchstone of truth about the past. Locke's plea for more ancient MSS found an answer in the forgeries. Bolingbroke also expressed this new empiricism. In his *Letters on the Study and Use of History,* published in 1752 but written in 1735, he complained that Herodotus "had neither original records, nor any authentic memorials to guide him, and yet these are the sole foundations of true history."[20] A symptomatic title of a history book was John Owen's *A Compleat and Impartial History of the Ancient Britons* (1743), which had the subtitle, carefully sequenced: "Faithfully Collected and Compiled from ancient Manuscripts, the best Historians and Antiquaries." William Warburton, however, was appalled by the shape affairs were taking. Though not objecting to the basic premise, he did not believe all MSS were of equal value, and saw discretion being swamped. In *A Critical and Philosophical Enquiry into the Causes of Prodigies and Miracles as related by Historians* (1727) he railed against

> an unnatural Fondness for any abortive Manuscript, that pretends but to relate to *English* Affairs. . . . Any uninformed senseless Heap of Rubbish, under the Name of a History of a Town, Society, College or Province, have long since taken from us the very Idea of a genuine Composition.[21]

Note the accusation of falsehood was here leveled at the MSS themselves. As the power of the MS was acknowledged, its authenticity became a proportionally urgent concern. Warburton took a Canute-like stance against movements he could not halt: nationalist, provincial, and local historiography, all of which bore directly on the forgeries. Warburton's next tirade introduced a new element: literature. He saw it as absurd that

> every Monkish Tale, and Lye, and Miracle, and Ballad, are rescued from their Dust and Worms, to proclaim the Poverty of our Forefathers; whose Nakedness, it seems, their pious Posterity take great Pleasure to pry into.[22]

The inclusion in this list of "ballad" alongside "monkish tale" was important. The implication was that ballads *were* being valued by historians. One of the most abundant kinds of extant MSS, particularly the farther back in time one went, was the literary MS—meaning, usually, the old poem.[23] Pepys had amassed a huge collection of ballads. The ways in which the ancient poem was valued as history will be dealt with shortly. Warburton's words could also have applied to literary editing. Anthologists gathered poems for their historical value. Only a few years before the publication of Warburton's *Enquiry* appeared the anthology *Old Ballads* (1723–25). Its editor stressed above all the historical value of the poems.

So the more revered the MS, the more the right of literature to be regarded as a potential source for historians. But such an inclusion brought problems. Literature, particularly poetry, could not shed its involvement with invention, with fiction, with lying. Historiography, by its very nature, could not openly endorse fiction. Confusion, speculation, and refutation were rife among theorists. Their guard was up. One year after Warburton's pamphlet, there appeared a translation by Richard Rawlinson of Lenglet Du Fresnoy's *A New Method of Studying History* (1728). The subtitle was revealing. Du Fresnoy offered a do-it-yourself historian's kit: "Recommending more easy and complete Instructions for Improvements in that Science than any hitherto extant: with the whole apparatus necessary to form a perfect Historian." It is precisely the construction of an "apparatus" of authentication that I am concerned with. Du Fresnoy believed most documents to be of value, though not of equal value. He graded in order of importance letters, memoirs, negotiations, panegyrics, secret histories, satires, and burlesques—what could be termed "genres" of history writing, categories particularly important with regard to Chatterton. In letters, said Du Fresnoy, we find "history in its purity."[24] But "purity" was difficult to keep a hold on. Du Fresnoy admitted that, in certain cases, what constituted a true fact could not be satisfactorily established. For instance

> a fact with all its circumstances well put together, related by judicious authors, although there may be in it something beyond probability, yet ought it rather to be believed than rejected.[25]

Clearly, a license was being given here for admitting fiction into history. Du Fresnoy seemed to have been aware of what he had sanctioned, for a flurry of chapters appeared on methods of detecting corruptions and hoaxes. There are titles such as "Judging of Historical Facts" and "Rules for the Discovery of Spurious Works." Du Fresnoy avoided mentioning literature directly. He had in mind political forgeries, such as fake char-

ters and bulls. Yet the tools of detection Du Fresnoy provided—the
weighing of internal and external evidence, eliciting of anachronisms,
analysis of style and orthography—would all be wielded with vehe-
mence in the controversies over the forgeries in the 1760s, 1770s and
1780s.

A pattern had emerged. A positive assertion of what went to make
historiographical validity or authority involved an immediate pit-stop to
examine inherent flaws or dangers in the system. Both movements were
conducive to the genesis of the forgeries. Thomas Innes, in the preface to
*A Critical Essay on the Ancient Inhabitants of the Northern Parts of Britain, or
Scotland* (1729), summed up the new spirit of authentication thus: "We
live in an age in which all ancient accounts of history, however con-
fidently delivered in the finest dress by modern writers, are brought
back to tryal."[26] But when Innes went on to give a more pragmatic
account of the new values, an invitation to literary forgery can be seen to
have appeared:

> In the course of ages, in proportion as the world came to be polished
> with letters, arts and sciences, and with the knowledge of the rules of
> chronology, all those high fabrics of antiquity, which the vanity or
> ignorance of former times had reared up, were the more easily over-
> turned, that they had no solid foundation nor support; particularly
> within these last two ages, when, by the discovery of so many monu-
> ments of antiquity, which in former ages had lain forgotten, and as it
> were, buried in the corners of old libraries, the true taste of solid
> antiquity hath been revived.[27]

Macpherson and Chatterton both acted as discoverers of "buried" MSS,
of literary "monuments," though more picturesque locations for the
discoveries were cited than "old libraries": the Highlands of Scotland,
and a chest in an attic room of a Bristol church.

Revaluation, revelation. Innes used the image of solidity where there
had been fragility. The MS, if correctly used, could produce scientifically
based data. Innes again:

> Men have begun, long since, to measure their belief of remote antiq-
> uities by the credit that the vouchers, on which they are grounded,
> have obtained, when, after being made public, they have passed the
> examination of the learned.[28]

True accountability. But also, if read so, a challenge to a forger: not only
to devise his "voucher," to create his version of the genuine article, but to
have it publicly scrutinized. Macpherson, Chatterton, and W. H. Ireland
all tried in their own ways to do this. It is worth bringing in Macpherson,

the "legitimate" historian, here. In the preface to *Original Papers* (1775), he detailed the path of his MS sources from discovery to publication. He presented the historian as a skilled discoverer and editor of his sources: the exact equivalent of the literary stance Macpherson took publicly to Ossian:

> It is needless to explain minutely, why papers of such value lay so long neglected and almost unknown. They are jumbled together in such a mass of confusion, that a great deal of time and industry, and, it may be said, a very considerable knowledge of the period to which they relate, were absolutely necessary, to give them the importance they deserve. They were placed in the Editor's hands, as materials for a history of this country, from the Revolution till the complete settlement of the family of Hanover on the throne. But when he examined them with precision, he found that the Life of James the Second threw a new and striking light, on almost all the transactions of his brother's reign. . . . to satisfy himself, as well as to authenticate his material to the public, he went to Paris to make still further discoveries.[29]

It is significant that Macpherson was one of few eighteenth-century authors to use the verb "authenticate." Note the image "new and striking light." The forgeries were born out of a spirit of controversy. Macpherson and Chatterton's imaginative visions presented radical views of the past. They were indeed "new and striking."

We can sum up by looking at the historians Toland and Carte. The second volume of Thomas Carte's *A General History of England* (1747–55) appeared in 1750. In the preface, Carte stressed his judicious, editorial use of contemporary documents to establish "the truth of facts":

> the accounts of transactions in ancient chronicles, have been examined in every circumstance, and compared with the rolls of parliament, and other records in different offices.[30]

But Carte pointed out immediately that MSS must not be blindly trusted. Literary sources were particularly suspect. In the preface to the first volume (1747), Carte claimed he had used for illustration "a multitude of passages in the works of the most ancient British poets."[31] I have not been able to locate these passages. No British poets are cited in the index. Carte's practice demonstrated visibly the precarious situation of the literary source. John Toland's *A Critical History of the Celtic Religion and Learning* (1740) also showed an ambivalence towards MSS. There was a relish for and reservation about the purity of ancient literary MSS. The ambivalence persistently raised the issue of literary forgery. Toland asked whether, besides the language and traditions of the Irish, or the monuments of stone and other materials which the country affords, there yet remain any Literary records truly antient and unadulterated, whereby the History of the Druids, with such other points of antiquity, may be retriev'd, or at least illustrated? This is a material question, to which I return a clear and direct answer; that not onely there remain very many antient Manuscripts undoubtedly genuine, besides such as are forg'd, and greater numbers interpolated, several whereof are in Ireland itself, some here in England, and others in the Irish monasteries abroad. . . . they have incomparably more antient materials of that kind for their history . . . . than either the English or the French, or any other European nation, with whose Manuscripts I have an acquaintance.[32]

Toland saw the genuine artefact threatened by imposture. Authority and authenticity resided again in the skill and integrity of the historian, not the data themselves:

The matter is certainly ready, there wants but will or skill for working of it; seperating the Dross from the pure Ore, and distinguishing counterfeit from sterling coin.[33]

This feat was to prove by no means easy. The ascendancy of the MS as historical source made literary forgery (in its broadest sense) an unavoidable issue. Forgery had intellectual currency. Ancient literature's acceptance into historiography was harshly contested, but an inexorable trend.

The Footnote

A second method designed to authenticate historiography was to employ footnotes for the citing of sources and expansion of points in the text. There were fewer reservations about the efficacy of this device, which was a mechanical and simple way of building an authenticating apparatus. The footnoting of imaginative literature by authors or editors was a practice at least as old as Spenser's *The Shepherd's Calender* (in Britain), and common enough by the eighteenth century for Pope to burlesque the format of a scholarly edition in the *Dunciad Variorum*. But the relation of the footnote and similar devices—the preface, dissertation, endnote—to history writing and historical literature had a special status: the establishing of factuality and its proof. In no other situation did the text rely so heavily on another, partial text, which was outside of it and existed concurrently. The format represented a display of accountability, a public declaration that all was sound. That was at least the ideal purpose of the procedure. As Robertson said, lauding the bibliography he provided for *The History of America* (1777):

> I have endeavoured to authenticate whatever I relate. The longer I reflect on the nature of historical composition, the more I am convinced that this scrupulous accuracy is necessary.[34]

Robertson's earlier *The History of the Reign of Emperor Charles V* (1769) used voluminous endnotes. He gave them the title "Proofs and Illustrations." Robertson relegated these notes to the end of his book, because as "critical disquisitions" they would hinder the flow of the narrative.[35] This dual purpose given to notes was important. They were not only "Proofs" to support the text, but independent or autonomous pockets of historical knowledge. The footnoting apparatus of the forgeries functioned in a similar way. The notes and the text were controlled by the overall vision of the forger—both participated in making history. Macpherson made a sanctioned assumption: the longer the note, the more powerful its authentication, and the greater its buttressing of the text. Bulk was equated with truth. Macpherson was not being renegade. William Hayley wrote the verse *Essay on History* in 1780. The poem occupied eighty-one pages, the notes seventy-four pages.

As prolixity was a loophole in the system, so was economy. Thomas Carte in the first volume of the *History* (1747) bore the same benevolent attitude to his reader as Robertson. He did not want the readability of the text restricted by long antiquarian digressions or pedantic displays of sources. His solution was not to defer the notes to the end:

> I have been careful to examine each fact, before I allowed it a place in the body of this work; and always quote the decisive authority upon which I relate it.[36]

The system creaked on that word "decisive." One source was now to carry the authority for all. Carte opted for

> seldom mentioning others of less weight, or later in time. I have thought it a very impertinent way of swelling a volume, and a very unfair treatment of a reader, to charge the notes with accounts I have been forced to reject, and put him upon the dry and tedious work of going through the task of writers unworthy of credit, and of forming judgements upon scraps and fragments.[37]

The text was readable, but its accountability was suspect. We only had the historian's word that he had consulted other sources. Each reference to the "decisive" source achieved the status of a stamp of authenticity. The forgeries and later historical poetry exploited this method of authentication. It was possible to cite a renowned historian, without necessarily giving the exact location of the information within that work. Hence it would be difficult to check on the veracity of the text. Even if a more stringent accountability was observed, a source could be chosen that most agreed with the imaginative version of events being given in the text. Typically, it was Macpherson, an arch exploiter of the device, who called it "imposture":

> To crowd a margin with the names of different writers, is an easy, and, perhaps, a harmless imposture. In the minds of the superficial, the expedient might establish an opinion of an Author's industry and knowledge: but it would have little effect on the judicious, from whose decision he has most to hope and fear.[38]

Philosophical Buttressing

Simultaneously with the design of a practical apparatus to authenticate historiography, a philosophical apparatus was being developed by Locke and Hume. It is to be expected that the empiricist philosophers had interesting and germane things to say about the authentication of history. History is, after all, the repository of human experience.

Locke's endorsement of the MS as the basic "voucher" of historical knowledge ended an interesting argument. Book four of the *Essay Concerning Human Understanding* is "Of Knowledge and Opinion." The relevant chapters are 15 and 16, titled "Of Probability" and "Of the Degrees of Assent." It is significant that Locke's treatment of historiography occurred in this context. He considered how we are persuaded to believe in something when we have no direct sensory experience of it. History was not the only embodiment of this situation, of course. But the importance of well-authenticated historical knowledge to contemporary culture is shown in the fact that Locke's argument in these chapters peaked in a discussion of historical perception.

In part 4 of chapter 15, Locke drew up the rules of probability: "The Grounds of Probability are two: Conformity with our own Experience; or the Testimony of others' experience."[39] The first rule required no elucidation. The second, which implied a process of communication or transmission, and therefore a medium, necessitated a subdivision:

> Secondly, the testimony of others, vouching their observation and experience. In the testimony of others, it is to be considered: 1. The

number. 2. The integrity. 3. The skill of the witnesses. 4. The design of the author, where it is a testimony out of a book cited. 5. The consistency of the parts, and circumstances of the relation. 6. Contrary testimonies.[40]

These rules, if transferred onto knowledge of the past, were seminal. Category 3 suggested eyewitnesses, memoirs, or memory. Category 4 referred to a literary medium, and quite possibly history books. Locke's rules prefigured Du Fresnoy's forgery detection manual. Locke was manufacturing tools of authentication, and the resources made available by him and others were exploited in the forgeries. In part 4 of chapter 16, history was mentioned for the first time, but not in a radical context. Locke said only that majority testimony should be believed: "if all historians that write of Tiberius say that Tiberius did so, it is extremely probable."[41] The spirit of the drive for authentication, which persistently revalued history and presented it in a new light, was not in that statement. Locke began to seek out the roots of historical knowledge, but he retreated. He then trod forward again: "when any particular matter of fact is vouched by the concurrent testimony of unsuspected witnesses, there our assent is also unavoidable."[42] The eyewitness stood at the point where history was made. The illustration of the point showed Locke's caution again. The example was timid and unprovoking:

> Thus: that there is such a city in Italy as Rome: that about 1700 years ago there lived in it a man, called Julius Caesar; that he was a general, and that he won a battle against another, called Pompey. This, though in the nature of the thing there be nothing for nor against it, yet being related by historians of credit, and contradicted by no one writer, a man cannot avoid believing it.[43]

But a radical attempt was being made to forge a link between the original eyewitness and the later historian by consideration of the transmission of a fact or an experience. Locke's decision to choose an example from classical history made the task more difficult, for large periods of time were involved. What is more, the written medium had to submit to the slippery phenomenon of oral tradition: the passing on of sense experience from one person to another by word of mouth only. Locke was skeptical about the efficiency of such a process. He invoked "Traditional Testimonies," only to refute their validity:

> any testimony, the further it is from the original truth, the less force and proof it has. The being and existence of the thing itself is what I call the original truth. A credible man vouching his knowledge of it is a good proof; but if another equally credible do witness it from his

report, the testimony is weaker; and a third that attests the hearsay of an hearsay is yet less considerable. So that in traditional truths each remove weakens the force of the proof; and the more hands the tradition had successively passed through, the less strength and evidence does it receive from them.[44]

Locke was dismissive of the purity of such transmission. The model he constructed (which influenced Hume profoundly), was of a chain of reportage whose original empirical data—"the being and existence of the thing itself"—diminished in an inverse relationship to time. It was odd perhaps that Locke did not insert the MS into the model, to see if the process of decay could be halted or at least slowed down. But then Locke was a philosopher dealing with empiricist ideas of knowledge: sensory experience. The credible man's "voucher" of knowledge was a kind of MS-equivalent, an ersatz empirical document. This concept was very relevant to Macpherson's Ossian, where the bard's spontaneous invocation of memory became the authentic mode for history's transmission. Yet Locke led himself into a logical contradiction. He asserted the precedence of initial spectatorship as authentic historical knowledge—"a credible man vouching his knowledge," or as he put it a few lines later, "a rational man contemporary with the first voucher"[45]—but Locke's evanescent model of transmission meant that this historiographical condition was inaccessible; its purity could not be proved. The conclusion to be drawn from his overall argument was that there was no such thing as historical truth. Locke realized where he had led himself, and hastily wrapped up the argument. His endorsement of MSS quoted earlier occurred in an apologetic context:

I would not be thought here to lessen the credit and use of history; it is all the light we have in many cases, and we receive from it a great part of the useful truths we have, with a convincing evidence. I think nothing more valuable than the records of antiquity; I wish we had more of them, and more uncorrupted. But this truth forces me to say, that no probability can rise higher than its first original.[46]

Locke found refuge in the authority of the MS or its equivalent, the "first original." Locke's progression had been consistent, a measure perhaps of the innovation of his inquiry. It was his insistence that the "first original" existed that was his great legacy. One of the central tasks of the drive for authentication was to attempt to recuperate this pristine condition where history, so to speak, commenced—where its making began. Locke was sceptical about salvaging that initial experience. He called for uncorrupted records, but was forced to admit that, pure or impure, probability could not go beyond them. His model was of an evanescent transmission of the past. It was left to Hume to reverse the polarity of Locke's perception.

Hume was a philosopher and practicing historian. His views on history in the *Treatise* (1740) are of vital importance. In book 1, part 3: "Of Knowledge and Probability" (vide Locke's "Of Knowledge and Opinion"), it becomes clear Hume was modifying Locke's views. Section 4 is "Of the Component Parts of Our Reasonings Concerning Cause and Effect." The context was causality. Hume declared:

> When we infer effects from causes, we must establish the existence of these causes; which we have only two ways of doing, either by an immediate perception of our memory or senses, or by an inference from other causes; which causes we must ascertain in the same manner, either by a present impression or by an inference from *their* causes, and so on, till we arrive at some object, which we see or remember. It is impossible for us to carry on our inferences *ad infinitum*; and the only thing that can stop them, is an impression of the memory or senses.[47]

Hume's model for sensory transmission did not involve decay. An empirical state of knowledge—memory or sense experience—had to be achieved. The chain ended there. The model was then applied to knowledge of the past: history. Hume chose Locke's example:

> We may choose any point of history, and consider for what reason we either believe or reject it. Thus, we believe that Caesar was killed in the senate-house on the *ides* of *March,* and that because this fact is established on the unanimous testimony of historians, who agree to assign this precise time and place to that event.[48]

Locke's cautious opening polemic was followed almost verbatim. Hume investigated further. He went beyond secondary sources to a more fundamental level. Unlike Locke, Hume believed that the *primum mobile,* that original object that was seen or remembered, could be recuperated. He drew Locke's model in reverse: an authenticating regression to the truth, instead of an atrophied progression away from it:

> Here are certain characters and letters present either to our memory or senses; which characters we likewise remember to have been used as the signs of certain ideas; and these ideas were either in the minds of such as were immediately present at that action, and received the ideas directly from its existence; or they were derived from the testimony of others, and that again from another testimony, by a visible gradation, till we arrive at those who were eye-witnesses and spectators of the event. It is obvious all this chain of argument or connection of causes

and effects, is at first founded on those characters or letters, which are seen or remembered, and that without the authority either of the memory or senses, our whole reasoning would be chimerical and without foundation. Every link of the chain would in that case hang upon another, but there would not be anything fixed to one end of it, capable of sustaining the whole; and consequently there would be no belief nor evidence.[49]

Hume did not distinguish between written and spoken testimonies. "Characters and letters" seems to refer to both modes as of equal value. Hume's great value was his confidence. The phrase "visible gradation" was a marvelous description of an apparatus of accountability and transmission. The forgeries explored imaginatively the idea of authentic regression into the past. Chatterton's perspectives of transmission were more "visible" than Macpherson's, but both forgers attempted a recuperation of that primary condition of spectatorship or participation, and that experience's preservation in memory or MS.

Later in the *Treatise*, Hume revalued his model. In section 13 of book 1 ("Of Unphilosophical Probability") Hume took Locke's stance at the beginning rather than the end of the chain of transmission and looked at time progressively. Locke's problem now confronted Hume. The "vivacity" of empirical knowledge was seen gradually to decay in proportion to the distance:[50]

It is evident there is no point of ancient history, of which we can have any assurance, but by passing through many millions of causes and effects, and through a chain of arguments of almost an immeasurable length. Before the knowledge of the fact could come to the first historian, it must be conveyed through many mouths; and after it is committed to writing, each new copy is a new object, of which the connection with the foregoing is known only by experience and observation. Perhaps therefore it may be concluded, from the present reasoning, that the evidence of all ancient history must now be lost, or at least will be lost in time, as the chain of causes increases, and runs on to a greater length.[51]

Hume seemed to have reversed his attitude to historical truth. Because his topic was still the authentication of history, however, he raised issues relevant to the forgeries: the potential loss of a nation's history; the transition from oral to literate culture, or from oral to written records. Macpherson's preface to the *Fragments of Ancient Poetry* brilliantly exploited the latter notion, as we shall see in chapter 3. Hume's solution to the problem of historical decay was again a modification of Locke's. Faith was put in literary sources, but Hume did not see these sources as necessarily polluted:

though the links are innumerable that connect any original fact with the present impression, which is the foundation of belief, yet they are all of the same kind, and depend on the fidelity of printers and copyists. One edition passes into another, and that into a third, and so on, till we come to that volume we peruse at present. There is no variation in the steps. After we know one, we know all of them; and after we have made one, we can have no scruple as to the rest. This circumstance alone preserves the evidence of history.[52]

Chatterton's vision was made up of interconnecting literary documents, of imaginative and non-imaginative kinds. These all worked to "preserve" history. It should be apparent that the forgeries were an imaginative putting into play of perplexing issues in contemporary historiography.

Authentication as a Reading Attitude: Fact and Fiction

Truth severe, by fairy fiction drest.

Thomas Gray, *The Bard* (1757)

A certain reading attitude was described and discussed by several eighteenth-century historians and theorists, which represented the most abstract and most desperate search for an authenticating procedure. The underlying motive beneath these discussions was the belief that the pure fact of history, and its verification, were in a precarious situation, unable to fend off the encroachment of fiction.

In *Letters on the Study and Use of History* (written in 1735) Bolingbroke stated that fables cannot be morally effective

unless [they] bear the appearance of truth. When they bear this appearance, reason connives at the innocent fraud of imagination; reason dispenses, in favour of probability, with those strict rules of criticism that she has established to try the truth of fact: but, after all, she receives these fables as fables; and as such only she permits imagination to make the most of them. If they pretended to be history, they would be soon subjected to another and more severe examination.[53]

Bolingbroke was dealing with literature's relation to history, with realism, that "appearance of truth." He could have been referring to the novel with his term "innocent fraud" (echoed by Hugh Blair's "fictitious histories"). But Bolingbroke stated that by application of those "rules" that "try the truth of the fact," the point where innocence became sin could easily be detected. In other words, where a pretence to be "real" changed to a pretence to be "historical." Bolingbroke did not say how the "appearance of truth" differed from the pretense to history, nor what his rules that "try the truth of fact" were. The shakiness in the reasoning actually undermined Bolingbroke's apparent complacency, and suggested that "the truth of fact" was by no means easy to prove, in literature or history. Thus authentication became a matter for the reader's acumen or intuition, his "reason." The difficulty of separating literature and history, fact and fiction, the pure and impure, was also expressed by Gibbon and Hume.

In *An Essay on the Study of Literature* (1764; originally written in 1759) Gibbon divided criticism into three categories: (1) what writers have said, i.e. textual scholarship, which includes "distinguishing supposed from genuine performances";[54] (2) what writers have said well, i.e. rhetoric; (3) what writers have said truly—a footnote here says: "Historically so; the truth of their evidence, not of their opinions."[55] The issue was factuality, the historical content of literature. Gibbon was under no illusions. He said this inquiry "opens an immense field, the enquiry into the circumstances and truths of facts."[56] He offered no guidelines for such an inquiry. Later in the *Essay*, he asserted that different kinds of historical fact exist:

> Among a multitude of historical facts, there are some, and those by much of the majority, which prove nothing more than that they are facts. There are others which may be useful in drawing a partial conclusion, whereby the philosopher may be enabled to judge of the motives of an action, or some peculiar features in a character: these relate only to single links of the chain. Those whose influence extends throughout the whole system, are so intimately connected as to have given motion to the springs of action, are very rare; and what is still more rarely to be met with is, a genius who knows how to distinguish them, amidst the vast chaos of events wherein they are jumbled, and deduce them, pure and unmixt, from the rest.[57]

Here was a very strong plea for an authenticating "genius," who would be very like the discriminating historian-editor demanded by Toland. Such a plea would not have been made unless "historical facts" were felt to be inextricably and unpardonably composed of elements of fiction. In the *Treatise*, Hume attempted to portray such a reader:

> Nothing is more evident, than that those ideas, to which we assent, are more strong, firm, and vivid, than the loose reveries of a castle-builder. If one person sits down to read a book as a romance, and

another as a true history, they plainly receive the same ideas, and in the same order; nor does the incredulity of the one, and the belief of the other, hinder them from putting the very same sense upon their author. His words produce the same ideas in both; though his testimony has not the same influence on them. The latter has a more lively conception of all the incidents. He enters deeper into the concerns of the persons: represents to himself their actions, and characters, and friendships, and enmities: he even goes so far as to form a notion of their features, and air, and person. While the former, who gives no credit to the testimony of the author, has a more faint and languid conception of all these particulars, and, except on account of the style and ingenuity of the composition, can receive little entertainment from it.[58]

The status of the text as history or romance now resided entirely in the reader's expectations: fact or fiction was, basically, the reader's invention. There was no question of applying rules to the text. Yet no clue was given as to what comprised the historian-reader's predisposition. Later in the *Treatise*, Hume's case became even weaker. Instead of a rationally argued method, the tool of authentication offered was simply a "feeling" about the text:

When we are convinced of any matter of fact, we do nothing but conceive it, along with a certain feeling, different from attends the mere *reveries* of the imagination. And when we express our incredulity concerning any fact, we mean, that the argument for the fact produces not that feeling. Did not the belief consist in a sentiment different from our mere conception, whatever objects were presented by the wildest imagination would be on equal footing with the most established truths founded on history and experience. There is nothing but the feeling or sentiment to distinguish the one from the other.[59]

There was some desperation in this attempt to distinguish fact from fiction. That desperation was caused by those developments in historiography under discussion that gave, intentionally or unintentionally, areas of "equal footing" to literature and history, and therefore to historical fact and imaginative fiction. Keith Stewart has noted that giving "an equivalence [to] fiction and history" posed for the eighteenth century "a persistent problem in generic definition, to say nothing of a problem in epistemology."[60] The forgeries grew from a climate in which history and literature, fact and fiction, were persistently under the scrutiny of the historical thinker. The attempt made to separate these seeming opposites often resulted in their being linked closer than ever. A "certain feeling" about authenticity was of little use to the scholars in the 1760s,

1770s and 1780s who strove to prove or disprove the authenticity of the forgeries. But the Humean "feeling" was a sanctioned authenticating device made available to later writers and scholars.

Adam Smith also expressed a spurious confidence that the fact-fiction border could be established and enforced. In his *Lectures on Rhetoric and Belles-Lettres* (1762), he discussed narrative in fable and history:

> It is of no consequence whether the incidents narrated be true or false. A well contrived story may be as interesting and entertaining as any real one. The causes which brought about the several incidents that are narrated may all be very ingeniously contrived and well adapted to their several ends.[61]

So fact and fiction were on "equal footing." But Smith went on:

> still, [as] the facts are not such as really existed, the end proposed by history will not be answered. The facts must be real, otherwise they will not assist us in our future conduct.[62]

Note the emphatic rhetoric: "The facts must be real." The conclusion to be drawn from Smith's reasoning was that historical fact was felt to be under threat from fiction. Bolingbroke's *Letters on the Study and Use of History* strove to prove that history was not "nothing better than a probable tale, artfully contrived, and plausibly told, wherein truth and falsehood are indistinguishably blended together."[63] Bolingbroke's anathema was historical fiction. The forgeries were born out of the issues that worried thinkers like Bolingbroke, Hume, and Smith; issues that centered on the relationship of history to fiction. Robert Wood, speaking of Homer in 1769, was, unlike Hume and the others, content to have "reality in fiction," and blend the historian and poet:

> I fear I may appear prejudiced to my subject, if I look for Nature in this imaginary province, and expect a regard for truth even in the Poet's fable; yet I cannot help thinking, that where his persons are most ideal, his scene is not less real; and that when his subject carries him beyond life, and his divine agents, or (in the language of criticism) his Machinery is introduced, the action is carried on with greater powers, no doubt, and upon a larger scale, but with the same attention to a just proportion, and generally in the same subordination to the invariable laws of time and place; a management which, though it cannot entirely command assent, softens extravagance, and leads the Reader so insensibly to fancy reality in fiction, by rendering both conformable to the same general rules of probability and consistence, that it is not easy to say where the Historian ends, or the Poet begins.[64]

That final comment would apply equally well to Ossian, who quickly earned the soubriquet "Scottish Homer."

Nationalist Historiography: The Origins of Society and the Ancient Bard

All that is really *known* of the ancient state of Britain is contained in a few pages. We *can* know no more than what the old writers have told us; yet what large books have we upon it, the whole of which, excepting such parts as are taken from those old writers, is all a dream.

Samuel Johnson, in a conversation reported by James Boswell, 29 April, 1778.

The eighteenth century was a great age of origin-seeking. The search was on for the roots of institutions, laws and, in particular, societies. Historiography could help to define a nation's identity, shaping it historically and showing its evolution to its present glory. In much poetry of the early eighteenth century, we can find this origins-and-progress format. Art, civilization, liberty, industry, or poetry were shown to follow a standard historical route: Greece, Rome, Florence, and Britain. Johnson's *Dictionary* was a nationalist enterprise. The British Empire was rapidly expanding. Among historians, the most difficult task in this aggrandizement was the portrayal of a nation's genesis: ancient society. It was no longer acceptable to begin with an account of the Flood or Brutus' landing in Britain (though, ironically, some of the history books cited in this chapter retained a mythical genealogy). Information was needed about the earliest times of British society. Therein lay a great problem: indigenous sources. Ancient documents—chronicles, genealogical poems, ballads, prose fragments—were the subjects of heated controversy. Some historians were so skeptical about the true age and validity of such sources that they discarded them altogether and either turned to the civilized and therefore "reliable" accounts of the Romans (Tacitus, Caesar), or refused to include a portrait of early society in their histories—this was the case with Robertson's *The History of Scotland* (1759). Those who were prepared to believe in a document's antiquity (dating methods were in a rudimentary state) were faced with an unavoidable problem. The document would more than likely be written in verse—either a verse chronicle or a narrative poem. Any writing in verse meant the existence of fiction. Such was nationalist zeal, however, that many historians were not deterred from portraying and discussing very earliest times. The enterprise was fraught with contradiction, confusion, and controversy. Much of the debate centered on the figure of the bard, the earliest poet. He was a phenomenon who could hardly ever be ignored. In any portrait of ancient society, the bard had an important role: the community's historian. It was unanimously agreed that the bard was society's first historian, Homer being the great precedent. Those historians who examined the issue rigorously realized the bard's true importance: as the author or likely author of the extant historical sources. The bard was the indigenous historian of a nation. His literary productions—poetry-history—were of crucial importance. Even in a theoretical inquiry, this matter had to be confronted. Adam Smith and Hugh Blair, in their different *Lectures on Rhetoric and Belles Lettres,* both discussed the history of historians, and both began with the poet. Reservations about the endorsement of the bard as historian were strong. There was a logical circle: information about the bard, supplied by the bard. Moreover, as a genre poetry always suggested indulgence in fiction or fictionalizing. Hume called poets "lyars by profession."[65] To quote Keith Stewart again:

> the conception of the bard as historian meant that bardic verse (and this could include anything from the *Iliad* to the outpourings of Ossian as well as ballads) might in varying degrees be accepted as history. . . . this is not to say that such poetically transmitted information was completely or regularly accepted as historical fact.[66]

Gibbon represents this ambivalent attitude: "we have no other way of coming at the knowledge of the heathen system, than by means of their Poets and Priests, both greatly addicted to fiction."[67] Or, earlier, John Lewis:

> in this my History I could speak of strange things more ancient and farther off from Man's Memory, but what has been written before are only extravagant stories, full of monstrous Fables imagined and devised by Poets, which are altogether uncertain and most untrue.[68]

These views were mainly relevant to Macpherson's Ossian, the fourth-century Caledonian prince and bard. Macpherson's forgery was a recreation of the situation of the bard-historian, and acted as an imaginative solution to many of the issues that have been raised. T. P. Peardon postulates, when discussing Ossian, "We can only conclude . . . that men were emotionally predisposed to accept as historic a picture of the ancient Celts which was really manufactured to fit their mood."[69] Few eighteenth-century historians would have agreed with Johnson that "we must consider how very little history there is; I mean, real authentic history . . . all the colouring, all the philosophy, of history is conjecture."[70] As T. P. Peardon notes, nationalist historians "combined the wildest theorizing with some substantial contributions to scholarship."[71] In other words, some history writing was itself often a form of historical fiction, an amalgam of fact and fiction, of righteous and profane procedures. This paradoxical quality of nationalist historiography grew from the same revaluation that fueled the drive for authentication. The quest was for the true picture of national origins. Battles of antiquity-seeking raged fiercely between the Scots and Irish, two nations who prided themselves on their "purity" and Celtic inheritance. The conflict had existed for centuries, but the terms of the struggle in the early eighteenth century had a new twist. Thomas Innes, in the preface to *A Critical Essay on the Ancient Inhabitants of the Northern Parts of Britain, or Scotland* (1729), said that Irish pretensions to "excel other nations in the antiquity of the settlement and monarchy of the *Scots* in *Britain*" had long been around.[72] Innes wished to dispel this charlatanry. He claimed he had consulted all extant "vouchers." He printed a catalogue of these MSS sources in an appendix, and he gave extracts from some of the verse chronicles. Innes' most ferocious attack on corrupt practices in historiography is fascinating. He said that the infamous practice of "running up" a nation's antiquity had *always* been a flaw of historiography. The fault went back much farther than the medieval historians such as Hector Boethius (whose account of the "ancient Scottish Constitution" Innes disproved). Such historians were to be criticized, but Innes, like Hume, looked farther back:

> The humour of running up the originals of nations to incredible heights, prevailed among almost all those, of whom we have any certain account: each nation vying with, and endeavouring to surpass one another in their antiquities. . . . The most part of other nations were possessed with the same humour, and the more they were ignorant of what passed before their own time, the more they were inclined to run up their antiquities to incredible heights. . . . It is then no wonder, that the inhabitants of *Great Britain* and *Ireland* were like to other nations in this. The time of the first planting of these islands, being in those ages, when they had no use of letters and by consequence no means of preserving the memory of past transactions, and less yet of calculation of dates or epochs, left them a fair field of expatiating in the dark ages of the remote antiquity, under the conduct of their ignorant and venal guides the bards, famous for flattering their patrons with ancient pedigrees, and whole nations with successions of kings.[73]

Hume and Innes both demonstrated a concern with the historiographical condition of the past. That condition was found to be less than perfect, but the regression back to it was one of the key features of the forgeries. The making of history belonged to the past as well as the present. Innes regarded ancient poetry as an unacceptable source (the verse chronicles he used were no more than that—bare facts arranged in lines of verse). He portrayed the bards as specific kinds of liars: genealogical fabricators. Genealogy was a conspicuous absence from Ossian.

The controversy about bardism was fired by primitivist sentiments. To confer a status of historiographical corruption on your ancestors was an act of cultural condemnation. Conversely, to portray early society as having achieved a state of historiographical integrity killed two birds with one stone. The nation was shown as inherently civilized; the extant MS sources being cited from those times were purified.

The ancient Scotland Innes pictured was not depraved, but neither was it over-refined. He presented the bard as the poet of oral culture only. Literacy, and therefore the first MSS, arrived with Christianity. This point was also hotly contested. Some believed pagan sources survived. Others posited an uncorrupted transition from oral tradition to written records. Innes payed lip service only to the idea of the bard-historian: "The Irish, in particular, agree, that the bards, to whom they give several names were the recorders and preservers of their ancient transactions."[74] But he had scorn for Celtic nations that "pretend, no less than the *Irish*, to have remains and fragments of poems and rhythms on their ancient heroes."[75] Macpherson was one such pretender. Ossian first appeared in *Fragments of Ancient Poetry* (1760). Even if ancient literary remnants were extant, Innes argued, they were still likely to be corrupt. The bards were forgers:

> What then may be thought of the ancient bards, or antiquaries of *Ireland* in times of paganism? And how far would their writings, if they had left any, deserve to be depended upon, when they left the spirit of imposture so deeply rooted in their posterity, that even Christianity could not correct it?[76]

As is shown below, a solution to the question had already been offered by the Irish historians, Keating and O'Flaherty. Innes attacked their use of literary MSS. Innes cited as proof of the dubious authenticity of ancient literary sources their very poor survival rate into modern times. Such a vacuum could be filled, of course, by the imagination:

> we see how little credit hath been given of late generally in all countries, where learning hath been improved, to rhythms or rhapsodies of bards or other forgers, since nothing of that kind, or very little, hath been thought to be transmitted to posterity, or published to the world.[77]

Ossian was published in the 1760s with great commercial success, and the process of transmission was imaginatively embodied in the forgery. Macpherson skirted the principles of accountability by withholding his "originals," though always stressing that they existed. Over thirty years before, Innes had accused Irish historians of this deception. His words anticipated exactly later attacks on the forgeries:

> the abettors of these high antiquities persevere to keep these pretended ancient monuments and documents of these antiquities from the eyes of the publick. . . . if these writings of their bards, or poets, etc. were made publick, whole and entire such as they are, they would be so far from finding any credit with unbiased persons, versed in ancient history, that on the contrary they would lose that small credit, which the confident assertions of their abettors procure them.[78]

Innes' accusation was justified. A general area of frustration for those involved in the historiographical debate over the bard and literary sources was the inability to find an outside reference. Especially for those who endorsed ancient MSS, polemic and logic became more circular, self-referring and, eventually, self-authenticating. In the history writing of Innes' enemies, the rational weighing of evidence was transformed into imaginative vision.

Roderic O'Flaherty's *Ogygia* (1685) was an early assault on Scottish historians. O'Flaherty looked at the roots of national identity, specifically whether the Scots were originally Irish, or vice versa:

> Writers of exceeding great veracity and authority, hold those Scots historians of the last and present century in the lowest estimation, and look upon them in the light of mythologists, who by a groundless equivocating construction of the similarity of names, have appropriated the merit of our transactions.[79]

Macpherson contributed directly to this controversy about cultural appropriation. His vision is of a Scottish Ossian, who was later stolen by the Irish bards. O'Flaherty focused his attack onto sources. He said that Scottish historiography, "not being deduced from ancient records, or reputable authorities, but the assertions of modern writers, supported solely by traditional and oral information, [is] questionable."[80] So O'Flaherty, like Innes, distrusted oral tradition. But unlike Innes, he endorsed ancient MSS. The ancient MS chronologies he claimed to have used were of unquestionable authority:

> no nation in the world with more assiduity has preserved its antiquities from the earliest eras therof, or transmitted to posterity with

greater precision its chronological and genealogical accounts, the achievements of its heroes, their propogation, the boundaries of their principalities, their laws—in short, everything relative to their antiquity.[81]

Hume's "visible gradation" was here not a natural process, but a consciously engineered cultural act. Irish national identity relied on its ancient historiographical integrity. Authentication was a process of national importance. Toland and Keating felt this so strongly that they sought to prove it by pure invention, historical fantasy. Toland, writing in 1718, expressed a strong belief that "there remain very many antient Manuscripts undoubtedly genuine, besides such as are forg'd, and greater numbers interpolated."[82] The problem of forgery could be overcome by appealing to O'Flaherty's notion of a pure cultural transmission: "In all conditions the Irish have been strangely sollicitous, if not in some degree superstitious, about preserving their books and parchments."[83] Toland went much further. He realized this idea in a mythical institution, a royal college at Tarah, in which took place

> a triennial revision of all the Antiquaries Books, by a committee of three Kings or great Lords, three Druids, and three Antiquaries. These were to cause whatever was approv'd and found valuable in those books, to be transcribed into the royal *Book of Tarah;* which was to be the perpetual standard of their history.[84]

So the royal assembly purged all contemporary historiography and preserved it in an historian's Bible. The Book of Tarah was not given as Toland's source for the information, nor was any other work. Toland indulged in fiction because the need for reliable, very ancient MSS was so great. That need was also frustrated by the presence of poetry. Geoffry Keating, in *The General History of Ireland* (1723), expanded Toland's vision, and incorporated poetry into the picture.

Keating's preface began with the standard rhetoric. He accused Giraldus Cambrensis' writings of being "a Forgery and Imposition upon Mankind."[85] Keating also made an important speculation:

> the Chronicles of *Ireland* receive an additional Value from this Consideration, that they were never supress'd by the Tyranny and Invasion of any Foreign Power.[86]

The equation was purity of culture with purity of MS. One could be gauged by the other. Macpherson, as we shall see, exploited the notion and its converse—cultural supression and extermination. Keating then discussed his sources in more detail. He committed himself wholly to unspecified literary sources:

It should seem surprising that the following History is diversified with so many Quotations out of ancient Poetry, to prove several Matters of Fact advanc'd, and to adjust the Chronology of the *Irish* History; it must be consider'd, particularly that the Authors of the *Irish* Chronicles Compos'd their Work generally in Verse, that their Records might be less subject to Corruption and Change, that the Obscurity of the Style might be a Defence to them, and that the Youths, who were instructed in that Profession, might be the better able to commit them to Memory.[87]

So authentication led to social stability in a mixed oral and literate culture. Such was Keating's commitment to ancient poetry as authentic records—"I shall receive them as the Principal Testimonies to consult in compiling the following History"[88]—that he sought a more spectacular authentication:

For notwithstanding that some of the Chronicles of *Ireland* differ from those poetical Records in some Cases, yet the Testimony of the Annals that were written in Verse is not for that Reason invalid, because all the publick Chronicles, as well in Verse as Prose, were submitted to a solemn Correction and Purgation, and therefore it is reasonable they should be esteem'd of equal Authority.[89]

The justification for the poetical making of history was the college at Tarah, which authenticated *all* records from that time. Keating fused ancient poetry and history into a self-authenticating system. Keating's fiction was, like the forgeries, a "vision," because he was concerned with history as process, with its inception and transmission. The aim was not simply to invent an ancient Irish academy. The only source Keating gave for his very detailed account of the college was "a Poet of great Authority, and very Ancient."[90] Keating invented a founder for the college, one Ollamh Fodhla, a pagan (like Ossian) and cultural philanthropist (like Chatterton's William Canynge):

He instituted the most useful Laws for the Government and Advantage of his People, and was so indefatiguable in his Studies, that he undertook to transmit to Posterity, in a very correct History, the several Travels, Voyages, Adventures, Wars, and other memorable Transactions of all his royal Ancestors. . . . and in order to purge and digest the Records of his Kingdom, he summon'd his principal Nobility, his Druids, the Poets, and Historiographers to meet him in a full Assembly at *Tara* once in every three years. . . . in Testimony of this, I shall produce the following Verses of great Antiquity and to be found in Writings of good Authority:

The learned *Ollamh* Fodhla first ordain'd,
The great *Assembly*, where the nobles met,

And Priests and Poets and Philosophers,
To make new Laws, and to correct the Old,
And to advance the Honour of his Country.[91]

In his desire to see history through poetry and not to allow the two to diverge, Keating offered an imaginative solution to the melée of confusion and contradiction surrounding the issue of the bard and the historical value of ancient verse. The benefits of Toland's authenticating historian, who could distinguish the "Dross" from the "Pure Ore," were given to the roots of society. Keating did not, like Macpherson, create the original history-poetry, but rather the post-bardic, academic purification of all extant MSS—a function of literate society. The whole of the very detailed description of the college is too long to cite. An extract is given here, while a fuller account is presented in Appendix 1. The wish-fulfilled purpose of the assembly at Tarah is that it represented, as Keating's imitator Charles O'Conor noted, a "Law, concerning the Authenticity of History."[92] Forgery and falsification of the facts of the past was a legal offence:

In this Assembly, the ancient Records and Chronicles of the Island were Perused and Examined; and if any Falshoods were detected, they were instantly Erased, that Posterity might not be imposed upon by False History; and the Author, who had the Insolence to abuse the World by his Relation, either by perverting Matters of Fact, and representing them in improper Colours, or by Fancies and Inventions of his own, was solemly Degraded from the Honour of sitting in that Assembly, and was dismissed with a Mark of Infamy upon him: His Works likewise were destroyed, as unworthy of Credit, and were not to be admitted into the Archives, or received among the Records of the Kingdom. Nor was this Expulsion the Whole of his Punishment, for he was liable to a Fine, or Imprisonment, or whatever Sentence the Justice of the Parliament thought proper to inflict. By these Methods, either out of Fear of Scandal or Disgrace, or of losing their Estate, their Pensions and Endowments, and of suffering perhaps some Corporal Correction, the Historians of those Ages were induced to be very exact in their Relations, and to transmit nothing to After Times, but what had passed this solemn Test and Examination, and was recommended by the Sanction and Authority of this Learned Assembly.[93]

It remains now to turn to less partisan historians. Again, there was no consensus about the status of bardic verse as history.

The bard was generally regarded as very important to his own and later times. As the first recorder of knowledge, the bard could be seen as the foundation of all learning and knowledge. As Hugh Blair said: "by this oral tradition of national Ballads, was conveyed all the historical knowledge, and all the instruction, of the first ages."[94] So the bard had monopolistic possession of civilization's values in relation to the past and present. "History appeared in *no other form* than that of poetical tales,"[95] Blair continued (my italics). Or Adam Smith: "The poets were the first historians of any. . . . the oldest original writings in Latin, Italian, French, English and Scots are all poets."[96] It was precisely this monopoly that was so disturbing. History *was* poetry, and the consequences of this had to be confronted. Poetry involved fiction. The most sought-after position was that of being able to resolve poetry into its factual and historical elements. Thus Hume's attack on Arthurian mythologists in *The History of England* (1763) revealed a characteristic ambivalence:

> poets, tho' they disfigure the most certain history by their fictions, and use strange liberties with truth where they are the sole historians, as among the Britains, have commonly some foundation for their wildest exaggerations.[97]

The bard's monopolistic position frustrated the effort to find a source outside of bardic verse from which to judge matters objectively. So many claims, like Hume's, that the "liberties" of the ancient poet have a "foundation" in fact, remained unsubstantiated.

The formula was a traditional one in epic theory: history served as the basis of the fable. It is no surprise, perhaps, that Ossian recited two epics (*Fingal* and *Temora*) and Chatterton's Turgot wrote one also (*The Battle of Hastynges*). The epic is looked at in more detail in chapter 2. But I have incorporated it into the discussion at this point because the epic was important to historians as well as to imaginative writers and critics. Thus the *Universal History* (1736) styled *The Iliad* "both a Poem and a History."[98] It was then left up to the "judicious historian" to resolve this hybrid into its component parts:

> What we have instanced in one Poet, may in the same manner be applied to others; For tho' their Works were interspersed with many fabulous Strokes, yet they might have furnished a judicious Historian, that could distinguish between Truth and Fiction, with good Materials for a History.[99]

This was as far as the argument went. We are left with ancient poetry being "both a poem and a history." Its potential as historical source was less secure, awaiting the perspicacity of a reader who could "distinguish between truth and fiction." This syndrome was recreated by Macpherson in Ossian. The way in which Ossian is history was worked out in the text and in Macpherson's editorial apparatus. Macpherson's vision was founded in the authentic resources of eighteenth-century historiography.

In 1759, the year Macpherson showed the first Ossianic poem to John Home, William Robertson published *The History of Scotland*. Robertson believed that records only became reliable in the thirteenth century:

> Everything beyond that short period, to which well attested annals reach, is obscure; an immense space is left for invention to occupy; each nation, with a vanity inseparable from human nature, hath filled that void with events calculated to display its own antiquity, and lustre. And history, which ought to record truth and teach wisdom, often sets out with retailing fictions and absurdities . . . relying upon uncertain legends, and the traditions of their bards.[100]

Macpherson can be seen to have reacted to these words positively, not negatively. In the "immense space" that was "left for invention to occupy," Macpherson created a unique form of historical fiction whose lifeblood was the contemporary debate over the value of fiction as history.

Social and Cultural History

In his *Lectures on Rhetoric and Belles Lettres*, first delivered in the 1760s, Hugh Blair referred to "a very great improvement which has, of late years, begun to be introduced into Historical Composition."[101] This improvement consisted of a new attention to

> laws, customs, commerce, religion, literature, and every other thing that tends to show the spirit and genius of nations. It is now understood to be the business of an able Historian to exhibit manners, as well as facts and events; and assuredly, whatever displays the state and life of mankind, in different periods, and illustrates the progress of the human mind, is more useful and interesting than the detail of seiges and battles.[102]

A new historical sympathy was evoked, a shift of focus away from political or military topics (as the traditionalist Gibbon put it: "wars and administration of public affairs are the principal subjects of history")[103] to the current of life beneath: manners and customs, the details of everyday life. Literature was a source of such information. A new and powerful yoking of literature and history had been created, one that inspired anthologists and literary historians such as Thomas Percy and Thomas Warton. The new view of ancient poetry as social history offered a way around the problem of fiction being corrupt history. A poem could err factually, but could still present authentic details of life in the past. Thomas Percy noted that "Sir Andrew Barton," in *Reliques of Ancient English Poetry* (1765), contained "some few deviations from the truth of history, to atone for which it has recorded many lesser facts, which history hath not condescended to relate."[104] We are not told what those "lesser facts" are, but we are assured they are "new." The same innovative spirit was present here that fired all the issues discussed in this chapter. The rise of social history enabled antiquarian knowledge to be absorbed into mainstream history writing. As Thomas Pownall said in 1782:

> The antiquary sets before our eyes, and puts into our hands, in a way that the historian does not, every component part and whole frame of the acting system. He makes his reader live as it were in the times, and through the scenes he describes.[105]

Of the two forgers, Chatterton was most involved with the minutiae of the past. But the new fusion of ancient literature and history was available to both Macpherson and Chatterton. As early as 1699, James Wright remarked to a friend: "old plays will be read by the curious if it were only to discover the manners and behaviour of several ages and how they altered."[106] In 1788, Joseph Priestley, applying the theory that anything written or done in an age must bear some marks and traces of that age, concluded that "even poets and orators may be considered as historians, and every law and custom as a piece of history.[107] It is appropriate to end this chapter with this view of the ancient poem as a "piece of history," and the ancient poet as historian. Before moving on to Ossian, we must now analyze the literary approach to these matters in the eighteenth century. For the forgeries, like all historical fiction, are literary as well as historiographical phenomena.

2

The Literary Impetus

in the warmth of a poetical enthusiasm, a poet has a counterfeit belief. . . .

David Hume, *A Treatise of Human Nature*

In chapter 1, it was shown how literature became inextricably entangled in historiographical developments, and how seminal the resulting speculations were in relation to the forgeries. In this chapter, a similar approach is taken toward eighteenth-century literature. The focus is on how writers and critics confronted the notion of historical fiction, that perplexing hybrid of fact and invention. There were marked trends at work, which, when combined with the movements charted in chapter 1, seem to make the appearance of the forgeries almost inevitable.

There is a huge amount of material to digest and process. As in the first chapter, a taxonomic approach is taken, though the controlling focus on historical perception should prevent compartmentalization or discontinuity. The cut-off point is 1760, when Macpherson's *Fragments* appeared. Because I am approaching the forgeries as a literary critic and not as a historian, there is need to exert a more rigid chronology here than was necessary in the first chapter. Historical literature written during and after the 1760s will be dealt with in later chapters, where I will be studying any influences coming from the forgeries. One marked omission from this chapter is the work of the anthologists prior to Bishop Percy, which, for reasons of clarity and continuity, I incorporate into chapter 4.

It is less easy to erect a chronological boundary at the opposite end of the century. History and literature have always been close relations, and trying to identify precisely where the "impetus" leading to the forgeries begins is impossible. However, the period under study is the eighteenth century, when significant advances in historical perception occurred. This self-consciousness, whether revealed in complex theory or flourishing practice, was the prime mover of issues relevant to the forgeries. Literature before 1700 is referred to only if it was an obvious agent or force in this awareness. Thus Milton's plans for an Arthuriad mark an appropriate place to begin discussion of the epic: not only because Milton was stimulating a debate about historical literature, but because Joseph Warton in the 1750s referred to Milton's proposals in a plea for the writing of more indigenous historical literature.

There was a revaluation of history and literature's interaction to be found in literary writings of the time that was the parallel of the rise of historical philosophy and theory in historiography. The "impetus" under scrutiny can be seen as an attempt by the eighteenth century to accommodate history into literature, to formulate methods and predict results. Could historical fiction be valuable history? By the time of Scott's novels (dealt with in the final chapter), a confident affirmative could be given. Carlyle concluded that the Waverley novels:

> have taught all men this truth, which looks like a truism, yet was unknown to writers of history . . . that the bygone ages of the world were actually filled by living men.[1]

Scott himself may have had worries about precise ramifications, but the rights of historical fiction had been established. Consider now one of Johnson's comments on Ossian:

> I look upon M'pherson's *Fingal* to be as gross an imposition as ever the world was troubled with. Had it really been an ancient work, a true specimen how men thought at the time, it would have been a curiosity of the first rate. As a modern production, it is nothing.[2]

Johnson rejected imaginative recreation of the past as a valuable historical exercise. The ancient, not the modern, had historical validity. But his view was not held by everyone, least of all, of course, by Macpherson and Chatterton.

The Epic and the Nationalist Quest

In the eighteenth century, there was a general reverence for literature that was known or believed to have a factual base—meaning, usually, a groundwork in history. In his *Essay on the Writings and Genius of Pope* (1756), Joseph Warton singled out for special praise *Elegy to the Memory of an Unfortunate Lady,* because it was based on Pope's own experiences. Warton then generalized:

> Events that have actually happened are, after all, the properest sub-jects for poetry. . . . If we briefly cast our eyes over the most interest-ing and affecting stories, ancient or modern, we shall find that they are such as, as however adorned and a little diversified, are yet grounded on true history, and on real matters of fact.[3]

Warton lauded historical fiction. The quantifier "little" was important. History should be the larger component in the hybrid. Departures from fact should not be extreme. Poetry's "proper subject" should be a faithful or at least serious rendering of "true history" or "real fact." Warton cited as examples *El Cid, King Lear, Romeo and Juliet,* and *Oronooko,* making an extraordinary claim for these stories:

> The series of events contained in these stories, seem far to surpass the utmost powers of human imagination. In the best-conducted fiction, some mark of improbability and incoherence will still appear.[4]

So well was history accommodated in these texts that their fictional content was effectively erased. The result was history, purged of the "improbability and incoherence" that earmarked all fiction. The stages of Warton's argument were revealing: a lauding of the factual content of literature, and so of the historical content; an emphasis on historical truth above fictional value. Warton went on to define history in specifi-cally nationalist terms, and made a very important plea for an increase in historical themes in literature. That was in 1756, less than four years before Macpherson created Ossian. Warton seemed to be prophesying the forgeries, not only in his nationalist sentiment, but in his idea that the best historical fiction should appear as genuine history. Lest one should wish to diminish Warton's theory as an aberration, it is worth going beyond 1760 briefly to note that Johnson subscribed to Warton's view in his *Life of Pope* (1779):

> The heart naturally loves truth. The adventures and misfortunes of this illustrious pair [Eloisa and Aberlard] are known from undisputed history. . . . so new and affecting is their story, that it supersedes invention, and imagination ranges at full liberty without straggling into scenes of fable.[5]

A few lines later, Johnson acknowledged the sagacity of Warton's study of Pope.[6] Johnson was being mutually complimentary, for Warton had borrowed from Johnson only a few lines before the passage from the *Essay* already cited. He first attributed the excellence of Pope's *Elegy*

> to this cause; that the occasion of it was real; for it is certainly an indisputable maxim "That nature is more powerful than fancy; that we can always feel more than we can imagine; and that the most artful fiction must give way to truth."[7]

The maxim "we can always feel more than we can imagine, and that the most artful fiction must give way to truth" was quoted from Johnson's *Adventurer* 92, where two of Virgil's pastorals were praised for their factual basis. Johnson did not, like Warton, ask for modern recreations of that situation. But between them, the two critics insisted that the best literature was a fusion of history and invention with, ideally, the veiling of the latter. The evidence for their speculations was very flimsy. Pope was not interested in adducing historical details in the *Elegy* or *Eloisa*. But the gap between precept and proof only indicated a very strong desire that things be this way. An identical case was the view of literature as social history, which valued old ballads for their pictures of "manners and customs," while never citing a specific example. Warton's and Johnson's formula was the crest of much previous turbulence, most of which eddied round the genre of the epic, the literary form most urgently raising the issue of the use and value of history—particularly indigenous history—in literature. Ossian's *Fingal* and *Temora*, and Chatterton's two versions of Turgot's *The Battle of Hastynges*, were native epics.

Spenser's *Fairie Queen* may have been the first English epic, but "English" here applied to language rather than subject. The poem's world was the pastoral never-never land, and it was not an historical landscape. Arthur, despite his Maloryean trappings, was still represented in eighteenth-century history books as a British hero, the Christian repeller of the pagan Saxons. However real Spenser felt his "fierce wars" to be, the anxiety that native history had yet to be glorified by the epic muse remained strong well into the eighteenth century. The first major figure to record this anxiety was Milton. The passage in *Mansus* describing the projected Arthuriad is famous. The poet hoped to

> recall hereafter into rhyme
> The kings and heroes of my native clime,
> Arthur the chief, who even now prepares,
> In subterraneous being, future wars,
> With all his martial Knights, to be restored,
> Each to his seat around the federal board,
> And Oh, if spirit fail me not, disperse
> Our Saxon plunderers, in triumphant verse![8]

Milton's interest in historical topics as subjects for major literature ran deeper than the passage from *Mansus* suggests. Milton had done much research. The Trinity MS records thirty-three proposals for British tragedies. None of the topics are from a time later than the Norman Conquest. Milton was considering recuperating the historiographical dark ages: periods, as was shown in the first chapter, about which little was known. None of Milton's projects achieved fruition, though many of the historical figures—Athelstan, Godwin, Harold, Vortiger, and, of course, Alfred—appeared in the poetry and drama of the late seventeenth and eighteenth centuries, including pieces by Chatterton and his disciple, W. H. Ireland. Surprisingly, Milton omitted Arthur from the list. Perhaps Milton had doubts about Arthur's reality, or about the inclusion in his tragedy of too much "machinery" (only proposals twenty-eight and thirty-one contain supernatural incidents). Whatever the reasons, Milton did not abandon plans for a native epic. He cast round for other English heroes, and proposal twenty-four suggests a candidate had been located. This proposal was unique in being the only one to posit a possible epic as well as tragedy:

> Alfred in disguise of a minstrel discovers the Danes negligence sets on with a mightie slaughter about the same tyme the devonshire men route Hubba & slay him.
> A Heroicall Poem may be founded somwhere in Alfreds reigne, especially at his issuing out of Edelingsey on the Danes, whose actions are well like those of Ulysses.[9]

An Afrediad replaced the Arthuriad, the Saxon worthy replaced the British. Milton thought of an English Ulysses, although he was unable to create him. Dryden felt compelled to complete the task, as did Pope. Neither poet succeeded, sharing in Milton's anxiety and frustration. The feeling in the middle of the eighteenth century was still that the incarnation of the national past had not been attained. Dryden related his abortive plans in *A Discourse Concerning the Original and Progress of Satire* (1693):

> I had intended to have put in practice . . . a work which would have taken up my life in the performance of it. This too, I had intended chiefly for the honour of my native country, to which a poet is particularly obliged. Of two subjects, both relating to it, I was doubtful, whether I should choose that of King Arthur, conquering the Saxons; which being farther distant in time, gives the greater scope to my invention, or that of Edward the Black Prince in subduing Spain, and restoring it to the lawful prince, though a great tyrant, Don Pedro the Cruel, which for the compass of time, including only the expedition of

one year, for the greatness of the action, and its answerable event; for the magnanimity of the English hero, opposed to the ingratitude of the person whom he restored; and for the many beautiful episodes, which I had interwoven with the principal design, together with the characters of the chiefest English persons; wherein, after Virgil and Spenser, I would have taken occasion to represent my living friends and patrons of the noblest families, and also shadowed the events of future ages, in the succession of our imperial line.[10]

Again, what was proposed was an Anglicization of the classical epic, a change not in form but content—from classical or mythical to native history. The forgeries participated in this transition, manifesting what the major poets of the century before them could not. Dryden blamed the foiling of his plans on lack of patronage and the encroachments of old age. But the choice of an historical topic was also clearly a problem, as it had been with Milton. Dryden's idea that a subject that was "further distant in time, gives the greater scope to my invention" anticipated an eighteenth-century debate about the historical theme of the epic, which reached a peak in the preface to William Wilkie's *Epigoniad* (1753). Distant periods, as Dryden notes, were regarded as more conducive to the fusion of fact and fiction than later ones. Macpherson shared this view, presenting the twilight world of the Celtic bard. Chatterton, who in so many ways advanced on Macpherson, had sufficient faith in his historical-fictional powers to recreate culture of the fifteenth century.

Only two years after Dryden's comments were published, Sir Richard Blackmore began a series of epic poems, which, from their titles, would seem to fit the historical bill perfectly: *Prince Arthur* (1695), *King Arthur* (1697), and *Alfred* (1723). Dryden's influence here was very direct, for in the preface to the *Fables* (1700), Dryden accused Blackmore of stealing his ideas and having "the baseness not to acknowledge his benefactor."[11] Theft or no theft, Blackmore was not a proficient enough poet to abate the nationalist thirst. Pope still planned a Brutiad. In his review of modern poets who had used the "Domestica Facta" with skill, Joseph Warton in 1756 made no mention of Blackmore. Blackmore did transfer English history onto tedious imitations of Homer and Virgil, but the history was only the thinnest veneer. Blackmore's real purpose (again taking a lead from Dryden) was to replace classical by Christian "machinery." The prefaces to *Prince Arthur* and *Alfred* expounded this point at great length. The space Blackmore gave to historical fact was small:

an Epick Poem is and ought to be a Fiction; it is the essential Property that distinguishes it from a true History, that is a Narration of Matters of Fact in Verse, such as *Lucan's Pharsalia*; and therefore, tho' true

Incidents may sometimes be related, yet they are brought into the Poem only as probable, not as real Facts.[12]

The "real" was reduced to the "probable." Little wonder then that later writers and critics felt that native history had been given insufficient attention. Thankfully, Blackmore's formula for the epic was not unanimously agreed upon. The consensus was Aristotelian: history should serve as the basis of the fable. Any attempt to be more precise than this proved a problem. In particular, writers were awed by the possibility that there might be as much history in a poem as fiction. In 1738, Henry Pemberton summarized Aristotle's dilemma of blending history and fiction on the one hand, separating them on the other:

> Aristotle has determined the truth of a fact to be no objection against it being a just foundation for a poem. For though he distinguishes the office of historian and poet by the historian's being limited to the relation of real facts, but the poet confined only to the representation of what might happen, and that his story contain a series of consequences either probable or necessary; yet any real fact, as it partakes of these conditions, may be fit subject for a poet.[13]

We are back again with "real fact" as poetry's subject. It was shown in chapter 1 how slippery a concept was "historical fact." Even taking the simplest definition, that of events, writers and theorists were still worried by the idea of an invented narrative in which most of the events actually happened. The identity of the poet was under threat, in danger of being consumed by the historian. Blackmore again:

> If therefore the Performance is not cast into a Fable devis'd by the Writer, from which artful Contrivance the Poet originally derives his Name, it would by no means be an Epick Writing. If *Livy* or *Thucydides* were turn'd into Verse by the most excellent Pen, let the numbers be ever so musical, and the Diction ever so splendid and admirable, they would no more become Poems, than a News-paper would be dignify'd with that Title, tho related in the most correct and beautiful Numbers.[14]

Anyone familiar with chapter 9 of Aristotle's *Poetics* would know that the poet was a maker of plots, not verses. Aristotle said that Herodotus versified "would be no less a kind of history than it is without metre."[15] But neither Aristotle nor Blackmore were applying strict logic. If the poet was defined as a maker of plots, an inventor of stories, the result of the poet's rewriting history was not a simple recasting of prose into verse. By Aristotle's own rules, the poet's making of history must have involved an injection of imagination and invention into the narrative.

A counter to the view that the poet's powers must remain distinct from, rather than coalesce or blend with the historian's, was Welwood's, in the preface to Rowe's translation of *The Pharsalia* (1718). Welwood saw no problem in calling Lucan's epic "properly an historical heroic poem, because the subject is a known true history."[16] Welwood went on to laud the power of historical fact:

> Now with our late critics, truth is an unnecessary trifle for an epic poem, and ought to be thrown aside as a curb to invention . . . but, to my taste, a fact very extraordinary in its kind . . . does not strike the less strong, but leaves a more lasting impression on my mind, for being true.[17]

The literary power of history, particularly national history, was felt increasingly as the century progressed. Pope is known to have considered writing an epic based on the founding of Britain by Brutus.[18] Though it was mythical history, the story was an important national tradition. But it was Pope's critic Joseph Warton who best displayed the pressure for the fictional making of the national past. In the *Essay on the Writings and Genius of Pope* (1756), written only a few years before Ossian's appearance, Warton made a passionate plea

> that our writers would more frequently search for subjects, in the annals of England, which afford many striking and pathetic events . . . we have been too long attached to Grecian and Roman stories. In truth, the DOMESTICA FACTA, are more interesting, as well as more useful.[19]

Having referred several times to Milton's precedent, and also to Pope's project, and despite having advised the budding poet

> in the choice of a domestic story, however, much judgement and circumspection must be exerted, to select one of proper aera; neither of too ancient, or of too modern a date[20]

the fact that Milton and Pope delved into the very earliest times of British history led Warton to conclude:"A full scope might have been given to a vigorous imagination, to embellish a fiction drawn from the bosom of remotest antiquity."[21] It was almost as if Macpherson were listening. Still, Warton did say "fiction" and not fact. Regarding early history, fact and fiction were often seen as synonymous. The advantages of choosing a historical topic from a remote period applied to any epic. A pretense that real history was being used could be maintained easily, because no data were available to check the narrative's veracity. This line of reason-

ing came to a head in the preface to William Wilkie's *Epigoniad*, published
a few years before Warton's essay, in 1753. Macpherson surely knew this
work by his famous blind countryman, who along with Ossian earned
the prestigous title "Scottish Homer." Wilkie was a staunch defender of
the view that poetry and history, fiction and the facts of the past, were
irreconcilable. Except, that was, concerning remote antiquity. Yet that
fusion, as shall be seen, was a sham one.

For Wilkie, the function of epic poetry was to excite admiration in the
reader, and the heightened effects necessary to achieve this relied on
hyperbole. Hyperbole was undermined by the "just and natural dimensions" of history.[22] There was no compromise possible: history and
poetry must clash. There must be a victor and a vanquished:

> there is nothing which poets ought more carefully to avoid, than
> interfering with such regular and well vouched accounts of things as
> would effectively confute their fable, and make the meanest reader
> reject it with contempt.[23]

The example pitched upon was the *Pharsalia*. Welwood's "historical heroic poem" was for Wilkie a discordant jumble of historical facts with
"unnecessary descriptions and trifling digressions,"[24] which Wilkie believed Lucan had to include both to justify his standing as poet and to
preempt rejection of the history in the poem by those familiar with its
details. Lucan and all epic poets who had chosen verifiable history as
their theme had learnt the same lesson: "that the true and fictitious parts
of their work refuse to unite."[25] The forgeries were sophisticated attempts to achieve this fusion. In Wilkie's opinion, only tragedy could
justifiably do this, because its aim was sympathy and identification with
a character and therefore it did not require hyperbolic effects. Tragedy
"may well be raised from subjects that are strictly historical."[26] As we
shall see, historical tragedies did flourish in the eighteenth century.
Macpherson's historical vision was shaped along tragic lines: loss, grief,
and decay. Wilkie's description of the historical complexion of tragedy
was important. The genre

> may be strictly historical without losing any real advantages, and
> attain its full perfection without the assistance of fable. I believe it will
> be easily allowed, that where truth and fiction are equally subservient
> to the purposes of poetry, the first ought always to be preferred; for
> true history carries a weight and authority with it, which seldom
> attend stories that are merely fictitious.[27]

Welwood described the epic along these lines. But for Wilkie, only
traditional history could become ascendant. Tradition consisted of all

those stories and myths from remote antiquity that were unverifiable. The history Wilkie recommended was actually fake history, having history's appearance, but no authenticity. Thus Homer could "feign" his facts at will:

> Homer, as he exceeds all other poets in merit, has likewise the advantage of them in point of good fortune; the condition of the age in which he wrote gave him an opportunity of celebrating, in his poems, events, which though they were in his days of no great antiquity, and consequently the more interesting, yet had fallen, through the want of authentic records, into so happy a degree of obscurity, that he was at full liberty to feign concerning them what he pleased, without any danger of confutation. This is an advantage which succeeding poets could not boast of; and therefore have found themselves under a necessity, either of taking their subjects from remote antiquity, as I have done, or, (which in my opinion, is worse) of attempting to mix fable with true history, which never can be done with success.[28]

Tradition, Wilkie insisted, was a mutant form of history, made of "stories which are already in some measure believed."[29] Tradition was folk history. So in order to be received into the hearts and minds of a nation, all poets

> as would have their fictions favourably received, must lay it down as a rule, to accommodate what they feign to established prejudices, and build upon stories which are already in some measure believed.[30]

Macpherson certainly did this, but the essential impulse behind the forgeries flowed back towards history instead of away from it. Fiction allowed the enhancement and exploration of the past and the processes of history. Compare the following two remarks. The first is Wilkie's conclusion. The second is Hugh Blair commenting on Ossian, written in 1763. Wilkie leaves history behind. Blair returns to it:

> Tradition is the best ground upon which fable can be built, not only because it gives the appearance of reality to things that are merely fictitious, but because it supplies a poet with the most proper materials, for his invention to work upon..[31]

> Aristotle means no more than that it is the business of a poet not to be a mere annalist of Facts, but to embellish truth with beautiful, probable, and useful fictions. . . . that Ossian has followed this course, and building upon true history, has sufficiently adorned it with poetical fiction for aggrandising his characters and facts, will not, I believe, be questioned by most readers. At the same time, the foundation which those facts and characters had in truth, and the share which the poet

himself had in the transactions which he records, must be considered as no small advantage to his work. For truth makes an impression on the mind far beyond any fiction.[32]

Blair's remarks from "at the same time" onwards indicate the special status of the forgeries. Macpherson and Chatterton did not patronize the past. Rather, they complemented it.

The "Historicist" School of Criticism

Wilkie's comment that Homer was fortunate to live when he did was an example of "historicist" criticism, a popular viewpoint that held that a writer could only be fully understood in relation to the age. As Pope put it in the *Essay on Criticism*:

> Know well each ANCIENT'S proper *Character*,
> His *Fable, Subject, Scope* in ev'ry Page,
> *Religion, Country, Genius* of his *Age;*
> Without all these at once before your Eyes,
> *Cavil* you may, but never *Criticize*.[33]
>
> (ll. 118–23)

This critical approach achieved fruition with two studies on Homer by Blackwell and Wood (*An Enquiry into the Life and Writings of Homer* (1735) and *An Essay on the Original Genius of Homer* (1769)) and with Johnson's notes to Shakespeare (1765). Historicism also spurred on the view that the writer was the product of the forces of his age, making literature and history interdependent. One result of this liaison was often to bolster the historical veracity and therefore the value of the work in question: to make it yield up its history, especially as embodied in the writer's own experience. Thus Blackwell argued about Homer:

> The Manners used in the *Trojan* Times were not disused in his own: The same way of living in private, and the same Pursuits in publick were still prevalent, and gave him a Model for his Design, which wou'd not allow him to exceed the Truth in his Draught. . . . IN SHORT, it may be said of *Homer,* and of every *Poet* who has wrote well, That *what* he felt and saw, *that* he described.[34]

Chapter 1 showed how great was the demand for sensory data of the past. Blackwell's notion of the ancient poet experiencing the past in his present could well describe Ossian (Blackwell was one of Macpherson's tutors at Aberdeen University). Macpherson also exploited the dubious logic of the historicist position. The supposedly extraneous historical information that acted as evidence for proving what the writer was doing was often gleaned from the text. The historicist view also clashed with those who believed literature yielded historical information about its own times. Pope and Johnson called Homer and Shakespeare the "mirrors" of their age. That "mirror" did not have to be made externally and held up to the text—the principle of historicism. The two approaches were often combined, historical knowledge of a period being used to indicate or, more importantly, authenticate the history that the text was itself supposed to generate. In the passage just cited, Blackwell's aim was to authenticate the historical value of Homer's writings. That quality made Homer a good poet. The value judgement must have been a great boost for Macpherson. Ossian presented the Homeric situation of the ancient bard whose poetry was made out of "what he felt and saw."

British Historical Drama

To Night our Author tells an English Story,
And brings your Ancestors to Life before ye.
Aaron Hill, Elfrid (1710)

Many historical dramas written in the eighteenth century took their subject matter from British history. Content is more important than form here, for there was no visible worry among dramatists about their method: their mode of access to the past, the way the past is made. There were a few exceptions, but in the main, history was a "given." Perhaps the great precedent of Shakespeare's history plays had something to do with this complacency. Several of Chatterton's fake authors produced historical dramas: the major ones are Rowley's *Aella* and *Godwynn*. Though these plays gained their uniqueness from their position and function within the forgery as a whole, one striking result of a reading of historical dramas of the eighteenth century is a realization of how conventional in their plots Rowley's plays are—even down to the customary attempted rape in *Aella*. It is likely then that Chatterton had read or seen some of the following plays. We can also expect that Macpherson knew at least those popular plays of the 1750s with Scottish themes: Home's *Douglas* (1756) and Mason's *Caractacus* (1759).

The dominant tone of the following dramas was nationalism. The royal and aristocratic heroes embodied the supposed virtues of Britain: courage, liberty, independent spirit. These plays were a mild response to the need to use indigenous history more attentively. All the plays used standardized melodramatic plots, a format that may have rubbed off on Macpherson. He, however, used such plots with great skill to explore historical points of view. A reflexive concern about history was not to be found in these plays. Few of them date their action, one indication that history was not the primary issue.

This lack of what we might term historiographical integrity was demonstrated by Dryden's preliminary remarks to *King Arthur* (1691). Several years earlier, in *Edgar* (1678), Thomas Rhymer had made a weak attempt to authenticate his plot: "The Histories examined, nothing in the Fable can seem Romantick or affected."[35] Dryden could not even maintain this posture:

> I employ'd some reading about it, to inform myself out of *Beda*, *Bochartus*, and other Authors, concerning the Rites and Customs of the Heathen Saxons; as I also used the little Skill I have in Poetry to adorn it. But not to offend the present Times, nor a Government which has protected me, I have been oblig'd so much to alter the first Design . . .[36]

King Arthur was actually a masque ("Dramatick Opera"), replete with machinery. But Dryden's remarks did show how far back in British history dramatists were prepared to delve, paralleling Milton's proposals in the Trinity MS. Periods as distant as Roman Britain furnished several plays before 1760.

Two plays by John Bancroft, published in the last decade of the seventeenth century, dealt with a theme Chatterton warmed to: the inability of the king to fulfil his role and duty. The heroes of *King Edward the Third* (1691) and *Henry the Second* (1693) were the king's advisers:

> delivering the Country from the Tyranny and Oppression it had long been afflicted with, and which in all probability threatened the total overthrow of the Establish'd Liberties of the Subject.[37]

A popular theme in the years following the Glorious Revolution. There was an obvious celebration of contemporary events: "Here English-Men with Pleasure may behold, / How much their Liberties were priz'd of old."[38] Not that such a celebration automatically made for shallow historical drama. In these plays, though, it seemed to.

Charles Hopkin's *Boadicea* (1697) was the first of several plays set in Roman Britain. There was some trumpery concerning sacrifices in a Druid temple, but Boadicea herself was rarely on stage, and the focus of the play was summed up in an apostrophe made by one of the Romans:

> Love, what a God art thou? no power Divine
> Enjoys an Empire uncontroll'd like thine,
> O're Land, and Seas, extends thy boundless sway,
> And Kings on Earth, and Gods in Heav'n Obey.[39]

Again, the dominance of a love plot need not extinguish serious historical interest. But in these plays it did. One craves for the historical astuteness of a Shakespeare. In *Antony and Cleopatra,* for instance, Octavius's short statement, "The time of universal peace is near" is a devastating historical perspective on the play's action.[40] The feeling that arises from these eighteenth-century dramas is that history was synonymous with unbridled and often barbarous passions: "fierce wars and loves" often culminating in a rape or attempted rape of a captive maiden (in *Boadicea,* for instance, the princess Camilla is raped). The motif was glaringly apparent in the title of Charles Gildon's *Love's Victim; Or, the Queen of Wales* (1701). Despite the author's claim to have been presenting "Domestic Virtue,"[41] one is hard pushed to find any. The queen is saved twice from rape by the arch-Druid, who commands great authority. Neither the Druid nor his shadow the bard receive any serious imaginative treatment in these dramas. Temples and sequestered oak groves abounded as props, but the denizens remained cardboard.

Nicholas Rowe's *The Royal Convert* (1708) was set in a period that had great potential: "about Twenty Years after the first Invasion of *Britain* by the Saxons,"[42] a period of turbulence and cultural conflict. The pagan-Christian interface was used by Macpherson with subtle skill. But any historical potential in Rowe's play was quickly stultified by the amorous escapades and usual paraphernalia of capture, escape, recapture, and the finale of multiple deaths. The triumph of Christianity was serendipitous. Nor did Mrs. Manley fare any better in *Lucius, the First Christian King of Britain* (1717). The play was undoubtedly influenced by *The Royal Convert,* and the plot followed similar lines. Lucius turned Christian to win the heart of the Queen of Aquitaine. Realistic, perhaps, but the entire role of the new religion in society was realized in terms of this romance. If Lucius succeeded in his amours, the Christian history of Britain effortlessly began. Few of these plays made a real effort to get inside history, being content rather to use it as a backcloth. In the prologue to *Elfrid; or, the Fair Inconstant* (1710), Aaron Hill announced "To night our Author tells an English Story, / And brings your Ancestors to Life before ye." The reference, however, was simply to drama's being a live medium. As works of historical fiction, these plays remained torpid.

One exception, before the work of Home and Mason in the 1750s, was Ambrose Philips' *The Briton* (1722). In the middle of the play, the British hero Vanoc and the Roman tribune Valens have a heated and protracted discussion of the rights and wrongs, benefits and drawbacks, of the Roman occupation of Britain. This incorporation of historical speculation may have been crudely done, a scissors-and-paste job, but the debate is serious:

Val. Did not the Romans civilize you?
Van. No!
    They brought new Customs, and new Vices over;
    Taught us more Arts, than honest Men require;
    And gave us Wants, that Nature never gave.
Val. We found you naked—
Van. And you found us free![43]

This attempt at giving history a dramatic immediacy was still very lame when compared to the forgeries.

Two years after the publication of *The Briton*, George Jeffreys announced in the prologue to *Edwin* (1724) "With Justice may we boast, in former Times, / Heroes and Bards, the Product of the Climes." Yet no bards appeared. By 1730, we find Henry Fielding burlesquing the dramatic presentation of native heroism:

> Britons, awake!—Let Greece and Rome no more
> Their heroes send to our Heroick Shore.
> Let home-bred Subjects grace the Modern Muse,
> And Grub-Street from her Self, her Heroes chuse:
> Her Story-Books Immortalise in Fame,
> Hickathrift, Jack the Giant-Killer, and Tom Tam.[44]

These lines are from the prologue to *Tom Thumb*. The cast featured King Arthur, who had the dubious honor only of being the last to fall in the parodic mayhem at the end. Fielding was not saying that native heroism was a worn-out literary subject. Rather that the formula—mainly the love plot—had become too trivializing. A change was needed. Fielding's satirical option was for folk and mythical history. That option was taken up seriously by Robert Dodsley in his prose plays *The King and the Miller of Mansfield* (1737), its sequel *Sir John Cockle at Court* (1738), and *The Blind Beggar of Bethnal Green* (1741). The setting was the never-never land of fairy tale and moral fable, which was precisely what the plays were, replete with *ipse dixit*, such as "If so happy a Miller, then who'd be a King"[45] and "he that acts greatly, is the true Great Man."[46]

The other option taken by some dramatists was more seminal. This was to inject the formula with a new artistic seriousness, not destroy it altogether. James Thomson's excursions into historical drama, *Edward and Eleanora* (1739) and *Alfred. A Masque* (co-written with David Mallet, 1740), advanced little on the established pattern. It was in the plays of William Mason and John Home that a new tone entered. Mason's *Elfrida* (1751–52) and *Caractacus* (1759), and Home's *Douglas* (1756), exploited the idea of eschatology, of an historical period and its heroism coming to an end. Historical and literary factors contributed to this innovation: the situation of Scotland after the abortive rebellion against the English in 1745 (both *Douglas* and *Caractacus* are set in the north) where a whole culture was rapidly disappearing; and the attempt to heighten pathos using this essentially epic device of historical catastrophe. Another impulse, and one that was left to Macpherson to consolidate, was to create a period in the past identified or characterized by its own history. When a family, culture, or nation feels itself to be in decline, the experiences of its past are likely to become an obsessive concern. History, to those concerned, is of paramount importance.

Mason's *Elfrida* (1752) reworked the story first dramatized by Aaron Hill in *Elfrid* (1710). But dark clouds had now gathered. Characters in the play tend to look backward. The smooth continuity to the future of the earlier plays was disrupted. Elfrida says to the chorus

> Meanwhile, my friends,
> Tune some harmonious lay. . . .
> Ye have been nurs'd amid yon Cambrian rocks,
> Where yet Posterity retains some vein
> Of that old minstrelsy, which whilom breath'd
> Thro' each time-honor'd grove of British oaks.[47]

There was here a regression to earlier times, and the transmitter was "that old minstrelsy"—the bards. They were now on the brink of extinction. The hero Athelwold was in similar danger. He too looked back:

> ye aged Oaks,
> Ye venerable Fathers of this wood,
> Who oft have cool'd beneath your arching shades
> My humble ancestors, oft seen them hie
> To your spread umbrage, from yon sultry field,
> The scenes of their honest labor. Shade, ah! shade,
> The last, the wretchedest of all their race.[48]

Major imaginative features of Macpherson's historical vision were present here: eschatology, regression, and recuperation of the past by the solitary hero. Home's *Douglas* (1756) was more sombre than *Elfrid*. The play opened with Douglas, a medieval border earl, supposedly seven years dead. Amorous goings-on were kept to a minimum. The earl returns in disguise. He is, like Athelwold, the last of his line, and the tension in the play is generated by the fragility of his position. Douglas eventually dies in a duel, and this "second" death signals the demise of his clan. The titular hero of Mason's *Caractacus,* published on the eve of Ossian in 1759, did very little to redeem his diminished status. He flees the Romans to seek sanctuary with the Druids, but their hallowed groves are only a temporary refuge. Mason cleverly combined two catastrophes: the king's (who is "last of the Britons")[49] and the Druids.' When the Romans capture Caractacus, they burn down the groves (probably the most famous incident concerning the Druids in Latin historiography). Mason recuperated the period of "old minstrelsy" invoked by Elfrida, but only to show it in decline. The play also had footnotes ("Illustrations"). Most of them cited classical sources for the plot, a standard method of authentication. Other notes were glosses. Some of these had the resourcefulness of the forgeries. The gloss on "Behold yon huge / And unknown sphere of living adamant," for instance, was

> This is meant to describe the rocking stone, of which there are several still to be seen in Wales, Cornwall and Derbyshire. They are universally supposed, by antiquarians, to be Druid monuments.[50]

An imaginary object was transformed, supposedly, into an extant relic.

In 1759, John Home met James Macpherson at Moffat. Macpherson was encouraged to produce one of the Gallic poems he claimed he had recovered from the Highlands. Ossian was born. Home may well have influenced the forger in literature and in real life.

The Novel

> the innocent fraud. . . .
>
> Bolingbroke, *Letters on the Study and Use of History* (1752)

> that little Art [Defoe] is truly master of, of forging a Story, and imposing it on the World for Truth. . . .
>
> *Read's Journal*, Nov 1, 1718

The eighteenth-century novel was a genre very obviously connected with history writing. The word "history" occurred in the title of most novels of the time, and by the 1760s, Hugh Blair had coined the label "fictitious histories" for the proliferating genre.[51] "History" here meant "life"—biography or autobiography—while retaining the connotation of "story" or narrative. In *Tom Jones*, Fielding posed as a biographer and an omniscient chronicler of events. This association between the eighteenth-century novel and history is usually regarded as a defensive posture, forced on the novelist because of the newness and untested nature of the form. Thus the pretense to factuality claimed by almost all novelists in this period is seen as a transparent device under which to cloak the fiction: in Bolingbroke's words an "innocent fraud."[52] The stance supposedly reflected the insecurity of the novelist, the inability to admit in public that all was invention. Anthony Burgess remarks on the "editor's" claim that *Robinson Crusoe* was "a just history of fact": "Defoe keeps a straight face, but everybody knows it is a novel."[53] The authenticating "apparatus" may often have been lightweight. But one should be careful not to be too dismissive. The interaction between the eighteenth-century novel and historiography could be very dynamic. Most novels appeared as documents: journals, memoirs, letters. The new authority of the MS was borrowed. Moreover, the content of the feigned MS could also be historical. The relevant novelist again was Defoe. He was a historical novelist of great skill. Anthony Burgess' comment does not reflect contemporary and modern reactions to some of Defoe's novels. As Ian Watt says:

> *Robinson Crusoe* itself was widely regarded as authentic at the time of publication, and it is still not certain to what extent some of Defoe's works, such as the *Memoirs of a Cavalier,* are fictitious or genuine.[54]

Memoirs of a Cavalier was indeed regarded by many as genuine for a good number of years. Not everyone knew it was a novel. Yet Burgess' description of a conventionalized game of bluff cannot be ignored. None other than Samuel Richardson took this position. When Warburton wished to prefix to *Clarissa* a declaration that the whole work was fiction, Richardson took offence. He wished "to avoid hurting that kind of Historical Faith which Fiction itself is generally read with, tho' we know it to be Fiction."[55]

Despite posing as history, eighteenth-century novels were ultimately limited by literary convention. The forgeries may have shared certain aims with novelists and poets. But in their zeal to get close to the past, the forgers were led to break conventions. Defoe came closest to this innovation, and to being the literary antecedent of Macpherson and Chatterton.

By 1718, *Read's Journal* had already earmarked Defoe's abilities, praising "that little Art he is truly Master of, of forging a Story, and imposing it on the World for Truth."[56] The terms used were revealing. One has to be careful, however, not to be led away into that treacherous region that regards all fiction as forgery. A distinction can be made between "forging a Story" and forging history, between the general authenticating desire to give a fiction verisimilitude and the authentication of the past. The latter does not exclude the former, but other devices are likely to be brought into play when the novelist wishes to violate the factual territory of history. Authentication becomes an epistemological concern. That, at least, was the situation before Scott. A self-consciousness about the nature of fiction was present in many eighteenth-century novels, particularly *Tristram Shandy*, and this was the legacy of *Don Quixote*. Sometimes this reflexiveness was manifested in terms of forgery. For instance, there was a playing around with hoaxes, imposters, charlatans, and disguises in *Peregrine Pickle* (1751). There was the inclusion of forged letters in *Clarissa* (1747). These possibly wry glances at the fiction-forgery idea had a Homeric precedent. In the *Odyssey*, the hero relishes lies and deception. The fantastical parts of the narrative are all narrated by him. When he returns to Ithaca, he dons a disguise. The forging of the past, then, needs to be seen as one orientation of the general fabrication of fiction. It is easy to see why N. M. Penzer's *Library of Impostors* (1926) folded after only two volumes. Penzer tried to limit himself to eighteenth-century fake travel literature, being only concerned with "the literary impostor—the man who wrote of places that he had never seen, of lands which existed in his imagination, or of countries as yet unexplored."[57] By these rules, many novels would be forgeries. One of the two texts chosen was a famous forgery: George Psalmanazar's *An Historical and Geographical Description of Formosa* (1704). The book was in fact a spurious memoir and geography text book. The other text chosen was a narrative: *The Life and Astonishing Adventures of John Daniel* (1751). This novel was no different in form from the many other fake travelogues of the time, such as *Robinson Crusoe* and *Gulliver's Travels*. Penzer's definition of forgery was too inclusive, and that is why I suspect the series folded.

Read's Journal was right to identify Defoe with forgery. He himself called fiction an "honest cheat."[58] The prefaces to his novels revealed much more than the "this story is true" bravado dismissed by Antony Burgess. The "editor" of *Moll Flanders* admitted that he had altered both the language and content of Moll's memoirs. What we read is not Moll's account, but a counterfeit, the editor's reworking:

> It is true that the original of this story is put into new words, and the style of the famous lady we hear speak of is a little altered; particularly she is *made* to tell her own tale in modester words than what she told it at first. . . . the pen employed in finishing her story, and *making* it what you now see it to be, has had no difficulty to put it into a dress fit to be seen, and to *make* it speak language fit to be read. . . . To this purpose some of the vicious parts of her life . . . quite left out, and several other parts very much shortened.[59]

Italics have been added to emphasize the connection between "making" and forging. *Roxana* (1724) was also a counterfeit. This time the editor apologized for "dressing up the Story in worse Cloaths than the Lady, whose Words he speaks."[60] A break with convention was claimed, which may however seem conventional. The story differs from most of the Modern Performances of this Kind . . . in this Great and Essential Article, Namely, That the Foundation of This is laid in Truth of Fact; and so the Work is not a Story, but a History.[61]

The authentication of this claim was based on the authority of sensory experience. The editor-writer became a transmitter:

> The Writer says, He was particularly acquainted with this Lady's first Husband, the Brewer, and with his Father; and also, with his Bad Circumstances; and knows that first Part of the Story to be Truth.
>
> This may, he hopes, be a Pledge for the Credit of the rest, tho' the Latter Part of her History lay Abroad, and cou'd not so well be vouch'd as the First; yet, as she has told it herself, we have the less Reason to question the Truth of that Part also.[62]

The conclusion was dubious. Personal reporting did not mean automatic factual veracity. Chapter 1 showed that there was a tendency to conflate the two: sensory data are the most authentic kinds of information. In fictional terms, Defoe combined two levels of authentication: the general one of verisimilitude, and the specifically historical one that what is presented to us is a record of the past. His aim was primarily to achieve the former: to convince the reader that nothing in the text was unbelievable. The other aim—to confirm that Roxana herself related the tale, that the narrative had an authentic teller—was more complex, and may in fact have clashed with the first aim. Ignorance, imprecision, and exaggeration may all be defining characteristics of a genuine memoir. Ossian was full of ghosts and phantoms. In *Roxana*, this level of authentication remained dormant. In the two novels properly "historical"—*Memoirs of a Cavalier* and *A Journal of the Plague Year* (1722)—Defoe pushed much further the possibilities and consequences of the narrator being read. Defoe satisfied many of the conditions of the new spirit of authentication in historiography. In other words, his historical fiction had historical value.

Defoe answered Locke's plea for more "first originals" of history. The first response was *Memoirs of a Cavalier* (1720), subtitled "a Military Journal of the Wars in Germany and the Wars in England from the Year 1632, to the Year 1648. Written Threescore Years ago by an English Gentleman," (the predating is similar to the subtitle of Scott's *Waverley*). Note the Humean gradation: the MS was made circa 1660, and itself was backward-looking. The displacement was crucial. The demand for "original" experience of history, it can be concluded, was greater than the demand for national history to be used by the modern writer. Defoe and the forgers confected the former, while actually indulging in the latter. The preface to *Cavalier* gave an elaborate account of how the MS has come to be in the editor's hands, including the citing of a memorandum by a previous owner. The really important material in the preface, however, was that relating to the method and value of historical fiction. In *Cavalier*, Defoe assumed a polemical stance, claiming the book to be: "a Confutation of many Errors in all the Writers upon the Subject of our Wars in England, and even in that extraordinary History written by the Earl of Clarendon."[63] Nor was the stance a mere counterfeiting of historians' rhetoric. I believe that historical fiction, the imaginative writer's power of recreation, was being pitted against orthodox history writing, especially as represented by the official received version of history. Historical fiction could, because of its ability to weave in and out of the recorded facts, explore and enhance them, set them in new, possibly subversive, perspectives, ultimately say something valuable about the making of the past; history as process. All this was happening below the surface, of course. The preface pointed out that the revisions to historical knowledge were not draconian: "almost all the Facts, especially those of Moment, are confirmed for their Part by all the Writers of those Times."[64] Defoe cleverly authenticated the hybrid form of historical fiction. The true history was authenticated by the established sources from which it had been taken. Where the narrative departed from the sources was precisely where the fiction was supposedly validated—as being, paradoxically, "factual" revision: new light on the past. Any imaginative writer wishing to take on an historical topic had, unless employing memory only, to read up on sources. The need to write imaginatively was to enhance, explore, or improve upon this primary information. That is, if the intention was not simply to use history as a backcloth.[65] The belief that modern historical fiction could improve on orthodox historiography in its portrayal of life in the past was established in the years after the forgeries, as is shown in chapter 6.

In *Cavalier*, the source material and the fiction remained largely separate. The cavalier had two voices: the autobiographer and the well-read, omniscient historian. It was the former identity that was supposed to give the soldier the right to refute previous historians. Empirical data were incontestable. For instance:

> I am the more particular in this Relation, having been an Eye-Witness of the Action, because the King was reproached in all the publick Libels, with which those Times abounded, for having put a great many to death, and hanged the Committee of the Parliament, and some *Scots*, in Cold Blood, which was a notorious Forgery.[66]

The blending of the soldier's imagined experience with real historical events was all rather too easy when it did occur. He consistently rubbed shoulders with the great, becoming a favorite of Gustavus Adolphus and the adviser to Prince Rupert. *Cavalier* was really a brief soldier's memoir, with overgenerous slices of royalist political history writing scissors-and-pasted into it.

Defoe refined his skills two years later in *A Journal of the Plague Year* (1722). By restricting the historical topic to only one year (1665), Defoe gave himself an opportunity for detailed exploration of the past. His aim was to make the past from the inside. *Plague Year* consisted of "observations or memorials . . . written by a Citizen who continued all the while in London."[67] Defoe was presenting a first-hand account of this momentous event. The narrator "H.F." was also a self-conscious historian, who investigated the transmission of information and its authentication. He used authenticating devices, citing statistics and documents such as bills of mortality. He even copied out a proclamation.[68] These MSS-in-MS appeared with great sophistication in Chatterton's forgery. There were also footnotes. Most of these glossed allusions or explained obscurities in the narrative. Some, however, gave historical data, such as a note on the city of Westminster: "A sort of enclave of the metropolis in which the king's writ did not run."[69] Hindsight was skillfully applied. In only the second paragraph, H.F. noted "We had no such thing as printed newspapers in those days . . . such things as were gathered [were] handed about by word of mouth only."[70] By defining his period at the outset as pre-newspapers, H.F. both drew in an authenticating perspective and enhanced further the value of eyewitness reports such as his own.

H.F. quoted statistics, but he did not always trust them. In fact, he believed that in the early days of the epidemic, the numbers of those dying of the plague was kept deliberately low to prevent panic. This policy he called "knavery" and "fraud."[71] Based on direct experience and the reports of others, he pitted "our received opinion"[72] against official sources. But H.F. was aware that "received opinion" could also be suspect. His own experience was inviolable, but not so those of others. In the main, a Humean "graduation" of oral transmission was to be trusted:

> I could give a great many such stories as these, diverting enough, which in the long course of that dismal year I met with—that is, heard of—and which are very certain to be true; or very near the truth; that is to say, true in the general: for no man at the time could learn all the particulars.[73]

Some reports however were "more of tale than of truth."[74] In other words, those reports were a historical fiction within the historical fiction. The investigation into what constituted a fact reached its climax in a debate about infection. H.F. noted physicians' wrangles over the cause of the "seeming propensity or a wicked inclination in those that were infected to infect others."[75] H.F.'s own views were striking. Instead of taking sides in the debate, he refuted the very source of the debate:

But I choose to give this grave debate a quite different turn, and answer it or resolve it all by saying that I do not grant the fact. On the contrary, I say that the thing is not really so.[76]

This was genuine radicalism. Deliberate infection, said H.F., never actually occurred. H.F.'s premise was that a fact *is* its reportage—the truth and its transmission are inseparable. The forgeries also were written from this premise: their great concern was authentication. H.F. looked at how the information the physicians wrangled over was made:

the thing is not really so, but that it was a general complaint raised by the people inhabiting the outlying villages against the citizens to justify, or at least excuse, those hardships and severities so much talked of, and in which both sides may be said to have injured one another . . . neither of which were really true—that is to say, in the colours they were described in.[77]

Other features of *Plague Year* anticipated the forgeries. Defoe almost matched Chatterton's detailed evocation of the social history of a city in the past: "the real condition of the people."[78] The two writers also shared a celebration of civic administration. The mayor and his aldermen were the heroes of *Plague Year,* as William Canynge was the hero of Chatterton's medieval Bristol:

everything was managed with so much care, and such excellent order was observed in the whole city and suburbs by the care of the Lord Mayor and aldermen and by the justices of the peace, church wardens, &c., in the outparts, that London may be a pattern to all the cities in the world for the good government and the excellent order.[79]

I shall have frequent occasion to speak of the prudence of the magistrates, their charity, their vigilance for the poor. . . .[80]

Defoe could not resist including some wry glances at imposture. Early in the epidemic, London was invaded by fake astrologers and quacks bearing "specious titles."[81] The most overtly fictional digression in the book, the tale of the three tradesmen who escaped to found a commune in outlying woods, involved much deception, "little fraud" and "sham" by the protagonists.[82]

Compared with the forgeries, *Plague Year* was still limited by its narrative convention, however. History was made from the inside, but the making was still retrospective, a narration in the past tense. The achievement of the forgeries was to regress a step further back to that truly "original" point where history was first made. H.F. was a voice of the present making the past. Ossian was a voice of the past making his present and past. The rendering of the spontaneous past by the forgers was a major triumph. H.F. noted that in his periods of rest during the epidemic he would be found "employed in reading books and in writing down my memorandums of what had occurred to me every day, and out of which afterwards I took most of this work."[83] The forgeries recovered that initial condition of "writing down": the white-hot experience. The first making, not the second. The original, ancient artefact, rather than the modern imitation. The demand for a historical relic was greater than that for a modern confection.

Poetry

O History, whose pregnant mines impart
Unfailing treasures to poetic art
William Hayley, *An Essay on History* (1780)

It is surprising that so few eighteenth-century poems before Ossian used national history with any degree of artistic depth. Often history appeared as mere statement, history-in-verse. The exceptions, notably poems by Gray and Collins, stand out all the more clearly. There were also anthologies of earlier verse, which are dealt with in chapter 4. One poem that can be given attention here, however, is "The Death Song of Ragnar Lodbrog." Sir William Temple first translated two stanzas of this Nordic poem in his essay "Of Heroic Virtue" (1690) and throughout the next century the poem was popular.[84] The poem is a monologue. The dramatic situation is of a captive warrior who, "being mortally stung by a Viper, before the Venom had reach'd his Vitals, broke out into the following Verses."[85] Here was the spontaneous voice of the past on the brink of extinction—the situation of Ossian. The death song was a traditional genre, but this skaldic fragment exerted a peculiar power by its being a fragment of ancient northern culture. Gray's *The Bard* was obviously influenced by "Ragnar Lodbrog," and Macpherson was probably influenced by both poems.

Leaving "ancients" for "moderns," the most common use of national history by eighteenth-century poets up to 1760 was as a rhetorical tool in an argument. Even then the mode of access to the past was usually heavily filtered by literary convention. Take Thomson's portrayal of early Britain in *Spring*:[86]

This to the poets gave the Golden Age:
When, as they sung in allegoric phrase,
The sailor pine had not the nations yet
In commerce mixed; for every country teemed
With every thing. . . .

(ll. 271–75)

Thomson foregrounded the literary filter (in this case Ovid's *Meta-morphoses*), then presented his own version of a national paradise. Primitivism was used to attack imperial smugness about the "civilizing" value of conquest and commerce. That history had become pure rhetoric was demonstrated very clearly when later in *The Seasons* Thomson reversed his position. In *Summer,* the ambrosial early culture became the Hobbesian state of nature. The early Briton was now "a savage, roaming through the woods and wilds/In quest of prey" (ll. 1759–60).[87] Thomson adopted a progressivist view, justifying the rise of the empire. Thomson's manner of making the past was summed up by the lines

The sage historic muse
Should next conduct us through the deeps of time.

(*Winter,* ll 587–88)[88]

The forgeries broke out of this artifice. The "historic muse" became the voice of the past or the MS. Ossian's world was a golden age only because he made it so.

Thomson's portrait of the British bard in *The Castle of Indolence* (1748) was also effete. He was "a Druid little wight, of withered aspect" and carried a "British harp."[89] He was not a historian. The essential feature of his verse was its "heavenly fire."[90] Even Gray's bard was not a historian but a prophet. There were few poems before 1760 that showed a serious historical concern. Pope's *Eloisa to Abelard* (1717), for instance, presented a voice from the past, but Pope's concern was not seriously with medieval history or with the poem as a possible historical document, a real letter from the past. Gray and Collins produced the seminal poems: Collins's *Persian Eclogues* (1742) and *An Ode on the Popular Superstitions of the Highlands of Scotland* (1749, publ. 1788), and Gray's *The Bard* (1757). Gray's short Norse odes were written after 1760 and so will be looked at in chapter 5. These odes could easily have been inspired by Macpherson's *Fragments,* bearing in mind Gray's enthusiastic reception of that work.[91]

The *Persian Eclogues* were not of course about British history. But they were important for several reasons. Collins pretended to be translating old MSS. The historical packaging was admittedly lightweight. The poems were said to have been completed in "the Beginning of *Sha Sultan*

Hosseyn's Reign."[92] It is hard to believe many readers would have taken this seriously. Yet the last of the four eclogues did make an interesting use of history. The scheme, significantly, was eschatalogical: two swains flee from the marauding Tartars. The pastoral paradise, an historical era, was being obliterated. The eschatological effect was peculiarly authenticated by the fact that this was the final eclogue. Collins anticipated a technique Macpherson used with great skill.

A fascination with cultural extinction was the dominant tone in historical literature of the decade or so before Ossian. This literature was also consistently the most interesting in its treatment of history. Collins' swains managed to survive the desolation of their world. When Gray chose a similar situation for *The Bard*, survival was only for the duration of the poem. The bard speaks and then commits suicide. The abyss he plummits into at the end of the poem is, symbolically, historical. Bardism is at an end. Edward I's intention has been fulfilled.[93] The dramatic situation in *The Bard* almost certainly influenced Macpherson. Yet the bard's speech, the voice of the past, was optimistic. The Tudors were seen to restore Welsh culture. The abyss was bridged by his prophecy. The Fall (enacted literally by the bard) was therefore used to justify the glory of later history. *The Bard* is referred to again in the next chapter, where the differences in technique and historical outlook between it and Ossian are highlighted. Regardless of whether or not Gray's bard was a historian, *The Bard* was the first poem to celebrate the ancient bard strongly and effectively. The bard is the dominating presence, high above Edward and his cowering myrmidons, plunging to their level only in suicide. Though most of the poem was the bard's speech, there was still a framework of modern narration, which provided "outside" views ("haggard eyes," "hoary hair"). Gray's poem was avowedly modern.

It is likely Macpherson knew *The Bard*. If he had read Collins' *An Ode on the Popular Superstitions of the Highlands of Scotland, Considered as the Subject for Poetry* (1749), it must have been in MS, for the poem was not published till 1788. This poem has been left till last, because it was specifically about adapting Scottish history to poetry, and it was an encouragement for such poetry.

A measure of the poem's effectiveness can be seen in that it inspired John Home (to whom it is addressed) to write *Douglas*. Collins' message was clear:

> Proceed, in forceful sounds and colours bold
> The native legends of the land rehearse;—
> To such adapt thy lyre and suit thy powerful verse.
>
> (ll. 185–87)[94]

Collins' Scotland was primarily the outsider's Scotland, full of dark, stirring legends and powerful myths, which "Tis thine to sing" (l. 53). Much of the Scottish history available to the poet was of "Fancy's land" (l. 9), inhabited by "airy minstrels" (l. 15), a "wizzard seer" (l. 54) and "gliding ghosts" (l. 60)—the last are part of Ossian's world. But there were other historical figures in the landscape:

> At ev'ry pause, before thy mind possest,
> Old RUNIC bards shall seem to rise around
>
> (ll. 41–42)

For Macpherson, there was no "seeming." Scottish history not only became the "subject for poetry": it became the poetry.

Pat Rogers remarked of Gray and Collins in *The Augustan Vision* (1974) "again and again we find the poet writing about ancient bards, rather than investing his own work with bardic qualities."[95] Rogers did not take Ossian into account.

Macpherson responded to the plea that national history be more seriously used by poets. His response was at one remove. That is, he responded even more strongly to historiographical demands for ancient MSS, bardic history, and sensory data of the past. It is in this light that his "forgery" should be seen: as an imaginative making of history by the past itself, a recuperation of the "first original." Mapherson invented Ossian to enable him to explore the literary making of history at its most authentic point: its source. This act of forgery created a unique form of historical fiction.

3

Ossian: The Voice of the Past

To understand fully Macpherson's making of history, it is necessary to look at his forgery as it evolved. Like Chatterton, the historical vision manifested itself accumulatively with each new item. The forgeries were a process. The focus of our analysis in this chapter will be on method: the mode of access to the past; the authenticating procedures used. The manner in which each new forged work related to previous ones and in hindsight to later ones was a crucial aspect of this method. Both forgers were extremely skilled in using devices such as inter-allusion, anticipation, and fulfillment. Macpherson began with "fragments" of ancient Erse poetry and progressed to complete and finished epics. Macpherson was given a free rein as to how his forgery appeared in print. It is possible then to study the evolution of his vision by taking each text in the order of original publication.[1]

The "Fragments"

In 1760 appeared *Fragments of Ancient Poetry, Collected in the Highlands of Scotland, and Translated from the Galic or Erse Language*. The anthology was fronted by a short preface. This text, then, introduced the forgeries to the world. Its importance requires a substantial amount of time to be spent on its study.

The opening of the preface established Macpherson's central strategy: "The public may depend on the following fragments as genuine remains of ancient Scottish poetry" (p. iii). One might wonder why, if the poems were genuine, such a statement was needed. But Macpherson's aim was authentication. The preface was the first part of the scholarly apparatus

73

of authentication that was to be erected around the imaginative text. Authenticity was of greater priority than commentary on the literary quality of the poems: "Of the poetical merit of these fragments nothing shall here be said. Let the public judge, and pronounce" (p. vii). It would have been a cunning move to have simply assumed authenticity and to have had the preface serve as literary criticism. The fact that Macpherson did the opposite shows his fascination with process, with the act of making.

Most of the preface, then, was ostensibly designed to prove the validity of the opening statement. The first paragraph told us that the exact date of composition of the fragments was not known. But Highland tradition "refers them to an aera of the most remote antiquity" (p. iii). As the next chapter will show, Macpherson was not being duplicitous in not giving precise dates, or in not saying how remote "remote" was. Added to external proof of the poems' ancientness, Macpherson noted "the spirit and strain of the poems themselves; which abound with those ideas, and paint those manners, that belong to the most early strata of society." (p. iii) So Macpherson used external and internal information. Not only did he predict the approach that participants in the controversies about the forgeries were to commonly take to the issue. Macpherson also anticipated the essentially dualistic format of his own and later historical fiction: the text (internal) and the annotation (external). Actually, as will be shown, there was no properly distinct border between the two. Both were controlled by the overall vision.

The reference to "manners" alluded to the view of ancient literature as social history. As yet this correlation was being used only as part of the dating exercise. We were not told what those "manners" consisted of. Authentication was weak. A few sentences later however, two verifiable and authentic institutions were brought into the argument: the Highland clans and Christianity. Because there was no mention of either in the poems, we are told, the poems necessarily predated these institutions. However suspect the logic, Macpherson cleverly incorporated an authenticating perspective. Once more Macpherson demonstrated a pioneering awareness of how history was made by ancient literature. He knew there were no rules as to the amount or type of social history a poem should embody. Thus he could make capital out of what was left out of the poems as much as what was included. As with so much else in the preface, the omission had an imaginative role to play in the vision. The rise of clans and Christianity signified the end of Ossian's pagan golden age. Hindsight could be applied here, because one of the ways the preface operated was to predispose us in certain ways to our reading of the texts. The relevance of these statements only became apparent later. A hint of a potential culture clash came in the remark that the poems were "coeval with the very infancy of Christianity in Scotland" (p. iv). Literate history rose from the ashes of prehistory. Note also that we are being taken back to the roots of society—the "very infancy." Macpherson was concerned with elemental history.

Macpherson's understanding that authentication did not rely on a plenitude of verifiable references within the text (indeed, many of them could function just as well in the notes) was shown in the reaction of two early commentators. Patrick Graham believed the Ossianic poems were literally like historical fragments that could be pieced together:

> these poems occasionally furnish many interesting views of the manners and mode of living which prevailed in that period of society, to which they relate. It would be amusing, and perhaps instructive, to collect these scattered traits, and to form from them a more precise picture of that state of society, in those ages, than has hitherto been exhibited.[2]

In Graham's eyes, Ossian made superlative social history. Lord Kames, on the other hand, put himself in the mind of the eighteenth-century writer of historical fiction:

> Can it be supposed, that a modern writer could be so constantly on his guard, as never to mention corn, nor cattle? . . . a man of such talents inventing a historical fable, and laying the scene of action among savages in a hunter-state, would naturally frame a system of manners the best suited in his opinion to that state. What then could tempt him to adopt a system of manners so opposite to any notion he could frame of savage manners? The absurdity is so gross, that we are forced, however reluctantly, to believe, that these manners are not fictitious, but in reality the manners of his country, coloured perhaps, or a little heightened, according to the privelege of an epic poet.[3]

When Joseph Warton asked for history to be used as the theme of national poetry, it is very likely he had in mind narrative. It is doubtful whether he understood the complexity that the essentially non-narrative issue of social history would create, and that Kames's comments reflect. The "manners" in Ossian's poetry, according to Kames, had replaced the historical fable that was unanimously regarded as the basis of an epic poem. Macpherson, to stimulate such a response, must have understood the different kinds of historical value Ossian's verse could create. Indeed, Patrick Graham's view of Ossian as social history was not put forward as the principal way history was made in Ossian. Ossian's main task, claimed Graham, was to relate, in verse, indeed, or in measured diction, for the ease of the memory, subjects of true history. . . . fictitious circumstances were altogether denied to him. The bard was, in fact, more properly a *historian* than a *poet*.[4]

Ossian only "seldom" descended to the details of everyday life. For Graham, Ossian was authentic history both at the level of events and of non-narrative social history.

Macpherson's "proof" that the fragments were of an age contiguous with the rise of Christianity constituted the crucial and most remarkable component in the preface. The source of the relevant information was literary: "a fragment of the same poems, which the translator has seen" (p. iv). The use of "seen" rather than "heard" implied the translator was working from MSS. The transition from oral to literate culture was precisely what this fragment was about. Its content was reported to us:

a Culdee or Monk is represented as desirous to take down in writing from the mouth of Ossian, who is the principal personage in several of the following fragments, his warlike achievements and those of his family. But Ossian treats the monk and his religion with disdain, telling him, that the deeds of such great men were subjects too high to be recorded by him, or by any of his religion.

(P. iv)

The subject of this imaginary poem was nothing less than the making of history. The first point to note is that the poem was being cited as history—that is, for its information relating to the age of the *Fragments*. History and poetry were fused at this level. Second, Macpherson was drawing on the real Ossianic poems of the Irish Fenian cycle. From Samuel Johnson's remarks to the proof by Derrick Thomson in 1952, it was known that Macpherson worked from genuine Gallic (presumably oral) sources.[5] In such poems, a confrontation between Ossian (or Oisin) and Saint Patrick was common. Their meetings could be violent. As Alfred Nutt says: "Ossian, in the ballads, is a pagan, defiant and reckless, full of contempt and scorn for the howling clerics and their churlish low-bred deity."[6] The relationship between Macpherson's Scottish vision and his Irish sources was to be worked out imaginatively and polemically with great subtlety in the later poems. The important point to note here is how Macpherson had modified the ethnically abrasive encounter between Ossian and the Christian. The context of the meeting was very interesting. The monk wished to record Ossian's songs, which chronicle "his warlike atchievements and those of his family." Ossian's verse was bardic history, the recording of felt experience, empirical data of the past—a Humean regression. The literate monk wished to preserve bardic history. He wanted to make a MS, a contemporaneous "voucher", the most authentic historical source possible. The monk would, if successful, have made a transition from oral to literate culture. It is striking therefore that Macpherson had Ossian refuse the request, thus denying the possible existence of a contemporary voucher (the MSS Macpherson supposedly discovered were never given dates, but they were meant to be a transcription from oral tradition made at some time after Ossian's demise). But Ossian's refusal prepared for the essential feature of the bardic voice—its spontaneity. The bard's poetry was stimulated by painful experiences; it could not be requisitioned, recited under artificial conditions. The empirical nature of bardic history ran deep. The monkish MS would have been impure. In these terms should Ossian's "disdain" be interpreted.

Even more important was the focus of the encounter: "the *mouth* of Ossian." The bardic voice: the voice of the past. The point where history and poetry fused, and history was created. This was the preparation we were given in the *Fragments,* which were to present us with Ossian's voice. It should be appreciated already how Macpherson exhibited a high degree of historiographical reflexivity—an understanding of the processes of history regarded specifically in terms of the role of literature in that making. Note that it was in the context of an imaginary poem that Macpherson chose to introduce Ossian to the world.

Also significant is the fact that the eschatology of Macpherson's vision was introduced in the figure of Ossian: "the last of the heroes" (p. v). As the last of the Fingalian heroes, Ossian was also the last of his species of bard. The notion of a poetic Fall concomitant with the historical one was undermined by the fourth paragraph, where it was argued that "the Bards" who composed the poems continued to exist uninterrupted through many centuries. In later poems, this sloppiness was cleared up. Macpherson's aim here was to construct a perspective of transmission, by which "such poems were handed down from race to race; some in manuscript, but more by oral tradition" (p. vi). Unadulterated transmission relied on purity of culture. The Highlands were pure—"a country so free of intermixture with foreigners"—and thus the poetic remains were "in a great measure incorrupted to this day" (p. vi). Macpherson provided an answer to those doubts that untainted literary records could be preserved.

The last salient feature of the preface was that it looked directly beyond the *Fragments* to as yet unwritten (or "undiscovered") material. Macpherson hoped that "many more remains of ancient genius" might be recovered. In particular, "an heroic poem," which related how Fingal rescued the Irish from the invading Danes (pp. vii–viii). The last three fragments were extracts from this epic. One of Macpherson's intentions was clearly to stimulate a public demand for Ossian. If the *Fragments* were well received, readers' appetites for more Ossianic verse would be whetted by the samples of the epic. The technique was repeated in *Fingal* (1762), in which an extract from *Temora* was presented. But there was also an imaginative level to the posturing. It was hinted, in the third paragraph, that all the *Fragments* may actually be part of the unrecovered epic: "there is ground to believe that most of them were originally episodes of a greater work which related to the wars of Fingal" (p. v). A unity was suggested. That unity was Macpherson's historical vision, the imagined Ossianic world and its transmission. Ultimately, the unity was Ossian, who was the author of the "greater work." A key feature of the forthcoming epic was given: "the author speaks of himself as present in the expedition of Fingal" (p. viii). Such was the pressure for empirical data of the past that Macpherson found a new genre: the memoir-epic. Ossian's bardic history "might serve to throw considerable light upon the Scottish and Irish antiquities" (p. viii). The preface closed with the Ossianic poem as history. We have been given essential clues as to how that history was made.

Fragment I was a dialogue between two lovers, Shilric and Vinvela. The dramatic nature of the poetry was immediately established: voices from the past: "What voice is that I hear?" is Shilric's first utterance (p. 10). The mood of the conversation was mournful. Shilric left to fight in the "wars of Fingal" (p. 10) and was not expected to return. Loss and grief were imminent. Shilric desired, as any warrior did, to be remembered—by a monument and in memory. This situation was realized in the next fragment, though strikingly inverted. It is important to note that the dialogue was a recreation of a spontaneous present in the past— the white-hot presentation of history as it happened, the "first original." As yet there was no place for the bard in the making. Although Macpherson eventually incorporated all the fragments into the Ossianic repertoire, at the outset, he used the poems to build up accumulatively the features of the bardic voice.

One such trait was established in Fragment II:

> I sit by the mossy fountain; on the top of the hill of winds. One tree is rustling above me. Dark waves roll over the heath. The lake is troubled below. The deer descend from the hill. No hunter at a distance is seen; no whistling cow-herd is nigh. It is mid-day: but all is silent. Sad are my thoughts as I sit alone.
>
> (P. 13)

This self-dramatizing resembled a soliloquy. The poetic genre most comparable to it is the dramatic monologue. In the sense that the voice of the past we hear was clearly not meant to be the poet's (Macpherson's), the fragments were dramatic monologues. It is preferable however to dispense with the term in favour of a descriptive apparatus more relevant and contemporary. In other words, the terms that have been presented so far in this study. Ossian made history through the bardic voice. That voice was an innovation in poetic form.

The voice in Fragment II was Shilric's. The poem was a sequel to Fragment I. Surprisngly, it was Shilric who mourned the loss of Vinvela. She died of grief at hearing, mistakenly, of his loss in battle. Her spirit returned: "She speaks: but how weak her voice!" (p. 14). Instead of the artificial dialogue form, which always suggests the poet is a presence outside of the poem, imposing the form, Fragment II was created before us. The maker was the speaker. Other voices had to be reported, subsumed in the spontaneous voice. In terms of the imaginative vision Macpherson was creating, the voice was taking on an authoritative status, an authenticity. Shilric was left, at the end of Fragment II, mourning his lover: "Let me hear thy voice, as thou passest, when mid-day is silent around! (p. 15). Macpherson imaginatively recreated oral culture from the inside.

The experimental nature of the *Fragments* was demonstrated in the number of times the "authentic" form of making—the spontaneous utterance—was transgressed. Fragments I, IV, XII, and XIV were dialogues. Fragments III, XIII, and VIII had a past tense, third-person editorial framework. Fragment XIII, the opening of the forthcoming epic, perhaps understandably maintained an orthodox narrative form (though in *Fingal* it was made apparent eventually that the whole of the narration was being uttered by Ossian; most of the fragments were eventually transformed in this manner). Fragments III and VIII, however, were less excusable. The first four sentences of Fragment III were a present-tense description of the landscape, identical to the opening of Fragment II. But then we read

> Sad, by a hollow rock, the grey-hair'd Carryl sat. Dry ferns wave over his head; his seat is an aged birch. Clear to the roaring winds he lifts his voice of woe.
>
> (P. 16)

The rest of the poem which is Carryl's utterance, should, strictly, have been in quotation marks, like Gray's *The Bard*. This was not to be the form of Ossian. Macpherson's role as a modern historical poet did not in later verse enter the poem, and such an imposition, was alien to his imaginative program. The reason he transgressed in Fragments III and VIII was to give us a privileged external view of the speaker. The ageing, bereaved Carryl was a type of the Ossian described in Fragment VIII.

The engraving of Ossian, which acted as frontispiece to *Fingal* (1762), followed that description closely.

Carryl, like Shilric before, and like Ossian later, mourned the loss of a loved one. Malcolm had been drowned sailing to or from the wars. The emphasis on voice remained dominant. Carryl pleaded with the returned spirit "let me hear thy voice," but agonizingly could not make out any words. Malcolm's loss was the loss of his voice, which gave him identity: "No more from the distant rock shall his voice greet thine ear" (pp. 17–18). Now Carryl's utterance had to speak for Malcolm's: "Hear my voice, ye trees! as ye bend on the shaggy hill. My voice shall preserve the praise of him, the hope of the isles" (p. 18). The most celebrated function of the ancient bard was his preservation of the fame of the warriors he served.

Fragment IV was a dialogue between two such warriors, Connal and Crimora. (She was the first of several versions of Virgil's female warrior, Camilla.) The motivating force was again the Fingalian wars. Connal's return home was first heard: "Whose voice is that, loud as the wind, but pleasant as the harp of Carryl?" (p. 19). The inter-allusions of the vision began to accumulate. The process of internal authentication was underway. We had just heard Carryl's voice. Also the first three fragments acted as a foil to the Fingalian wars. The cost of the wars to those left behind had been counted. Now Connal informed his lover "the war, my love is near" (p. 20). An invasion threatened the homeland itself. The preface had informed us that Fingal, his family (which included Ossian) and his military achievements were the central topics of Ossianic poetry. So far Fingal had been a presence in the background. Now he was brought tantalizingly close. Battle would take place on the morrow. We expect the next fragment to be a sequel, to show us finally the wars at first-hand.

The fulfilment of this expectation in Fragment V incorporated new elements into the voice, which prepared the reader for the ultimately "authentic" utterance of Ossian in Fragment VI. For the first time, history became a topic. The poem was the utterance of an anonymous friend of Connal. The reader had leapt in time beyond the battle prophesied at the end of Fragment IV. That battle, and the fall of Connal and Crimora, were now history. Specifically, they were now the memory of the speaker, who had been an eyewitness:

Here was the din of arms; and here the groan of the dying. Mournful are the wars of Fingal. O Connal! it was here thou didst fall. Thine arm was like a storm . . .

(P. 24)

Here was a past-tense narration existing within the voice of the past. Macpherson broke through the conventions of past-tense narrative. His primary concern was to create the spontaneous experiencing of the past. Within this spontaneity, regression took place. History was a deeply felt emotion springing from personal loss: empirical data. The dramatic situation of the speaker of Fragment V was one that Ossian was often to be in—seated, alone, by the graves of loved ones:

> The grass grows between the stones of their tomb; I sit in the mournful shade. The wind sighs through the grass; and their memory rushes on my mind.
>
> (P. 25)

We see now why Ossian could not create poetry for the monk. Bardic verse was, to borrow Wordsworth's famous dictum, "the spontaneous overflow of powerful feelings." These feelings, however, were always about the loss of the past. "Memory" was the first word Ossian uttered in Fragment VI:

> Memory, son of Alpin, memory wounds the aged. Of former times are my thoughts; my thoughts are of the noble Fingal. The race of the king return into my mind, and wound me with remembrance.
>
> (P. 26)

Unlike the bard of Fragment I, Ossian was more than a spectator of the Fingalian wars. He was a participant, the "Son of the noble Fingal," as the opening of Fragment VI told the reader. Or rather, he had been these things. The Ossian the reader was to know as poet had "the cheeks of age" (p. 26). To him the glory of Fingal could only be history, it could not be the immediate present of the first four Fragments. From now on, the material promised in the preface—"the wars of Fingal"—was bardic history. Fingal and others were recalled by Ossian, they were made by his voice. As the wars resulted in many real wounds, now the wounds were inflicted on Ossian's memory. He remembered the family:

> One day, returned from the sport of the mountains, from pursuing the sons of the hill, we covered this heath with our youth. Fingal the mighty was here, and Oscur, my son, great in war.
>
> (P. 26)

The situation quickly turned to tragedy. A fugitive maiden implored their aid. Their response was immediate, but in the ensuing mayhem she was killed. The mini-plots of the *Fragments* were sensationalist and repetitive, though as will be shown later, Macpherson used this repetition to explore different ways of making the past. Ossian's first memory then was not of the Fingalian wars proper. Rather, he remembered the heroism of his son Oscur, who felled the pursuing villain. Oscur was given precedence, because "Oscur my son was brave; but Oscur is now no more" (p. 30). Oscur was Ossian's only son. His death accounted for the situation of Ossian as "last of the heroes."

Little wonder then that the next poem (Fragment VII) related "the mournful death" (p. 31) of Oscur. It is significant that this poem was the first item of the forgery produced by Macpherson.[7] The essence of Ossian's position and his bardic utterance was revealed in the second paragraph:

He fell as the moon in a storm; as the sun from the midst of his course, when clouds rise from the waste of the waves, when the blackness of the storm inwraps the rocks of Ardannider. I, like an ancient oak on Morven, I moulder alone in my place. The blast hath lopped my branches away; and I tremble at the wings of the north.

(P. 31)

The change in tense marked a causal connection. Ossian was driven to a past that reminded him of his forlorn situation in the present.

Oscur's death was not in battle, but in the star-crossed conflict of rival love. Oscur killed his best friend in a dual over Dargo's daughter. Unable to bear the responsiblity, he deceived the maiden into killing him, and on realizing this, she committed suicide. More important than the fatuity of these events was the authenticating capital Macpherson made out of them. The moment of Oscur's death ("Her arrow flew and pierced his breast" [p. 35]) was momentous enough to stimulate the first footnote:

Nothing was held by the ancient Highlanders more essential to their glory, than to die by the hand of some person worthy or renowned. This was the occasion of Oscur's contriving to be slain by his mistress, now that he was weary of life. In these early times suicide was utterly unknown among that people, and no traces of it are found in the old poetry. Whence the translator suspects the account that follows of the daughter of Dargo killing herself, to be the interpolation of some later Bard.

(P. 35)

Much can be said about this footnote. Macpherson wrote as an editor. The *Fragments* were, of course, a spurious anthology of ancient poetry. This aspect of Ossian, and the similarities between Macpherson and the genuine anthologists, will be looked at in chapter 4. Macpherson authenticated the veracity of Oscur's death by bringing in historical information. A detail of Scottish social history was given. As no source was cited, of course, the details could not be checked. It was suggested that ancient poetry was itself a source. A logical circle was set up, uniting history and poetry ever more firmly. Macpherson anticipated footnotes used by real anthologists and by historical writers, including Chatterton and Scott. The ostensible purpose of the notes was to illustrate further the Fingalian custom of dying an honorable death at the hand of a worthy killer. Macpherson's conclusion that the suicide of Dargo's daughter must be an interpolation was a remarkable one. Macpherson was aware of the inevitability of forgery in ancient MSS, as Toland, Locke, and Innes were. Macpherson's interpolation was therefore realistic, and also had the effect of authenticating the interpolation-free remainder of the text. Also, the whole question of a modern editor's interference in the received MS text was shot through with the notion of imposture. Macpherson himself was eventually branded a duplicitous interpolator and embellisher. His fake interpolation in Fragment VII was a forgery-in-forgery.

Macpherson put complete faith in oral tradition, even though he was aware of its pitfalls. Ossian was usually but not always a protagonist in his own narrative. Some information, such as Oscur's death, must have been transmitted to him. Similarly, the "son of Alpin," who had been Ossian's companion in Fragments VI and VII, was the "authentic" equivalent of the monk of the preface: the mode of transmission. Such listeners were not always present in Ossian's poems, though there were enough of them to carry the point.

Fragment VIII was the final poem acknowledged to be Ossian's. (Macpherson had not yet informed the reader directly that the forthcoming epic *Fingal* was Ossian's.) So the reader was permitted to see the bard from the outside:

> By the side of a rock on the hill, beneath the aged trees, old Ossian sat on the moss; the last of the race of Fingal. Sightless are his aged eyes; his beard is waving in the wind. Dull through the leafless trees he heard the voice of the north. Sorrow revived in his soul: he began and lamented the dead.
>
> (P. 37)

Like Homer, Ossian was blind. Unlike Homer, he was perched on the brink of an historical abyss: "the last of the race of Fingal." One of the jobs of *Fingal* (1762) and *Temora* (1763) was to fill out this eschatalogical model with much more historical detail. The job of the *Fragments* was to establish the authenticity of the bardic making of history. Ossian spoke to the reader. The past spoke to him: at the end of this fragment, Ossian lamented "no more I hear my friends" (p. 40). In the poem Ossian recalled for the first time the martial valor of Fingal, and described him defeating the rebel Gaul. Ossian's final poem prepared us for the extracts from *Fingal* that comprised the final three fragments. The end of the narrative celebrated Fingal's compassion and mercy (which for many early readers of Ossian meant an ascendancy over Homer's heartless heroes). He gave up the captive Gaul to his suppliant daughter. Ossian's parting words were cleverly engineered:

> Such, Fingal! were thy words; but thy words I hear no more. Sightless I sit by thy tomb. I hear the wind in the wood; but no more I hear my friends. The cry of the hunter is over. The voice of war is ceased.
>
> (P. 40)

"The voice of war" was an artfully ambiguous phrase referring to Fingal's voice and to Ossian's own, which was making a temporary disappearance, having established its proper form. The next four fragments (up to the first extract from *Fingal*) had non-martial themes. Macpherson used the sequence of his poems to experiment with authentication and modes of access into the past.

Several features of Fragment IX suggested a break with its predecessors. The narrative was not spontaneous or requested, but demanded. The bard was an employee:

> Why seek we our grief from afar? or give our tears to those of other times? But thou commandest, and I obey, O fair daughter of the isles!
>
> (P. 41)

The young Ossian was also the bard of Fingal, and in later poems he was ordered to sing. Another way in which Fragment IX was different was in the datum from a footnote: "This fragment is reckoned not altogether so ancient as most of the rest" (p. 42). Macpherson had cleared a space for himself in which he could attempt some virtuoso maneuvers with his voices and plots. In Fragment IX, the story was told of a tragic misunderstanding. Two friends were deceived into dueling over the lover of one of them. In Fragment X, the same plot situation occured. But this time it was created from the inside by the maiden. She awaited her lover (they were to elope) only to discover he and her brother had killed each other in a duel. This fragment, like the early ones, was wholly in the spontaneous present, with no recalled narrative. The maiden ended by prophesying the return of her spirit to this spot: "sweet shall my voice be; for pleasant were they both to me" (p. 49). In Fragment XI, the maiden's plight became part of a narrative again. Her voice was transmuted from spontaneity to recreation by a bereaved narrator; we were given now a quoted speech rather than the speech itself. Her death was the death of her voice: "Before morning appeared, her voice was weak. It died away. . . . Spent with grief she expired" (p. 53). The father's agony on seeing his children's spirits was also described in terms of voice: "they walk in mournful conference together. Will none of you speak to me?" (p. 54). Armyn, as "the last of his race" (p. 50) recalling the loss of his family, was a type of Ossian.

Ossian's presence was also prepared for in the hoary, aged father of the dead Morar in Fragment XII. Morar had "left no son," (p. 58) making his father the last of the line. Fragment XII, a dialogue, had neither a romantic nor martial narrative. The focus was purely on personal loss, a situation in which the past dominated the present.

The most notable feature of the three extracts from *Fingal* (Fragments XIII, XIV, XV) was their seeming incongruity and inconsequentiality. Fragment XIII had no spontaneous bardic voice, and Fragments XIV and XV had themes unrelated to Fingal's expedition to Ireland (they would in fact be introduced into *Fingal* as episodes). Moreover, Fragment XIV contained bizarre anti-authenticating stage directions inserted between speeches in the dialogue: "[He gives her the sword: with which she instantly stabs him]" (P. 65). As an editor's interpolation, suggesting what might be supposed to have happened in a lost part of the text, it is difficult to decipher Macpherson's intention, other than to conclude he was trying out a disastrous experiment. Fragment XIV ended like Fragment XV, abruptly. But if Macpherson was trying to create an unfinished poem, a "fragment," the parenthesis that ended Fragment XIV failed to accomplish this. It has been apparent, of course, that none of the fragments resembled genuine, incomplete relics, other than in name and shortness. Fragment XIII would probably have served its purpose of advertising and authenticating *Fingal* better if it had been the only extract. Though the Irish leader Cuchulaid went to give battle to the invading Scandinavian Garve, it was the arrival of Fingal that everyone awaited. He "alone can fight with Garve" (p. 60). Only Ossian's "voice of war" could tell us of this fight.

"Fingal": The Voice of War

In 1762 was published *Fingal, An Ancient Epic Poem, in Six Books. Together with several other Poems, composed by Ossian the son of Fingal. Translated from the Galic Lanugage, by James Macpherson.* By "several" was meant actually fifteen other poems. After the success of the *Fragments*, Macpherson expanded his material liberally. With the inclusion of *Temora*

(1763), he added two epics, twenty shorter poems, and voluminous dissertations and prefaces to the humble beginnings of Ossian in the *Fragments*. Obviously there is little point in expending on this abundance the exhaustive analysis afforded the *Fragments*. What needs illumination are only the ways in which the new poems develop on the *Fragments*. There is no need to point out what they have in common.

The authenticating apparatus assembled before the text of *Fingal* was formidable indeed: an advertisement, preface and dissertation. Only Walter Scott fifty years later rivaled this prolixity of extra-textual authenticating material. The advertisement stressed the existence of manuscript "originals":

> there is a design on foot to print the originals, as soon as the translator shall have time to transcribe them for the press; and if this publication shall not take place copies will then be deposited in one of the public libraries, to prevent so ancient a monument of genius from being lost.
>
> $(A_2$ recto)

That last statement, although bogus (it was not until 1807 that the supposed Gallic "originals" were published)[8] captured exactly the spirit of the anthologists of the time, such as Percy and Evan Evans. Ancient poetry could be a historical "monument" (according to Johnson's *Dictionary* "Anything by which the memory of persons or things is preserved"). Macpherson used the language of Locke, Toland, and Innes when they discussed MSS—the "vouchers" of authentic history. A collector of national ancient poetry was thus seen as recuperating the remote history of his country. The anthologist was a species of nationalist historian. Macpherson donned this role with relish. He entered the lists of historiographical combat cautiously and cleverly, however. He noted in the preface that the plot of *Fingal* (the poem):

> is so little interlarded with fable, that one cannot help thinking it the genuine history of Fingal's expedition, embellished by poetry. In that case, the compositions of Ossian are not less valuable for the light they throw on the ancient state of Scotland and Ireland, than they are for their poetical merit.
>
> (Preface, A_4 recto)

Near-identical assertions to the last sentence had been made in the preface to the *Fragments*. But here the authentication of the poetry's function as history was given a double bolstering: first as MS "monument" (done weakly in the *Fragments*); second as the basis of an epic poem. Macpherson did not deny all "embellishment," but stated that there was very little. "History" in the first sentence of the quoted passage referred to events in the narrative. In the second sentence, the suggestion of "ancient state" was of two kinds of history: the traditional "events" type, and the new social history. Macpherson had now argued himself into a position from which he could give the background of this "ancient state" of Celtic Britain, which the poems supposedly would illuminate. His first point was that Ossian was a Scot, and that the Irish appropriated Ossian to themselves, meaning that the Irish Ossian poems were "spurious pieces" (Preface, A_4 recto). Macpherson was pre-empting his opponents' polemic, exactly as nationalist historians did—accusing their rivals of forgery. The forgery was understandable, said Macpherson, because the Irish and Scots had been closely related since the Roman invasion. So far it appears Macpherson's nationalist senti-ment had little to do with the poems, other than glamorizing their antiquity for the Scots. However, in the "Dissertation concerning the antiquity etc. of the poems of Ossian the son of Fingal," which followed the preface to *Fingal*, the relevance to the historical vision of Macpher-son's participation in nationalist historiography became clear.

The "Dissertation" opened with a refutation of the idea that anything certain could be known about "the antiquities of nations" (p. i). Early society lacked important events, as it lacked "the means of transmitting them to posterity" (p. i). Macpherson concluded, like Innes, that there was "much of the marvellous in the origin of every nation" and that ingenious "systems of history" were built on "few facts" (p. i). Macpher-son counterfeited perfectly the very reasoning that would be thought to have disproved the authenticity of Ossian. But Macpherson had been careful enough to establish an authentic historian's voice. (Many of those most actively involved in denouncing or defending Ossian in the 1760s, 1770s and 1780s were historians.) He could then proceed to show that ancient Scotland was the exception to the rule. Many facts were known about the foundation of Scotland, its origins. The model used was not complex. The original inhabitants of Britain were the Celts, who had migrated from Gaul. When the Romans invaded, the Celts retreated, first to Scotland, then later to Ireland. For Ossian to be Scottish, of course, the Scots had to be the older nation. The Scots were ruled by Druids, who eventually became tyrants. This view of the Druids was popular and could be found in Stukeley or Toland. So far Macpherson had done nothing spurious. The historical world Ossian inhabited was founded in sanctioned contemporary speculation about the origins of Britain and its nation countries. To us, much of this ratiocination is suspect, but such a condemnation is of little consequence to this study. It was shown in chapter 1 that speculation of a free kind *had* to be sanc-tioned, because there were so many obstacles to recuperating such remote ages. As Macpherson exploited prolixity of speculation, he also exploited the brief reference. In the margin of the "Dissertation," the names of classical historians were desultorily scattered: "Plin. 1.6," "Caes. 1.5.," "Tac. Agric. 1.i.c.2.," "Caesar," "Pomp. Mel.," "Tacitus," "Dio. Sic. 1.5." (p. ii); "Strabo. 1.7.," "Caes. 1.6.," "Liv. 1.5.," "Tac. de. mor. Germ." (p. iii); "Caes. 1.6." (p. iv); "Tacitus. de mor. Germ.," "Abbe de la Bleterle Remarques sur la Germaine" (p. xiii). The area given to invention within the established authenticating specifications was large, and Macpherson made use of it.

Readers were told that the power of the Druids over the Caledonians began to decline "in the beginning of the second century" (p. iv). Soon after, turbulent events erupted. Macpherson's account of these events was a superb imagining of large-scale social and cultural history, the decline of one culture and the rise of another:

> The continual wars of the Caledonians against the Romans hindered the nobility from initiating themselves, as the custom was, into the order of the Druids. The precepts of their religion were confined to a few, and were not much attended to by a people inured to war. The Vergobretus, or chief magistrate, was chosen without the concurrence of the heirarchy, or continued in his office against their will. Continual power strengthened his interest among the tribes, and enabled him to send down, as hereditary to his posterity, the office he had only received himself by election.
>
> On occasion of a new war against the *King of the World,* as the poems emphatically call the Roman emperor, the Druids, to vindicate the honour of the order, began to resume that ancient privilege of choosing the Vergobretus. Gormal, the son of Tarno, being deputed by them, came to the grandfather of the celebrated Fingal, who was then Vergobretus, and commanded him, in the name of the whole order, to lay down his office. Upon his refusal, a civil war commenced, which soon ended in almost the total extinction of the religious order of the Druids. A few that remained, retired to the dark recesses of their groves, and the caves they had formerly used for their meditations. It is then we find them in the circle of stones, and unheeded by the world. A total disregard for the order, and utter abhorrence of Druid-ical rites ensued. Under this cloud of public hate, all that had any knowledge of the religion of the Druids became extinct, and the nation fell into the last degree of ignorance of their rites and ceremonies.
>
> (Pp. iv–v)

The Fingalian line, and Ossian's world, were thus founded (no sources were given for this account). One dictatorship replaced another. On Macpherson's scale of values, however, a benevolent military aristocracy was preferable to duplicitous priesthood. We see now the significance of the statement in the preface to the *Fragments* (p. iv) that there were "few

traces of religion of any kind" in the poems. The Fingalians rid themselves of religious institutions. The Ossianic pagan world was, basically,
institution-free. As it was preceded by Druidism, so it was followed by
Christianity. From Fingal's grandfather to Oscur spanned only five gen-
erations. The Fingalian rule lasted for little more than a century, putting
Ossian's existence in the late third and early fourth century A.D., the
time of the arrival of Christianity. This was the only time Macpherson
was explicit in his dating. Because the Fingalian heroic world lasted for a
relatively short time, Ossian's recreation of it was further authenticated.
His memory alone encompassed over half the epoch. The oral transmission of the remainder was unlikely to be grossly corrupted. Macpherson
noted the reliability of oral tradition in other cultures. For instance, "All
the historical monuments of the Germans were comprehended in their
ancient songs" (pp. xii–xiii). The notion was a popular one, as was shown
in chapter 1. The purity of oral transmission was necessary, not only for
Ossian's own making of history, but for the passage of his poems to
modern times. Macpherson never said when his supposed MSS were
made. He let the issue remain ambiguous, retaining MS and oral authority for the poems. As an editor, he "admired the poems, in the
original, very early, and gathered part of them from *tradition* for his own
amusement" (p. xiv) (my italics). The final perspective Macpherson incorporated into the vision was that of evanescent Highland culture
following its decimation by the British after the 1745 rebellion, in which
"the taste for ancient poetry is at a low ebb" (p. xv). As Ossian was
poised on an abyss, so was Macpherson. Both strove to recuperate their
past through poetry, before it was too late. Both processes occurred at
the same time in the published Ossian.

The final significance of the detailed historical exposition in the "Dissertation" was that it gave to the authentic bardic utterance established in
the *Fragments* historiographical dress. The reader could appreciate Ossian's historical position. Ossian's grief was not only for the loss of his
family, but for the world which they ruled. Personal and historical
eschatology were fused in the voice of the bard. Macpherson created a
situation in which regression was inevitable, in which the past—history—dominated the present. As the historian of oral culture, the bard
embodied this situation. As the last of the heroes, Ossian was the history
of his culture. He was its making.

Fingal, *An Epic Poem*

Fingal gave the Scots and Britain an "original" native epic to rival the
precedence of Homer. The standard trappings of the epic were all

present: an *in medias res* opening, war councils and debates, long similes, the delayed involvement of the hero. For most of the first three books, Ossian's spontaneous voice was absent, and the poem answered perfectly those eighteenth-century pleas that national history become the subject of poetry. But even in the conspicuous absence of Ossian as reciter and protagonist, the importance of the voice of history—the past as poetry—within ancient Celtic society was consolidated. The action of the poem was already twice-removed from the reader. In the various songs that existed within Ossian's voice, the further past was recuperated. Poetry and history were inseparable. "Pleasant is thy voice, O Carril" said the Irish chieftain Cuthullin to his bard, "Pleasant are the words of other times" (p. 18). Carril's song had a social function. In a lull in the fighting, he entertained the warriors, as he equally inspired them to fight. For Macpherson's Celts, entertaining song consisted of plaintiveness, the "joy of grief":

> raise the voice on high and tell the deeds of other times. Send thou the night away in song, and give the joy of grief. For many heroes and maids of love, have moved in Innis-fail. And lovely are the songs of woe, that are heard in Albion's rocks; when the noise of the chase is over, and the streams of Cona answer to the voice of Ossian.
>
> (P. 16)

This reference to Ossian was, of course, to the young Ossian who was soon to enter the poem as protagonist, and who was the chief bard of Fingal. Thus in the poem's action, Ossian was not the only bard, and it was shown how ubiquitous was the making of the past by song—ubiquitous and ancient. Celtic culture had long been this way. Carril was ordered to

> raise again thy voice; and let me hear the song of Tura: which was sung in my halls of joy, when Fingal king of shields was there, and glowed at the deeds of his fathers.
>
> (P. 89)

Thus, in Carril's narration, Fingal's youth was transmitted to the present relative to the action of the poem, and to us. It was however the old Fingal, still mighty in battle, whose arrival was awaited by the beleaguered Irish.

When Fingal arrived in book 3, he brought with him his family. One of them was Ossian. Battle commenced. Ossian fought. As he entered the fray, so Ossian's spontaneous voice from the present was raised for the first time. The innovative form of *Fingal* as a memoir-epic was strikingly introduced:

Myself, like a rock, came down. I exulted in the strength the king.
Many were the deaths of my arm; and dismal was the gleam of my
sword! My locks were not then so grey; nor trembled my hands of age.
My eyes were not closed in darkness; nor failed my feet in the race.

(P. 44)

Ossian's authorship, his presence as maker, was revealed. For the remainder of the poem, the presence was always close, the spontaneous
voice always imminent. History was never allowed to be a "given," a
narrative that could simply exist without any authentication. History had
to be made, created. Fingal's description of his ancestors was archetypal.
They were the subjects of "the song of bards" (p. 44).

Ossian's poetry was a process. It happened before us. The past he
recalled all had an equal status. In book 4, Ossian related to his companion Malvina the story of his courtship of his wife. The story was not a
digression, which implied it had a subordinate status to the epic martial
events. Ossian remembered his wife because at the point he had reached
in the narrative, the young Ossian was thinking of her. She was in the
thoughts of both Ossians, in the past and in the present. Evirallin had
died shortly before the expedition to Ireland. The Ossian of the present
recalled the times previous to her death. It was very likely that the
Ossian in the narrative ("Of Evirallin were my thoughts" [p. 51]), who is
visited by her ghost, was remembering exactly the same events. Macpherson's experimentation with perspectives of time was complex. In the
first edition of *Fingal*, he tried to help his reader by marking with an
asterisk the point where "the poet returns to his subject" (p. 51). In other
words, where Ossian ceased to speak of other things and returned to
narrating the epic.

The complex shifting of time and historical point of view is illustrated
best by the incident at the end of book 5, when Ossian met his Irish
counterpart Carril. The two bards complimented each other profession-
ally:

"Hail, Carril of other times; thy voice is like the harp in the halls of
Tura. Thy words are pleasant as the shower that falls on the fields of
the sun. . . ."

"Ossian, king of swords," replied the bard, "thou best can raise the
song. Long hast thou been known to Carril, thou ruler of battles!"

(P. 72)

Ossian requested a song: "But sit thou on the heath, O bard, and let us
hear thy voice" (p. 72). This was at the end of book 5. At the opening of
book 6, the perspective changed to Ossian in the present. Carril's song

was reported: "He sung of the companions of our youth and the days of former years" (p. 73). Ossian again requested Carril's voice, as he had done at the end of book 5, but the context was totally changed. Now Ossian was addressing Carril's spirit: "Why dost thou not speak to me in my grief. . . ?" (p. 74). The past lived in the present.

"Comala" to "Berrathon": Shorter Poems

Accompanying *Fingal* in the anthology of 1762 were fifteen short poems, including an extract from *Temora*, the second promised epic. It is only necessary when looking at these poems to note significant or salient points of interest. With the formula of Ossian established in *Fingal*, Macpherson provided more, easily palatable Ossianic material, episodes from the Fingalian past as Ossian remembers them. Macpherson still retained his ability to use the sequence of the poems as an authenticating device. The striking examples of this maneuver will be pointed out.

Oddly, in the first short poem, "Comala," Macpherson broke the authentic mode in favour of a "Dramatic Poem." The piece showed Fingal defeating a Roman general, Severus. The salient development to note is the long first footnote prefixed to the piece. This footnote authenticated the history in the narrative by presenting the "background." No sources for this information were given. The poems were usually said to continue the story or dramatize it in some way. In *Temora* and in later editions of Ossian's poems, Macpherson added an "Argument" to do the job of the long footnote. These arguments anticipated in their function Bishop Percy's prefaces in the *Reliques* (1765), as the next chapter will show.

Another battle with the Romans was said to be the "foundation" (p. 95) of the next poem, "The War of Caros." Percy strove to prove that most of his *Reliques* had a "foundation" in history. Macpherson was not totally deceitful in his claim. Like Chatterton, he built his vision on "foundations" that were in his own time legitimate. Chatterton's may have been more solid, but a note of Malcolm Laing's on "The War of Caros" made an important point:

As the expedition of Severus in 208, and the usurpation of Carausius in 286, are the only events extant in the Roman history of Britain, during the third century, the preceding drama contains Fingal's triumphant return from a victory over Caracalla; and the present poem describes the encounter of Oscar, his grandson, with the usurper Carausius.[9]

"The War of Caros" contained a striking incident. Oscur was visited by the ghost of Trenmor, the founder of the race, the "Vergobretus" of the "Dissertation." He held a private conference:

> Many were his words to Oscur; but they only came by halves to our ears; they were dark as the tales of other times, before the light of song arose.
>
> (P. 101)

This was the farthest back in time Ossian regressed: to the dark ages of his culture. Trenmor, the founder, was born in the pre-history of Ossian's world. Note the way that pre-history was described: "before the light of song arose." Some kind of poetry still existed—"the tales of other times"—but not in any form comprehended by Ossian.

There is little to note about the next four poems: "The War of Inis-Thona," "The Battle of Lora," "Conlath and Cuthona," and "Carthon." The opening of "Carthon" was representative of the vision: "A tale of the times of old" (p. 127). The opening was repeated for "Cath-Loda," which appeared in *Temora* (1763). When Macpherson revised the sequence of the Ossianic repertoire for the 1773 edition of Ossian's works, he placed "Cath-Loda" first, so that "A tale of the times of old" was the reader's introduction to Ossian's poetry.[10]

The three poems "The Death of Cuthullin," "Dar-thula," and "Temora" served the same function as the final three fragments. They prepared us for the newly discovered epic, *Temora*. "Temora," like Fragment XIII, was the opening of the epic. "The Death of Cuthullin" was "an episode introduced in a great poem, which celebrates the last expedition of Fingal into Ireland" (p. 144). The new epic would tell of "last" things; a truly apocalyptic poem. *Temora* picked up chronologically where *Fingal* left off, and sealed Fingal's involvement in Irish affairs. Only three years after Fingal expelled the Danes from Ireland (in *Fingal*), insurrection broke out, and the usurper Cairbar claimed the throne. The theme of *Temora* was a final righteous expedition by Fingal to reestablish the royal family of Ireland. The maiden Darthula's story wove in and out of this history. Her lover, who was also Cuthullin's nephew, was killed by the jealous Cairbar. She died disguised as a warrior. Macpherson noted that the account of her death in the poem differed from "the common tradition" (p. 155). In other words, the MSS of Ossian were supposedly being compared with the rival literary transmission of oral history. Ossian was reckoned to be the more authentic source, because suicide (the manner of her death in the traditional account) was unknown "in those early times" (p. 156), a repeat of Macpherson's note to Fragment VII. Again Macpherson anticipated the collational editorial procedures of Percy.

Collation is a device essential to Macpherson. In "Temora," the death of Oscur was completely changed from that in Fragment VII. He now died treacherously at the hands of Cairbar. Macpherson explained the inconsistency by declaring that new, more authentic Ossianic pieces had been located by him since 1760. Fragment VII was now styled the work of a later bard and was quoted in a footnote. Clearly, when Macpherson decided that *Temora* would tell of "last" things, Oscur's death had to be included. His death secured the demise of the Fingalian order. His death in Fragment VII had no martial status.

One might wonder why "Temora" was not the final poem in *Fingal*. That is, leaving the reader in expectation of the new epic. The explanation must be that he was less certain than in the *Fragments* that the commercial backing for yet another volume of Ossian would be forthcoming. So "Temora" was placed in the middle of the anthology of 1762, and was followed by seven further poems. Of these the most important were "The Songs of Selma" and "Berrathon."

"The Songs of Selma" was a unique Ossianic poem in that its subject was poetry. Ossian recalled one of the annual bardic festivals held by Fingal. As a note explained:

The bards, at an annual feast, provided by the king or chief, repeated their poems, and such of them as were thought, by him, worthy of being preserved, were carefully taught to their children, in order to have them transmitted to posterity.

(P. 209)

The festival at Selma was Macpherson's equivalent of Keating's college at Tarah. Ossian's fellow bards Minona, Ullin, and Armin uttered Fragments X, XII, and XI respectively. The manner in which Macpherson worked the fragments into the poem—in other words "authenticated" them in terms of Ossian's repertoire—was ingeniously done. First, each fragment was given a definite creator, a bard. For Fragment X, Minona assumed the voice of the maiden, in effect reciting a dramatic monologue. Fragment X was thus a voice-within-voice-within-voice, and was at four removes from the reader. But there was a more direct, empirical relationship between the bard and her song. The story in Fragment X was not invented, it was history. The tragedy of Colma (the maiden who was anonymous in Fragment X was given a name) and Salgar was known to all those assembled: "Often had they seen the grave of Salgar, the dark dwelling of white-bosomed Colma" (p. 210). Similarly with Fragment XII, the dialogue between Ryno and Alpin. This time the bard acted as straight transmitter or recorder, thus authenticating oral transmission. The reader was told that one day Ullin overheard Ryno and Alpin mourning for Morar. In other words, Ullin heard Fragment XII.

Now, to celebrate Ryno and Alpin as well as Morar (all are dead), he recalled their words. The relation of Armin to Fragment XI was simple: he was the bereaved father who uttered the poem, and who did in fact reveal himself in the first paragraph of the fragment. This fragment was uttered spontaneously. Ullin's song reminded Armin of the death of his own children, and he could not repress his grief.

So the *Fragments* were transformed into felt experience, within Ossian's world. Each song stimulated a powerful emotional reaction in the listeners. Armin's reaction was his song. After Minona's song, Ossian remembered "Our tears descended for Colma, and our souls were sad" (p. 212). The significance of "The Songs of Selma" to Goethe's Werther was not only the tragedies they told of. The intense emotional response of the assembled heroes struck a chord in the lachrymose Werther's heart. He and Lotte wept bitterly, "and their tears flowed as one" with the ancient Fingalians.[11] Also, of course, the suicidal Werther was attracted by Ossian's spontaneous voice, which at the end of "Songs of Selma" was at its most evanescent yet: "Let the tomb open to Ossian; for his strength has failed" (p. 218).

"Berrathon" was the final poem in the 1762 volume. If *Temora* had not appeared, "Berrathon" would have been the last poem of all. Macpherson was prepared for this contingency. He made imaginative use of "Berrathon's" apocalyptic position:

> The poem is reputed to have been composed by Ossian, a little time before his death; and consequently it is known in tradition by no other name than Ossian's last hymn.
>
> (P. 257)

The bardic form was not abandoned. A tale was still told. Ossian remembered a triumphant expedition to Scandinavia, and his own heroism. However, Ossian's spontaneous voice dominated the poem. As a footnote spelled out the poem "is almost altogether in lyric measure" (p. 258). Ossian dramatized his own death. "Berrathon" was the equivalent of "The Death Song of Ragnar Lodbrog" (comparison with Gray's *The Bard* is reserved for "Colna-Dona," which was properly Ossian's final poem, appearing at the end of the 1763 volume.) Ossian perched on the abyss. The only reference he made to the society around him was contemptuous: "The sons of little men" (p. 260). Readers were never given any details about the world that succeeded Ossian's. "Tradition is entirely silent concerning what passed in the north, immediately after the death of Fingal and all his heroes" (p. 260). The abyss was definite: a Fall. The footnote concluded that the post-Ossianic world's actions "were not to be compared to those of the renowned Fingalians" (p. 260).

Characteristically, Ossian wished to expire in song: "Another song shall rise. My soul shall depart in the sound" (p. 267). "The voice of Ossian has been heard" (p. 269), he asserted. "My fame shall remain, and grow like the oak of Morven" (p. 270). It is questionable how Ossian's words at this point have been transmitted to us. The beginning of "Berrathon" told us Ossian's trusty companion Malvina was dead. But then Ragnar Lodbrog's speech had survived. The mere fact that we are hearing Ossian's voice peculiarly authenticates his prophecy, and thus his voice.

"Temora": Last Things

In 1763 Macpherson published his third and final "anthology," entitled *Temora*. The volume contained an epic poem of that name (in eight Books) and five shorter poems.

The dissertation prefixed to the volume was even more massive than its predecessor in *Fingal*. The reason for this expansion was revealed in Macpherson's claim that "what renders Temora infinitely more valuable than Fingal, is the light it throws on the history of the times" (p. xviii). To authenticate the claim, even more background information had to be given. Much of the historical speculation in the dissertation was there simply to make up the authenticating bulk and was, imaginatively, superfluous to the vision.

As in *Fingal*, Macpherson also exploited economy of reference. The margin of the dissertation contained references to "St. Heirom," "Dio. Sic," and "War de antiq. Hybern. prae" (pp. v, vii, x). The last reference was particularly important. The allusion was to Sir James Ware, one of the historians cited in chapter 1. In *Fingal* there were no references to eighteenth-century historians. But in *Temora*, Macpherson used Ware to attack Keating and O'Flaherty, who believed in the superior antiquity of Ireland:

> we may, on [Ware's] authority, reject the improbable and self-condemned tales of Keating and O'Flaherty. Credulous and peurile [sic] to the last degree, they have disgraced the antiquities they meant to establish . . . [they are] idle fabulists.
>
> (P. xi)

The relevant new material in the dissertation was that about Scottish-Irish relations. Macpherson participated in the historiographical tug-of-war by claiming the Scots had the greatest antiquity: they were the "original" Celtic nation, and Ossian was their spokesman. He became more precise. "Temora," we are told, was the name of "the royal palace of the first Irish kings of the Caledonian race" (p. xxvi). In other words, the first King of a united Ireland was a Scot. His name was Conar. He pacified the warring tribes and they elected him ruler:

> Conar, the first king of Ireland, was the son of Trenmor, the great-grand-father of Fingal. It was on account of this family-connection, that Fingal was engaged in so many wars in the cause of the race of Conar.
>
> (Pp. 30–31)

The Irish kingdom was only one generation younger than its Scottish counterpart. Far from there being antagonism between Selma and Temora, there was familial love. *Temora* the epic poem showed Fingal restoring Caledonian rule to Ireland. The implication was that even though Fingal's own line expired, it lived on symbolically in Ireland. Macpherson used Irish history skillfully. By stressing the involvement and importance of Ireland in his historical vision, Macpherson borrowed the authenticity of the Irish Fenian poems, most of which were thought to be the work of "Oisin" or Ossian. He borrowed that authority by establishing a causal relationship between the Irish and Scottish Ossian. First, Macpherson performed a dating exercise on the Irish poems:

> I have just now, in my hands, all that remain, of those compositions; but, unluckily for the antiquities of Ireland, they appear to be the work of a very modern period. Every stanza, nay almost every line, affords striking proofs, that they cannot be three centuries old. Their allusions to the manners and customs of the fifteenth century, are so many, that it is a matter of wonder to me, how any one could dream of their antiquity.
>
> (P. xxiii)

The cornerstone of Macpherson's argument was the fact that in the Irish Ossianic poems, Fingal was a Christian; whereas, according to Macpherson, he was clearly a pagan. Macpherson anticipated or rehearsed the kind of analysis that would be applied to his and Chatterton's work to prove or disprove its authenticity. Historical and literary values were fused. *Fingal* and *Temora*, Macpherson's two epics, both took place in Ireland. Macpherson's ingenuity exerted itself at this point:

> the Irish became acquainted with, and carried into their country, the compositions of Ossian. The scene of so many of the pieces being in Ireland, suggested first to them a hint, of making both heroes and poets natives of that Island.
>
> (Pp. xxxiii–iv)

Macpherson made a virtue out of the Innes-style view of the ancient bards as forgers, as "makers." The same exercise was performed on the Scottish clan bards, the genealogical fabricators:

> A succession of bards was retained in every clan, to hand down the memorable actions of their forefathers. As the aera of Fingal, on account of Ossian's poems, was the most remarkable, and the chiefs the most renowned names in tradition, the bards took care to place one of them in the genealogy of every great family—That part of the poems, which concerned the hero who was regarded as ancestor, was preserved, as an authentic record of the antiquity of the family, and was delivered down, from race to race, with wonderful exactness.
>
> (P. xvi)

No Highland expedition had this time been necessary to recover those "authentic records." Throughout his notes, Macpherson simply claimed that "originals" of Ossian's poetry had come into his possession. To put the issue beyond doubt, however, he appended to the volume "A Specimen of the Original of Temora Book VII." He succumbed to the pressure to be accountable. Of course his opponents were not satisfied with the Gallic extract, because the true "original," the MS, still remained hidden. Also Macpherson was hard pushed to explain why *all* his Gallic originals were not published. He said that publication of the MS of *Fingal* "was unnecessary, as a copy of the originals lay, for many months, in the bookseller's hands, for the public's inspection" (p. 226). As the next chapter will show, it was not the anthologists' practice to publish the whole of their sources. This led Percy into many problems. Macpherson again concurred with, or even anticipated, "legitimate" procedure. The full Gallic text of Ossian was published in 1807. It has yet to be established whether this text is a mere translation of Macpherson's English into Gallic.

Macpherson also had a legitimate answer for those who should wonder why Ossian's making of history followed the rules of the epic. The first footnote to *Temora* stated that Ossian, like Homer, learned these rules from nature. Two years later, in the *Reliques*, Percy noted that "nature and common sense had supplied to these old simple bards the want of intricate art, and taught them some of the most essential rules of Epic Poetry."[12]

The tone of *Temora* the poem was gloomy and evanescent. Oscur was killed, Fingal's enemy Cathmor was portrayed as great and magnanimous, and victory brought little joy. Fingal was waning: "The days of my years begin to fail: I feel the weakness of my arm. My fathers bend from their clouds, to receive their grey-haired son" (p. 17). Nowhere did Ossian show us the death of Fingal. At the end of *Temora* we saw his death as ruler. He abdicated, passing on his spear (the Fingalian equivalent of the crown) to Ossian. Ossian was therefore the new king, but he never dwelt on this topic. The fate of the Fingalian world after the action of *Temora* was a blank. As Macpherson said earlier, tradition (Ossian) "is entirely silent." All we know is that Ossian was surrounded by "little men." Macpherson created a vacuum to stress the eschatological scheme of things: Ossian perched on an abyss. Chronologically, history ceased to be a topic for him with *Temora*.

A comparison of Ossian with Gray's *The Bard* is unavoidable. The poem best suited for such a comparison is "Colna-Dona," the final poem of the 1763 volume. In terms of Macpherson's original creation, "Colna-Dona" was Ossian's final utterance. (The only point to note about the other shorter poems ("Cathlin of Clutha," "Sulmalla of Lumon," "Cath-Loda," and "Oina-Morul") is that "Sulmalla" and "Cath-Loda," like "Colna-Dona," purported to have sections missing. In other words, Macpherson resurrected the notion that he had found fragments, damaged texts. The missing portions were marked by asterisks.) "Colna-Dona" described how Fingal "dispatches Ossian and Toscar . . . to raise a stone on the banks of the stream of Crona, to perpetuate the memory of a victory, which he had obtained in that place" (p. 218).

The poem's major incident was the erecting of a monument. The passage which described this act needs to be quoted in full. Ossian, like the bard in Gray's poem, stood on an abyss and made a prophecy:

> I took a stone from the stream, amidst the song of bards. The blood of Fingal's foes hung curdled in its ooze. Beneath, I placed, at intervals, three bosses from the shields of foes, as rose or fell the sound of Ullin's nightly song. Toscar laid a dagger in earth, a mail of sounding steel. We raised the mould around the stone, and bade it speak to other years.
>
> Oozy daughter of streams, that now art reared on high, speak to the feeble, O stone, after Selma's race have failed! Prone, from the stormy night, the traveller shall lay him, by thy sides: thy whistling moss shall sound in his dreams; the years that were past shall return. Battles rise before him, blue-shielded kings descend to war: the darkened moon looks from heaven, on the troubled field. He shall burst, with morning, from dreams, and see the tombs of warriors round. He shall ask about the stone; and the aged shall reply, "This grey stone was raised by Ossian, a chief of other years."
>
> (Pp. 220–21)

This prophecy was totally unlike that in *The Bard*. There the self-authenticating vision saw the Tudors restoring the glory of Wales in Britain. The abyss was bridged, the Fall was temporary. But Ossian only saw the future looking back. He saw history. There was no feeling, as in *The Bard*, that the future could ever compete with Ossian's time. The monument would "speak" to the future traveller. It would make history: "the years that were past shall return." History relative to the traveller encompassed Ossian's past, present, and future. But when he asked about the stone, the climax of his experience, he was not told what the stone celebrated, but that it "was raised by Ossian." What was remembered was the act of remembering. History was three times in the making: for the traveller, for Ossian who erected the monument, and for Ossian who recalled the incident.

No footnote informed us that this was a real monument being presented. A convenient way of preparing for Chatterton is to note that he used real monuments, real people, and real places in his vision. He advanced beyond Macpherson's making of history to a more modern form of historical fiction.

4

Literary Archaeology: Macpherson, Percy, and the Anthologists

there is a design on foot to print the Originals. . . . copies will then be deposited in one of the public libraries, to prevent so ancient a monument of genius from being lost.

Macpherson, Fingal (1762)

Macpherson goes on very successfully in picking up subscriptions, for his proposed translation of the ancient Epic Poem in the Erse Language: Tho' hardly one reader in ten believes the specimens already produced to be genuine.—How much greater attention would be due to an editor, who rescues the original itself from oblivion. . . .

Thomas Percy in a letter to Evan Evans, (1763)

a number of most curious relicks have . . . been lost. . . .

William Owen, The Heroic Elegies and Other Pieces
of Llywarch Hen (1792)

My concern with the forgeries of Macpherson and Chatterton is not with authenticity but with authentication. However, chapter 3 showed how Ossian appeared in the form of several anthologies of ancient poetry. It is known that Chatterton also planned various compilations of "antiquities" and Rowleyan works (see Appendix 2), though unlike Ossian, the historical vision of Chatterton did not evolve spontaneously in that form. The purpose of this chapter is to explain and speculate on the status of Ossian as a counterfeit anthology, and to relate the forged to the "legitimate" work of the anthologists. As might be expected, the issues involved were by no means clearly defined at the time. Macpherson's and Percy's methods were often very similar. Study of the *Reliques* (1765) also acts as a bridge to Chatterton, the subject of the next chapter. As the title to this chapter suggests, the controlling focus is on national history. Historical and literary inquiries about the past were inextricably affiliated.

The anthologists were interested in the transmission of the past through poetry. The literary making of history began with the MS: it had the same empirical status as historiography. The real problem lay in dating. Even if a MS could be dated with reasonable accuracy, the poem preserved could be of an earlier time, as Percy claimed for his folio MS. Thus arose the thorny question of regression and transmission. The issue was more often than not eschewed rather than pursued. An even more pressing problem, but one equally prone to neglect, was authorship. Any decision about who had written a piece necessarily involved ascribing a date, but also made the historical complexion of the piece a weightier concern. The author's own experience was brought into play, and thus the empirical (sensory) status of what was described in the poem. Was the subject matter contemporaneous with the poem's composition (making the poem "occasional," relative to the author) or was it historical recreation? The latter category involved regression. The old poem was historical at two removes. Editors tended to evade this possibility, applying an all-embracing label, "historical." Percy groped towards some understanding. Macpherson and Chatterton were far advanced in their insight into these processes. The last chapter showed Macpherson's intensely realized vision of regression and transmission. The forgeries offered imaginative solutions to major literary-historical problems of their time.

A Collection of Old Ballads

The eighteenth-century anthology that anticipated both Macpherson and Percy in tone and method was Ambrose Philips' three-volume *A Collection of Old Ballads* (1723–1725). There is no direct evidence that Macpherson had read Philips, but Percy certainly had. He sent an edition to William Shenstone, asking his friend to select the best ballads for possible inclusion in the *Reliques*. Shenstone's enthusiastic reply became known as the famous "Shenstone's Billets."[1]

Philips revealed his colors early on in the preface:

It was the Custom of these Song Enditers thus to transmit to their Children the glorious Actions which happen'd in their Days. And I believe it never was used more than amongst the English in Times of Old. For we may very reasonably suppose, that one half at least of their Works are lost; and we have still one half of whatever is remarkable in History, handed down to us in Ballads.[2]

The standard flaws characterized this argument: imprecise dating and vagueness of definition. "Times of Old," like its ubiquitous counterpart, "ancient," could refer to any time as recent as the seventeenth century. No distinction was made between oral and literate times. Fuzzy chronology (or no chronology at all) on an editor's part could allow his poets to retain bardic qualities *and* be literate, a MS source. Philips' "Song-Enditers" wrote about the "remarkable" of "their Days." Philips presented the ballads as a resource for the historian:

> several fine Historians are indebted to Historical Ballads for all their Learning. For had not Curiosity, and a Desire of comparing these Poetical Works with Ancient Records, first incited them to it, they would never have given themselves the Trouble of diving into History; And in this I have endeavoured to make our old Songs still more useful, by the Introductions which I have prefix'd to 'em; and in which is pointed out what is Fact and what Fiction.[3]

Philips acted as another "fine Historian" (his predecessors were not named, incidentally) who by comparing the poetry with the records separated the components of the hybrid "Historical Ballad." He wished to perform that judicious task of deciphering fact and fiction in ancient poetry that was so desperately required at the time. In this context, his editorial format was born. The crux of the issue rested obviously on the word "Historical," which was not defined. Chapter 2 pointed out the difference between "historical," meaning "genuinely old," and "historical," meaning "having subject matter set in or describing the past." The problem for the anthologists lay in the chronological gap between the author and his subject matter. A ballad telling of events in the fifteenth century need not have been written at that time. The point was crucial, marking the change from recording to recreation: historical fiction. The historical validity of the latter was suspect, so the easiest way to avoid undermining the historical value of the ancient poem was to destroy the gap by ignoring authorship altogether (especially easy with the anonymity of the ballads), or to assume contemporaneity and thus empirical status for the subject matter. The focus on the ballad, the "proof" of its historical value, could then be on the factuality of the events in the narrative. Philips used this approach; it is how he understood "historical." Macpherson and Chatterton realized how much more complex the situation was. They were aware of the gap between the composer and the content of his product, of the gradations and regressions of the past created. Percy, despite his grasp of social history and his invention of a composer for the ballads—the minstrel—was less aware of the process. Macpherson had Ossian indulge in the supernatural, knowing that this breach of factuality did not disprove the fact that it was Ossian's voice we were hearing. The forgers had a subtle grasp of the "external" and "internal" factors involved in literary history. Philips was only concerned with the ballads as records of orthodox history—political and military narratives. Other kinds of topics were therefore not "historical." "Cupid's Revenge," for instance, was censured as "the Invention of some Poet, who would not give himself the Trouble of turning History over, to find out a proper subject."[4] Preceding each poem by an introduction became the standard procedure for anthologists and historical poets later in the century. Philips established this format with the declared intention of presenting the factual and fictional portions of his ballads. The emphasis, however, was always on the former quality. So great was Philips' desire to authenticate this factuality that he also established editorial dissimulation. He rarely pointed out what is fiction. Most of his introductions gave a "textbook" or authoritative account of events that were either the prelude to or "background" of the supposed historical content of the poem. The last chapter showed how Macpherson used the device. More often than not, the introduction stood as its own authentication. Sometimes no comparison with the text was made, or the text was said simply to agree or to support the introduction. No proofs for these claims were given. When an inconsistency was pointed out (which was not very often) its fictionality could be reduced to probability or conjectural truth, whose validity later researches would authenticate.[5] Philips also understood like Macpherson the value of bulkiness in an authenticating apparatus. The introduction to "The Battel of Agincourt" was longer than the poem.[6] He could also go to the opposite, frugal extreme, saying of a poem only that "the Account is, I believe, as authentick as any we have extant."[7] Or "I know no Story of [Robin Hood] more probable, than what is related in the following ballad."[8] Or even

> An Introduction to this Ballad ["The Banishment of the Dukes of Hereford and Norfolk"] is almost unnecessary; our Poet has either copied so closely from History, or the Historians have borrow'd from our Poet in such a Manner, that I scarce find one Point in which they differ.[9]

Philips, Macpherson, and Percy were all on common ground here. Literature was history. The making of the past was rarely broken down any further, even to the extent of a few working examples. Philips' bias away from fiction toward fact was so strong that he could even sacrifice the historian to the poet. Regarding the Queen's relations with her second husband in "Queen Eleanor's Confession," he said "if we may give any Credit to the following Song, the Historians are palpably mistaken."[10] The paradoxical idea that imaginative literature of the past could be a more authentic source of history than history writing itself was a striking confirmation of how deeply literature had been absorbed into historiography. Both forgers took this controversial stance.

Philips' legacy was his stated belief that old ballads were valuable indigenous history and the editorial method he devised to prove this claim. It must be realized that many eighteenth-century anthologies were organized along polemical lines. Old ballads and romances needed to be defended by their editors. The most common defense was to laud their artless simplicity and their historical value. Philips saw himself as instigating a revival of interest in national history:

> History, especially our own, has for many Years been too much neglected, and the generality of *English-Men* are such strangers to ancient Facts and the Customs of their Kingdom, that they are easily misled by any Six-penny Pamphleteer. . . . [*Old Ballads* exists] for the Instruction of those who have not Leisure or Inclination to search Historical Transactions; and who may, I hope, learn as much from these Abridgements, as may give them a tolerable Insight into the History of their Country.[11]

By Percy's time, a new note of urgency had entered the recovery of national literature. Fired on by the notion of social history, which made all old literature historically valuable, and by an increased awareness of the fragility and potential for decay of the MS, the editing of ancient poetry became literary archaeology. A task of national importance, each new poem rescued from oblivion was seen as the restoration of a "monument" of antiquity.

Thomas Percy

In Joshua Reynolds' portrait of Percy (painted in May 1773) the bulky bound volume labelled "MSS" being held looms at least as large as the prelate himself. That fact is significant. But there is a further pointed irony. The MSS volume, as explained below, may well have been a forgery. There is an immediate correlation with the forgers, particularly Chatterton, and their involvement with MSS.

If we believe Percy's testimony, the folio MS was a literary "find," akin to the narrator's in *The Castle of Otranto*, or Macpherson's on a Highland expedition, or indeed Chatterton's in a Bristol church. According to J. Furnivall, the first editor of the MS in 1867, Percy recorded the discovery on the fly leaf of the binding that he later had made. He was visiting his friend Humphrey Pitt at Shiffnal in Shropshire, and saw the MS "lying dirty on the floor under a Bureau in the Parlour . . . being used by the maids to light the fire."[12] Percy begged the remnants off his friend and later had them bound. Joseph Ritson heard the same tale of discovery by word of mouth in the early 1790s.[13] Furnivall's description of the resulting volume was not Reynolds' tome with "MSS" conspicuously declared on the spine: "The Manuscript itself is a 'scrubby, shabby, paper' book—about fifteen and a half inches long by five and a half wide, and about two inches thick."[14] In the preface to the *Reliques of Ancient English Poetry* (1765), Percy omitted these details. He dated the MS as "about the middle of the last century," (Furnivall puts it at 1650), though it contained "compositions of all times and dates, from the ages prior to Chaucer, to the conclusion of the reign of Charles I."[15] Such a period was covered by the word "ancient." Percy stressed that the MS was the source for most of the pieces selected. But he was dissembling. Of the one hundred seventy-six poems in the first edition of the *Reliques,* only forty-five were taken from the folio MS. The majority were from printed sources. Percy's desire to foreground the authority of his MS seems stronger in needing the help of dissimulation. That is how the Reynolds portrait should be interpreted. Percy wished his editorial and scholarly identity to be dominated and defined by the MS.

The MS was only truly authoritative when it was made accountable. It was too much to expect an editor to publish the MS original of all his poems. But his integrity, and the authenticity of his sources, had not to be doubted. Macpherson's suppression of his "originals" was his opponents' strongest weapon, despite the publication of the Gallic extract from *Temora.* Percy also guarded his folio MS very jealously. He would only have done this if his published "transcriptions" were at variance with the originals. That was indeed the case. Percy sowed the seeds of his own downfall when he described his use of the MS at the end of the preface to the *Reliques.* He said the mutilated condition of parts of the MS obliged him to interpolate. All interpolations were to be set off by quotation marks. They were to be made accountable. But when it came to the poems, Percy was less than faithful to this formula. Quotation marks rarely appeared. Accountability was gone. This was Joseph Ritson's major bone of contention, as shall be seen. The image of the fabricating, surreptitious Percy reduced the gap between the fraudulent Ossian and the legitimate *Reliques* even further. Especially when Johnson's theory that Macpherson embellished real Gallic ballads was confirmed by Derrick Thomson in 1951.[16] Percy's alterations were interesting in two ways. First, once Percy was persuaded by Shenstone to be a man of taste as well as an antiquarian and thus to alter his sources to accord with modern literary taste (Shenstone was inspired, ironically, by the poetical success of Ossian),[17] he ran the same risks as Macpherson of lauding while concealing MS authority. Second, it needs to be known whether Percy's inventions were in any sense historical fiction: that is whether his interpolations supported his keen interest in history. Before an answer can be found, it is necessary therefore to look at Percy the literary archaeologist.

The title "Reliques" was indicative of a major shift from the "Old Ballads" of Philips' day. The word suggests solidity, an artefact or "monument"—the tangible MS as an historical and cultural remnant. Yet in the preface to the *Reliques*, Percy presented the historical value of the poems as only one of their functions:

> such specimens of ancient poetry have been selected as either shew the gradation of our language, exhibit the progress of popular opinions, display the peculiar manners and customs of former ages, or throw light on our earlier classical poets.[18]

Unlike Macpherson in the preface to the *Fragments*, Percy devoted a good deal of space to praising the literary graces of the ballads (a trend begun by Addison's famous "Chevy Chase" papers). Percy acted as the man of taste. As he said in the "Essay on the Ancient Metrical Romances" prefixed to the third volume, he was not one of those antiquaries

> who have revived the works of our ancient writers, [and] have been for the most part men void of taste and genius, [who] therefore have always fastidiously rejected the old poetical Romances, because founded on fictitious or popular subjects, while they have been careful to grub up every petty fragment of the most dull and insipid rhymist.[19]

Percy rejected an indiscriminate salvaging of the literary past. But despite this refined pose, the antiquarian Percy of Reynolds' portrait was more strongly present than might seem. The first declaration of the program of the *Reliques* was in the "Dedication to the Countess of Northumberland":

> these poems are presented to your LADYSHIP, not as labours of art, but as effusions of nature, shewing the first efforts of ancient genius, and exhibiting the customs and opinions of remote ages: of ages that had been almost lost to memory, had not gallant deeds of your illustrious ancestors preserved them from oblivion.[20]

Though obsequious, this was the literary archaeologist speaking. The recovery of ancient poetry was the restoration of social history. It can be

appreciated how clearly Macpherson understood the ties between editing and national history, and how subtly he exploited them. Three years
before the *Reliques,* Macpherson had said he would soon be publishing
the originals of *Fingal* (1762), "to prevent so ancient a monument of
genius from being lost."[21] When one reads Percy's correspondence with
his scholarly acquaintances in the years around 1760, it is startling how
Macpherson always seems one step ahead, a reference to him always
imminent.

Michael Lort of Cambridge noted of the early 1760s: "Macpherson
with his Galic poetry has set all the English antiquarians agog after the
Welsh, in hopes to find something equal to it."[22] The anthologists
participated in the nationalist historical warfare. The major Welsh anthologist of Percy's day was Evan Evans. In a letter of 1761, he described
to Percy the aim of his literary labors. Note how similar in rhetoric and
sentiment the words are to many statements cited in chapter 1:

> seeing that our poetry and antiquities have been so undeservedly
> disregarded by our own countrymen, 'tis no wonder that strangers
> have been so rude to us to deny and call in question all our antient
> monuments, even some which are attested by the contemporary
> Bards themselves—I have made it my business for some years past to
> transcribe some of our old MSS . . . to contradict our disingenuous
> adversaries, who as they know nothing to the purpose of the matter,
> peremptorily condemn our histories as fabulous and fictitious.[23]

Percy's support for Evans was wholehearted. All he requested was that
the remains of imaginative literature receive the first attention. In his
first letter to Evans, Percy praised the Welshman's "pains you have taken
to rescue the productions of your ancient Bards from oblivion."[24] The
catalyst to this literary archaeological statement was, needless to say,
Ossian. Percy noted "the Scotch, they are everywhere recommending
the antiquities of their country to public notice, vindicating its history,
setting off its poetry." It is hard to believe that is not a veiled reference to
Ossian. Macpherson had got there first, making Ossian's poetry a possession of national history. In October 1761, Percy stressed to Evans that
indigenous poetry should be recovered first. His motives were not
governed by standards of taste:

> I would not have any ancient historical monuments perish, or be
> wholly neglected: They may come into use, upon a thousand occa-
> sions that we cannot at present foresee. . . . But I think the first care is
> due to these noble remains of ancient genius, which are in so much
> greater danger of perishing because so much harder to be under-
> stood.[25]

The note of urgency was strong. The past was being lost. The linguistic distance between us and our ancient ancestors widens, affecting literature particularly harshly. Percy's words also reflected the awareness of the fragility of the MS, its propensity to decay. As Evans noted elsewhere, "one century makes a great havoc of old MSS."[26] In other words, the anthologists appreciated more than historians that eschatology was built into their labors. Their evanescent sources were balanced precariously on the brink of an abyss: the destruction of history. In a comment to George Paton in 1768, Percy conflated the editor and the original author:

> what I chiefly want to recover are those fine old Historical Songs, which are only preserved in the memories of old People, etc; these are in so perishable a state that I apprehend it is nearly as much merit to retrieve them from that oblivion which they are falling into, as to compose them at first: I mean that the person who does this will almost deserve as well of the World as the original Composer.[27]

Percy's "etc" presumably referred to MSS. The statement could be a gloss on Ossian. Macpherson exploited the association between the demise of Ossian's world and the decay of oral tradition in late eighteenth-century Scotland, aligning Ossian and himself, the "editor," as makers of the past.

Percy tried to inspire Evans to conduct a literary excavation, whose treasures had once again been rifled by Macpherson, albeit fraudulently:

> How strongly is one's curiosity piqued by the mention you make . . . of the Epic Poem wrote in 570 [the *Gododin*] . . . what a noble field for literary application to rescue such a fine monument of antiquity from that oblivion; to which every revolving year of delay will more certainly consign it, till it is lost for ever. . . . *Macpherson* goes on very successfully in picking up subscriptions, for his proposed translation of the antient Epic Poem in the Erse language [*Fingal*]: Tho' hardly one reader in ten believes the specimens already produced to be genuine—How much greater attention would be due to an editor, who rescues the original itself from oblivion, and fixes its meaning by an accurate version.[28]

Fingal appeared only a few months later, several years before the *Gododin*.[29] Chapter 2 showed how great was the pressure for a poem of national history: the epic. Macpherson saw that the value of the "original" or ancient, primary epic was superior to the modern imitation. An editor could uncover a national Homer. The modern poet, on the other hand, could only copy the Greek Homer or other precedents. Note how the discovery of the *Gododin* was reported by Evans' friend Lewis Morris: "We have found an epic Poem in the British called Gododin, equal at least to the Iliad, Aeneid or Paradise Lost."[30] Ossian deserved a place in the list.

So Macpherson shared with the anthologists the aim of restoring the history of a nation through its poetry. Ancient poetry contains authentic, elemental, empirical information of the past, vastly superior to a later poet's recreation of the same events. History is made in the anthology. The editor is as much a contributor to the making as his authors. When advising Percy on a policy of selection for the *Reliques*, Shenstone stated in 1762 that "mere *Historical*, without *poetical* merit is not a sufficient recommendation."[31] Percy was not totally convinced. As in *Old Ballads* and Ossian, the aim of most of the introductions to poems in the *Reliques* was to prove the poem's factuality. The major difference between Percy and Philips was that Percy had a committed belief in social history, the non-narrative view of the past. It is necessary to go outside of the *Reliques* briefly to demonstrate how strong was Percy's allegiance to this school of thought.

In the preface to the Chinese novel, *Hau Kiou Choaan* (1761), Percy presented the novel as the superlative organ of contemporary social history:

> A foreigner will form a truer notion of the genius and spirit of the *English*, from one page of *Fielding*, and one or two writers now alive, than from whole volumes of *Present States of England*, or *French Letters concerning the English Nation*.[32]

Literature is again placed above historiography. In similar vein, Percy declared his faith in all old MSS in a letter to Lord Hailes in 1765. Percy outlined an ambitious project:

> I propose to read over all our antient historians, and to examine all the MSS in our public Libraries that have any sort of relation to my subject, with a view of gleaning all those little minute incidents &c. which have been rejected by our more formal Historians, yet which perhaps are not only more curious and interesting, but serve to give us a truer insight into the causes of great revolutions, and important events, than those which Politicians more formally assign—Whatever throws light on the History of Manners, I shall sieze as my proper prey.[33]

Percy regarded poetry as a major source of those precious "little minute incidents." This view buttressed much literary endeavor in the late eighteenth century. Thomas Warton underpinned his *History of English*

Poetry with the claim that "our national poetry" had the virtue of "faithfully recording the features of the times, and of preserving the most picturesque and expressive representations of manners."[34] Substantiation of the view, or any precise indications of the "manners" preserved, was not required. Percy's monumental scheme dwindled into *The Household Books of the Earl of Northumberland in 1512* (1768), designed to show ancient domestic economics at work. But Percy had a dualistic vision of history to apply to his reliques: the formal and the informal, events and "manners."

So Percy could authenticate the historical value of the poems in two ways. Like Philips, he presented the "textbook" account of events the poem was supposed to be dealing with. Fictionality was not delineated. Of the first poem, "Chevy Chase," Percy told the reader it "had originally some foundation in fact."[35] Logically, therefore, much of the poem was fiction. But Percy was not concerned to point this out. Macpherson had been equally reticent. Neither did Percy say what portions of the ballad were fact. Like Philips and Macpherson, Percy made suspect statements. He said of the protagonists of "Sir Patrick Spence": "their catastrophe is not altogether without foundation in history, though it has escaped my researches."[36] Or of "Edom O' Gordon":

> Whether this ballad hath any foundation in fact, we have not been able to discover. It contains however but too just a picture of the violences practised in the feudal times all over Europe.[37]

Note here that Percy had a second mode of authentication in reserve. Any ballad, regardless of the veracity of its narrative, could present (consciously or unconsciously) details of social history. Philips did not have this secondary option. The logic is of course notoriously circular. The proof of the authenticity of the "manners" remained the text itself. Percy did not always play this trump card. For instance, "George Barnwell seemed to relate a real fact; but when it happened I have not been able to discover."[38] A Humean "feeling" sufficed. But regarding "Sir Andrew Barton," Percy allowed social history to compensate for errors in orthodox history. The ballad had

> some few deviations from the truth of history: to attone for which it has probably recorded many lesser facts, which history hath not condescended to relate.[39]

Neither did Percy "condescend to relate" what those "lesser facts" were.

Bearing Percy's historical outlook in mind, attention can be focused on his interpolations in the *Reliques*. We might expect Percy's inventions to have added to the poem's historical worth, injecting those "manners"

that give the truest insight into the past. This is not the case. The ballads
that were most heavily changed between the folio MS and the *Reliques*
were "Sir Cauline," "The Child of Elle," "Edom o' Gordon," "The Rising
in the North," "Northumberland Betrayed by Douglas," "Sir Aldingar,"
"The Heir of Linne," "Sir Andrew Barton," "King John and the Abbot of
Canterbury," "King Arthur's Death," "Gil Morrice," and "The Marriage
of Sir Gawaine." A comparison of the originals with Percy's versions
reveals that most of his interpolations were completions of the narrative
(Percy wanted reliques but not fragments) or adjustments in sentiment.[40] Very few descriptive details of more than quiescent, conventional quality were added. There was the odd tinselled trapping. In
"Sir Cauline" for instance, Percy added to the effect of the duel: "Till
helme and hauberke, mail and sheelde,/They were all well-nye brast" (ll.
105–06).[41] A Macpherson or a Chatterton would have seized on such
details and antiquated diction, offering glosses in a footnote. The only
time Percy came close to this kind of authentication was in "Gil Morrice."
Percy claimed in the introduction that by his "additional strokes," "the
colouring here is so much improved and heightened."[42] The only
"stroke" that had any significance was baron's "siller cup and mazer
dish" (l. 95).[43] Percy glossed the dish as "a drinking cup of maple."

So Percy's fabrications did not make the past in accord with his theo-
ries about the relations between literature and history. He did not, like
Macpherson and Chatterton, create interesting historical fiction. Nor did
Percy see like them the possibilities for authentication in the foregrounding of the author. Percy did not exploit his own invention: the minstrel.
This figure was designed by Percy as the medieval successor to the bard
of oral times. He was not a historian proper, but his songs might have
historical topics, and in any case, they absorbed the social history of the
minstrel's own time. Percy did not follow up the most promising facets
of his model. Near the end of the "Essay on the Ancient English Minstrels," which followed the preface to volume one of the *Reliques*, he
presented the minstrels as oral poets in literate times: "what copies are
preserved of [their rhymes] were doubtless taken down from their
mouths."[44] Percy could have been influenced here by Macpherson's
preface to the *Fragments*. Ossian refused to allow the monk to record his
bardic voice. Macpherson exploited the interface between oral and literate cultures. Percy had grave problems. His minstrel was an anonymous
poet, composing at any time between the Norman invasion and the
sixteenth century. He rarely appeared in his own poems, thus making it
difficult to claim that what is described in the poems was the minstrel's
own experience. At times Percy would speculate and shrug aside these
obstacles. He stated that the second part of "The Rising in the North"

was "written by some northern bard, soon after the event" and therefore "history coincides with this ballad."[45] Generally though, even speculation was absent and did not play a part in making the historical value of the poem. The first rule of annotation (or authentication) Percy laid down in a letter to George Paton was "to mention (where it can be done) the Authors of the several Songs or Ballads, or at least their Antiquity, or any Tradition concerning them."[46] Authorship and date. Neither were forthcoming in the *Reliques,* except regarding very recent poems with known authors. As we noted in relation to *Old Ballads,* the issue was regression: the difference between a poet telling of what he "felt and saw" (to recall Blackwell on Homer) and recreating some event of a time beyond his experience. The latter undoubtedly had a lesser status as history than the former: imagination as against empiricism. That is the reason Macpherson and Chatterton displaced their imaginations into the past. Percy's three remaining rules of annotation were all to do with history:

2. To explain the History or Story referred to in some of the Historical Ballads; where necessary.
3. To inform us . . . where the particular Scene or Place lies. . . .
4. Miscellaneous; either explanatory, or Digressive: particularly to illustrate any Allusions to the old Manners, Customs, Opinions, or Idioms . . . [that] are now wearing out so fast, that if not preserved in such publications as these, they will be utterly unknown to posterity.[47]

Percy would have been dismayed to learn that many of those precious "allusions" to social history were in fact historical recreations, and not contemporaneous with composition. We remember Johnson's dismissal of Ossian: "As a modern production, it is nothing." Only Macpherson and Chatterton saw the virtues in regression and its crucial role in the making of history. We create the past, we know it, through what Hume called "visible gradations." Percy and the other anthologists could not appreciate that the next poem they unearthed might rescue several historical periods simultaneously. The literary monument was itself a conduit.

My aim is not to diminish the problems Percy faced, or play down the positive aspects of the *Reliques.* To the young Chatterton, the anthology must have enshrined poetry of the middle ages in a scholarly garb, and not many years later, they had a profound effect on the young Walter Scott. Percy stated that the minor details of life in the past were every bit as important as military and political events, and that one could obtain that superior information from a traditional poetical genre like the ballad. Macpherson was limited solely to Ossian's voice. The *Reliques* helped in forming Chatterton's versatile and sophisticated vision. Their influence can only be properly understood in the next chapter.

Other Anthologists

The rest of this chapter will look briefly at the relations of the forgeries to other anthologists of the late eighteenth century.

Evan Evans' *Some Specimens of the Poetry of the Antient Welsh Bards* eventually appeared in 1764, one year before the *Reliques*. The work was awaited eagerly by Percy and was to influence Gray and Chatterton. Evans like most of his colleagues was a social historian. He provided notes "to give the Curious some Idea of the Taste and Sentiments of our Ancestors."[48] The direct Macphersonic equivalent of this anthology was the *Fragments*, published four years earlier. Indeed, Evans used as an epigraph the same quotation from Lucan that was prefixed to the *Fragments*.[49] Evans stressed that he was not imitating Macpherson. He had conceived the *Specimens* long before 1760. But he had to admit Macpherson had convinced people the Dark Ages could shine poetically. Evans regarded the poems characteristically as "monuments of genius."[50] Macpherson used the same term. David Herd in *The Ancient and Modern Scots Songs* (1769) omitted the authenticating apparatus of notes, but he could still claim the poems as "the most natural pictures of ancient manners."[51] The desire was to humanize the past, something the forgeries did very literally. In 1770, the year of Chatterton's death, appeared *Ancient Scottish Poems*, edited by another of Percy's correspondents, Lord Hailes. Hailes's main source was the Bannatyne MS, though he admitted he had introduced forty old poems from other sources "to make such a selection as might illustrate the manners and history . . . of Scotland during the sixteenth century."[52] So "ancient" referred to only a couple of centuries ago. Indeed, most anthologies presented poems of medieval and later times, a movement of which Chatterton was certainly a part. Few literary archaeologists dug as deep as Ossianic times. Evans dated his MS as fourteenth-century, and the oldest of the poems as twelfth-century. But some still believed genuine primeval poems existed. In 1741, a speaker in a work called *The Polite Correspondence* said

altho' the Songs of the ancient Druids have been swallow'd up in Oblivion, yet there are still some Remains of British Poetry twelve hundred Years old, I mean the works of Taliesin a British Bard.[53]

That there had existed very ancient poets called Taliessin, Llywarch Hen, Aneurin, Oisin, and so on was uncontested. But whether their compositions survived in their original form was a different matter.

John Smith's *Galic Antiquities* (1780) professed to have located very ancient Scottish poems. But the full title of the anthology raises suspicions:

> Galic Antiquities: consisting of a History of the Druids, Particularly those of Caledonia; A Dissertation on the Authenticity of the Poems of Ossian; And a Collection of ancient Poems, Translated from the Galic of Ullin, Ossian, Orran etc.[54]

Macpherson would have smiled to see he had spawned imitators. Many of the anthologies being cited begin with compendious dissertations, most of them spiced with nationalist sentiment and extolling the poetical and historical virtues of the poems that follow. Smith's Gallic poems are so obviously Ossianic pastiches that they are reserved for chapter 5. There are doubts too about Edward Jones' *Musical and Poetical Relicks of the Welsh Bards: Preserved by Tradition and Authentic Manuscripts, from Remote Antiquity; Never before Published* (1784). We are not told how remote "Remote" is, though presumably oral culture was referred to in the title. The pieces were not particularly Ossianic, but in the preface Jones authenticated his sources by describing an ancient Welsh college called the "Gorfedd." An assembly of scholars met regularly at the institution. Their job was to "extinguish falsehood and establish certainty in the relation of events."[55] Jones created the Welsh equivalent of Keating's Irish college at Tarah. It is significant that this fictional academy, replete with imaginary poetical sources, should reappear in this wholly literary context. In Joseph Cooper Walker's *Historical Memoirs of the Irish Bards* (1786), which though not an anthology cited many ancient poems, the triennial assembly at Tarah was used to prove that in Ireland more than anywhere "many volumes of well-authenticated records have escaped the ravages of time and foreign spoilers."[56] Walker tried to reclaim Ossian to Irish soil after the theft by Macpherson. Walker cited several Fenian poems that went into Charlotte Brooke's *Reliques of Irish Poetry* (1789). Specific dating was again absent. Brooke ascribed nearly all the Fenian poems to an Irish Oisin, but admitted the original compositions were heavily corrupted by later bards.[57] Brooke included in her anthology two of those renowned cantankerous exchanges between Oisin and Saint Patrick. But the fourth relique, "Moira Borb," began with the line "A Tale of Old," which was of course lifted from Macpherson's "Carthon" and "Cath-Loda." Whether the poem was fake or Brooke was translating with a Macphersonic cadence only enhanced the importance of Ossian in relation to contemporary anthologizing.

The Welsh "Gorfedd" occurred again in the "Essay on Bardism" in William Owen's *The Heroic Elegies and Other Pieces of Llywarch Hen, Prince of the Cumbrian Britons* (1792). (There was also a brief mention by Southey in the introduction to A. S. Cottle's *Icelandic Poetry* of 1797.) Owen, like Charlotte Brooke, printed the Gallic originals of his translations. Macpherson was attacked for suppressing his sources, giving only a snatch of the Erse *Temora* at the end of *Fingal* (1762). Percy printed the original texts to *Five Pieces of Runic Poetry* (1763), but not the *Reliques* (with the exception of "The Marriage of Sir Gawaine," which is dealt with below). Owen can be cited to consolidate the anthologist's role as literary archaeologist:

> There were many celebrated Bards amongst the ancient Britons, whose productions have been partly preserved to the present time; but it is to be regretted that a number of most curious relicks have also been lost through the viccissitudes of destructive warfare; and what remain moulder away apace. . . . fearing that a total oblivion should, at some short period hence, be the fate that awaits these monuments of genius, the Editor, anxious to give the world some notice of their existence, has it in view to lay them before the public.[58]

Joseph Cooper Walker described the enemy of the MS as "the ravages of time and foreign spoilers.'[59] As was noted earlier, the editor stood on the brink of the abyss: he battled against time. The anthology can be seen as his museum. That word actually occurs in the titles of certain anthologies, such as James Johnson's *The Scot's Musical Museum* (1787) and Edward Jones' *The bardic museum of primitive British poetry* (1802). John Smith believed that Macpherson had preserved exactly the spirit of the evanescent Scottish Highlands whose culture was rapidly diminishing under English rule after the 1745 rebellion.[60]

The climax of the debate about the authenticity of primeval British poetry was Sharon Turner's *A Vindication of the Genuiness of the Ancient British Poems of Aneurin, Taliessin, Llywarch Hen, and Modlin* (1803). This remarkable document is reserved for appendix 3, because though it aimed to provide once and for all a detailed method of authenticating ancient poetry, it in fact performed a marvelous gloss on the forgeries, an irony best placed near the end of this study.

The best known of the anthologists who did not try to vie with Macpherson in antiquity were John Pinkerton and Joseph Ritson. In the 1780s and 1790s, they produced a score of editions of Scottish and English songs, ballads, and romances. Neither editor was free of some involvement with the issues under discussion.

In *Ancient Scottish Poems* (1786), Pinkerton refuted Ossian, though like Evan Evans, honoring Macpherson's genius and calling him the "Homer of the Celtic tongue."[61] In his first two anthologies, *Scottish Tragic Ballads* (1781) and *Select Scottish Ballads* (1783), he had put the point more lyrically. Though the ancient bards were extinct "they have left a spirit of poetry in the country where they flourished, and Ossian's harp still yields a dying sound among the wilds of Morven."[62]

Pinkerton was a "man of taste." As he said in *Ancient Scottish Poems* (1786)

> the editor has in no instance sacrificed the character of a man of taste to that of an antiquary; as of all characters he should least chuse that of an hoarder of ancient dirt.[63]

Yet Pinkerton did not deny the poems their historical value. He declared the purpose of *Scottish Poems* (1792) to be "to redeem our ancient history and poetry from neglect."[64] He saw the fifteenth-century poem *The Bruce* (1790) as "mostly real history" and its author, Barbour

> the earliest historian of Scotland, who has entered into any detail, and from whom any view of the real state and manners of the country can be had.[65]

Pinkerton's enthusiasm for literary merit led him, like Percy, to interpolate and invent. Most egregiously, he offered in *Scottish Tragic Ballads* a sequel to *Hardyknute*, already perhaps the most notorious forgery in Scottish literature after Ossian. *Hardyknute* first appeared in 1719. Supposedly a newly discovered ancient poem, its authors were popularly thought to be Elizabeth Wardlaw or Sir John Bruce. In 1740, Robert Dodsley published the poem as "Hardyknute: A Fragment. Beeing the First Canto of an Epick Poem; with General Remarks, and Notes." The format was obviously important in relation to the forgeries, though none of the "Remarks" and "Notes" says anything about history. Pinkerton could not resist attempting by his own imaginative powers to restore the ballad to "its original perfection," saying he had obtained the new stanzas from "the memory of a lady in Lanarkshire."[66] Joseph Ritson's suspicions were aroused.

Shortly after the publication of Pinkerton's *Selected Scottish Ballads* (1783) Ritson wrote a savagely denunciatory letter to *The Gentleman's Magazine* signed "anti-Scot." It was Ritson who first stamped the character of forgery onto dubious editorial procedures. He accused Pinkerton of pure invention, and gave him a place in a gallery of Scottish impostors:

> The distinguished honour which your native country has acquired by literary imposition upon her neighbours renders a function with those illustrious worthies, William Lauder, Archibald Bower, and James Macpherson, no small compliment to the ingenious Mr Pinkerton.[67]

(The various lists of impostors produced in the late eighteenth century are dealt with in Appendix 4.) Ritson turned literary imposture into a national trait. It was not simply that Pinkerton's work was "palpable and bungling forgery" or "studied and systematic forgery."[68] What really rankled Ritson was the public acclamation of such work: "The history of Scotch poetry exhibits a series of fraud, forgery and imposture, practised with impunity and success."[69] Johnson was not surprised by the popularity of Ossian in a nation who "loved Scotland better than truth."[70] Seen in this light, Macpherson was simply being a Scot guaranteed aid by literati who were, according to Ritson, "addicted to literary imposition."[71]

These accusations were made in the "Historical Essay on Scottish Song," which opened Ritson's *Scottish Songs* (1794). But though "anti-Scot," Ritson was a scholar first. In *Ancient Songs* (1792) he had already shown serious misgivings about the methods of his countryman Percy. Ritson disagreed with Percy's portrayal of the minstrels. Ritson believed they were musicians and performers and did not compose their own songs. Thus he doubted the authenticity of Percy's minstrel ballads—the ones Percy claimed were taken from the folio MS. This led to suspicions about the MS:

> The MS is doubtless the most singular thing of the kind that was ever known to exist. How such a multifarious collection could possibly have been formed so late as the year 1650, of compositions from the ages prior to Chaucer, most, if not all of which had never been printed, is scarcely to be conceived by those versed in ancient MSS. a similar instance perhaps not being found in any library public or private. This MS to increase its singularity, no other writer has ever pretended to have seen.[72]

Percy became a proto-Macpherson, "withholding" a MS that may not exist. Note that Ritson's disbelief centered on regression, one of the major traits of the forgeries. Ritson did not believe in or did not understand the process. When Percy had posed for Reynolds in 1773, the folio MS had been vicariously displayed to the public. Bertrand Bronson in his fine study of Ritson believes the reaction was transparent: "the folio conspicuously held in the crook of his arm, hardly produced conviction in the minds of doubters."[73] Particularly those scholars interested in the contents of the folio and not its awesome exterior. By the time Ritson published *Ancient English Metrical Romances* in 1802, he had inspected the folio MS, but this had only confirmed his belief that Percy had indulged in covert invention:

> To correct the obvious errours of an illiterate transcribeër, to supply irremediable defects, and to make sense of nonsense, are certainly essential dutys of an editour of ancient poetry; provideëd he act with integrity and publicity; but secretly to suppress the original text, and insert his own fabrications for the sake of provideing more refine'd entertainment for readers of taste and genius, is no proof of either judgement, candour, or integrity.[74]

Percy's fault was dissimulation, lack of "publicity," not allowing his revisions to be judged against the originals. Macpherson faced exactly the same charge, though he had the added veil of translation to shield him. Chatterton created originals as well as transcriptions, but, as will be shown, he ran very high risks when he became accountable to experts. In the fourth edition of the *Reliques* (1794), Percy finally printed the original version of "The Marriage of Sir Gawaine." He hoped the corrupt and incomplete state of the original text would prove

> how unfit for publication many of the pieces would have been, if all the blunders, corruptions, and nonsense of illiterate Reciters and Transcribers had been superstitiously retained, without some attempt to correct and amend them.[75]

But Ritson seized on Percy's failure to print all the other originals:

> The purchaseërs and peruseërs of such a collection are deceive'd and impos'd upon; the pleasure they receive is derive'd from the idea of antiquity, which, in fact, is perfect illusion.[76]

There was the dichotomy again between the genuine and the fake: real antiquity versus illusory, recreated antiquity. This chapter began with Percy alluding to that dichotomy to place himself and his fellow anthologists on the other side of the fence and Macpherson on the wrong side. The chapter ends, significantly, with Percy subject to the same sentencing. He was now rubbing shoulders with Macpherson. But then that was always the case.

5

Chatterton: Literary Transmission

"I would by no means borrow and detain your MSS"
"those papers . . . how have they been transmitted?"
Horace Walpole in letters to Chatterton

Chatterton's vision was a sophisticated advancement on Ossian. I say "advancement" and not "modification" because there was a clear progression between the two forgeries. Most obvious was the bringing forward of the historical setting. Thomas Rowley was a fifteenth-century figure, some twelve hundred years later than his Celtic counterpart Ossian. Rowley belonged to civilized, sophisticated urban culture: a *literate* world; the MS world before the invention of the printing press. Ossian existed in an oral culture. Macpherson's great achievement was to create and authenticate Ossian's spontaneous utterance. But Chatterton's world was peopled by authors, not speakers. The voices of the past we hear were always mediated by a literary mode. This dominance of the MS was actually a liberating force. Responsive to historiographical developments, Chatterton broadened the scope of history to allow any document a position of value. The resulting diversity of materials creates problems for the critic. Macpherson's vision was the bardic voice: history as poetry. But Thomas Rowley wrote non-literary as well as imaginative works. Moreover, he was not the only author in Chatterton's vision: Canynge, Iscam, and others all made contributions. The net result of this composite authorship is difficult to classify in literary terms. There were over seventy "items," including letters, biographies, genealogies, heraldries, chronicles, even a painter's bill. The unifying factor that embodied the imagined world was the MS and its making of history. The transmission of the past was literary. Chatterton was more intimately concerned with the tangible and verifiable materials of historiography than Macpherson. Oral transmission, which Macpherson labored with great ingenuity to authenticate, played no part in Chatterton's vision.

Ossian's world was itself dominated by the past. Chatterton's vision also involved a regression of perspectives. But the "gradations" were far more solid and verifiable than in Ossian. Thomas Rowley was an anti-quarian, scholar, and poet. He wrote works that were, in terms of the vision, contemporary and factual (such as a biography of his patron William Canynge). For instance, we learn historical facts about Rowley's Saxon hero Aella in the treatise "A Discourse on Brystowe." But Aella's life was also dramatized in Rowley's tragedy *Aella*. Chatterton's vision showed the making of historical fiction out of historical fact. Ossian was not so sophisticated. Indeed, many features of Chatterton's forgery were so different from Ossian as to be antithetical. Chatterton's vision was Christian, and it grew from verifiable events and institutions: medieval church building, the War of the Roses. Ossian belonged to a pagan, pre-institutional world, in which concrete details of life and society were kept to a bare minimum. Chatterton was more the pioneer of modern historical fiction in the way he mixed fiction with large amounts of documented source material and authentic historical fact.

Bristol Affairs

Unlike Ossian, Chatterton's forgery was not published in his lifetime. The only items he saw in print were "Bridge Narrative" (*Felix Farley's Bristol Journal*, October 1, 1768), "Elinoure and Juga" (*Town and Country Magazine*, May 1769), "Antiquity of Christmas Games" (*Town and Country Magazine*, December 1769), "The Court Mantle" (*Town and Country Magazine*, March 1769) and six of the seven Ossianics, (*Town and Country Magazine*, March to December 1769). So we can only speculate on the form the forgery would have appeared in had Chatterton been given, like Macpherson, a free hand concerning publication. There is certain extant evidence to suggest Chatterton was thinking of a series of mis-cellaneous historical anthologies, again developing on Macpherson's practices (see Appendix 2). But in the absence of conclusive data we must be thankful for Donald Taylor's chronological ordering of the forg-ery in the bicentennial Oxford *Works* (1971).[1] Taylor enables us to see the forgery as an evolving vision and to treat it sequentially as we did with Ossian. Unlike Ossian, however, Chatterton's genius and diversity means that almost every item is worthy of study. Only a few very minor pieces have been omitted for the sake of coherence (this includes the many sketches of buildings). I omit the parentheses Taylor placed round titles that he has provided for the untitled works. Difficult Rowleyese words are glossed in footnotes. A "C" after the word denotes Chatterton's own gloss. A "T" denotes Donald Taylor's gloss.

Chatterton's vision was English, Macpherson's Scottish. The title of the first work in the Chatterton forgery was "Bristowe Tragedie or the Dethe of Syr Charles Bawdin" (*Works*, 1:6–20), and was a ballad by Thomas Rowley describing the execution of a local hero by Edward IV. This was local history. Municipal histories, of which Whitaker's *History of Manchester* (1771) was one of the best known, were becoming popular. As will be shown, as the vision developed it became parochial history, recreating Chatterton's own parish of Redcliff in the middle ages. Chatterton's concern was to give Bristol and Redcliff an important and rich past. Ossian's was a whole world on the brink of extinction. The Bristol knight, Charles Bawdin, was also on the point of death. But he was being killed by the forces of real national history that for a time channeled themselves through Bristol. The city was made to figure significantly in the York-Lancaster conflict (known as the Roses War) of the fifteenth century. Chatterton anticipated Thomas Warton's belief, stated in *Specimen of a History of Oxfordshire* (1783), that "what is local is often national."[2] The poem described an event at which Rowley was a spectator. He was history's hallowed eyewitness. This primary "prism" or "gradation" of Chatterton's historical vision was set in a period of civil warfare and national upheaval. The influence of Macpherson could be seen again. He used the Fingalian Wars as the great historical events against which the *Fragments* and many of the minor poems authenticated themselves. Yet Macpherson's Fingalian Wars were imaginary. The York-Lancaster conflict was not. Chatterton even had Edward IV and the future Richard III present at Baldwin's execution (as, according to Chatterton's sources, they were).[3] Chatterton, like Scott after him, was not afraid to introduce real historical characters into an imagined account.

The poem was a voice of war, but spoke through a definite literary genre: the ballad. The fact that Chatterton used such a genre is particularly important. Macpherson strove to make Ossian's voice unique. His innovative prose-poetry represented the uniqueness of Ossian's bardic utterance: poetry-history. Before Chatterton began to commit his vision to paper, however (in 1768), Percy published the *Reliques* (1765). The *Reliques* were a strong influence on Chatterton, not only as a source for Rowleyese diction. Percy popularized the medieval world through the medium of the ballad. His scholarly apparatus strove to prove that such a minor literary genre could perform the valuable task of preserving a nation's social history. As Chatterton's first footnote showed ("the following Transaction happen'd in Bristol the 2nd year of King Edward

4th" (*Works*, 1:6)) the ballad was offered as historical proof of King Edward's ruthlessness. Thomas Rowley was introduced, effectively, as a poetic journalist.[4]

There were only five footnotes to "Brystowe Tragedie," but because they were the first of their kind, they are worth scrutinizing. If these notes are compared to the prefaces to Ossian's poems and Percy's *Reliques*, we see that Chatterton was closer to the latter. The literary merit of the ballad was stressed, and in such a way as to challenge conventional literary history. The ballad was "a Specimen of the Poetry of those Days, being greatly superior to what we have been taught to believe" (*Works*, 1:6). Notes 2, 3, and 4 reinforce the statement. Ossian clearly did challenge conventional notions of literary history, but Macpherson did not introduce Ossian under that banner. Percy's purpose (followed by other anthologists) was to show that among the dross of the Dark Ages some literary gems existed. Beneath Chatterton's claims that the ballad rivals Homer (*Works*, 1:17) was the eighteenth-century drive to find a truly native hero. Ossian, of course, fulfilled the desires of many. Chatterton here began to present his own idea of heroism. Bawdin was a Bristolian, Christian, and martyr to his beliefs.

The historical background given in footnote 5 (*Works*, 1:20) was the equivalent of a Macphersonic or Percyean introduction to a poem. There was more than bravado in Chatterton's quoting the chronicle Stowe. As Donald Taylor is at pains to point out in his own notes, much of what Chatterton presented as historical fact was actually taken from verifiable sources. With Ossian, the proportion of "fact" of this kind was much less, and Macpherson rarely foregrounded sources so conspicuously as to quote them. The sudden switch in footnote 5 from the citing of Stowe to imaginary evidence (the "Parchment Roll," which told of an earlier MS possessed by Canynge) was typical of Macpherson's procedure however. No reason was given why this MS was "more Authentick" than Stowe. The essential point to note is that Chatterton would manufacture this document later in "England's Glorye Revyved." In other words, he authenticated a later work. We can call this technique inter-allusion. The "conclusion" to note 5 also had a direct precedent in Macpherson's appeal for subscriptions to recover an Ossianic epic made at the end of the preface to the *Fragments*. Chatterton was one stage earlier, in that he was not yet published, but he was trying to stimulate a desired audience:

> if Gentlemen of Fortune wou'd take the Trouble of looking over the Manuscripts in their Possession, which are only valued for their Antiquity, it might possibly throw Light upon many obscure Passages in and help to establish a more Concise History of our Native Country, than even *Camden's Brittania*. (*Works*, 1:20)

The initial "sell" of "Brystowe Tragedie" was literary. But the essential function of the ballad was presented as historical. Chatterton was asking for the very things the rise of social history in the eighteenth century sought to achieve: the elevation of antiquarianism, the "small details" of the past, to mainstream history writing; the building up of the national from the local. Chatterton tried to provoke the kind of MS-hunting activity that Macpherson was paid to undertake. Another aspect of Chatterton's advance on his predecessor, however, was that MS recovery was to be an integral imaginative part of the vision. Thomas Rowley undertook an expedition to recover MSS that was very similar to the real one of Macpherson.

So "Brystowe Tragedie" related an important event in Bristol's past. Taylor shows (*Works*, 2:816) that Chatterton used exact topography. Like Defoe, Chatterton relished such details. The poem described a social spectacle, a rich and colorful pageant at which, we can deduce, Rowley was an onlooker with Lancastrian sympathies. His presence in his own poem was not conspicuous. He was like a *Reliques* minstrel, making interjections mainly of a moral kind (for instance, in the final stanza). There was no attempt to create the dramatic, spontaneous form of Ossian because such an authentication was not needed. Rowley's was a literate world. The richness of detail also marked Rowley off from Ossian. There was a parade of those "minute circumstances" that were declared by anthologists to present authentic social history. Almost any of the stanzas describing the execution procession could be quoted. For instance:

> The Freers of Seincte Augustyne next
>   Appeared to the syghte,
> Alle cladd ynne homelie russett weedes,
>   Of goodlie monkysh plyghte:
>
> Ynne diffraunt partes a godlie psaume
>   Moste sweetlie theye dydd chaunt;
> Behynde theyre backes syx mynstrelles came,
>   Who tun'd the strunge betaunt.
>
> (ll. 269–76)

Chatterton was not indulging in a simple costume-parade form of historical fiction. The vision was to refute that idea as it unfolded. For instance, take the last stanza of the procession passage:

> And after them, a multitude
>   Of citizenns dydd thronge;
> The wyndowes were alle fulle of heddes,
>   As hee dydd passe alonge.
>
> (ll. 297–300)

These were the common people of history, spectators like Rowley, but unlikely to be remembered. Note Bawdin's prophecy: "Oh, fickle people! rewyn'd londe!/Thou wylt kenne peace ne moe;" (ll. 181–82). Chatterton had a Shakespearian grasp of social history that went far beyond Macpherson's.

The creation of speeches for historical figures had a venerable history stretching back through historical drama to classical historiography. There was an obvious indulgence in such poetic licence in the confrontation scene between Bawdin and the King (11.305–44). Even if Rowley had been a spectator of the execution, it was highly unlikely he could have heard the shameful whispers between Edward and his brother:

> Kynge Edwarde's soule rush'd to hys face,
>   Hee turn'd hys hedde awaie,
> And to hys broder Gloucester
>   Hee thus dydd speke and saie:
>
> 'To hym that soe-much-dreaded dethe
>   'Ne ghastlie terrors brynge,
> 'Beholde the manne! hee spake the truthe,
>   'Hee's greater thanne a kynge!'
>
> (11.333–40)

The scriptural allusion (Pilate's proclamation to the condemned Jesus in John 19.5) made Bawdin a Christ figure. The essential values of Chatterton's vision were strikingly introduced. Social history broke the dominance of monarchs and battles over the making of the past. That cashiering was enacted in the lines quoted: Bawdin was "greater thanne a kynge!" Chatterton's fifteenth-century Bristol was governed by a Christian middle class. Chatterton's was not a proletarian vision. Rowley, Canynge, and the rest were very important Bristol citizens. They were legislators and town-planners. But they were citizens nonetheless—an active, functioning part of a society. They were not remote aristocrats. Chatterton's vision was of the current beneath political and military history, and of the interaction between the two. Fingal was a benign ruler, but an absolute king nevertheless. Bawdin's being "greater thanne a kynge" showed again how Chatterton moved on from Macpherson.

The next piece to be composed was "Ynn auntient Dayes, when Kenewalchyn Kynge" (*Works*, 1:21–22). A problem of the unpublished nature of the forgery is that some pieces, like this one, were not "edited" by Chatterton and have no designated author. The language is Rowleyese, so we can assume the author was Rowley or someone of the same period. The poem began a biography of St. Warburgh, who later became the Saint of Redcliff, Chatterton's own parish. Another hero was created whom we see "cast asyde his Earles estate" (1.5) because he "Saw something further, and saw something more" (1.8). The poem was unfinished. We do not learn much else about the man. Unlike Macpherson, Chatterton produced genuine literary fragments. Unless he also edited the work, however, one cannot be sure fragmentation was Chatterton's intention. This poem could have been an experiment in the genre of poetical biography. The first words "Ynn auntient Dayes" made clear readers were seeing the past at second remove. No doubt Chatterton would have glossed the reference to "Kenewalchyn Kynge," had he edited the piece, giving some exact dates. Taylor (*Works*, 1:817) tells us the setting is the seventh century: Anglo-Saxon times. Thus the allusion to Ursa in line 14 ("Since valorous Ursa first wonne Brittayne Isle") suggests the author had particular sympathies for that period (Ursa is Horsa who with Hengist conquered England). "Brystowe Tragedie" was poetical reportage, empirical data of the past. "Ynn auntient Dayes" was, relative to Rowley's time, poetical history: historical literature. Many of the observations made about "Brystowe Tragedie" can still be applied. The poem dealt with factual events. Chatterton was still working from sources. But the double perspective, the regression or "gradation," needs to be grasped.

Chatterton's system of perspectives had not yet become dynamic. In "The Tournament" (*Works*, 1:23–26) the proper transmission of the past was still being prepared for. "Tournament," with its martial topic, prepared for the epic "Battle of Hastynges I" that followed it. The subheading was Macphersonic:

One Cento of an ancient Poem called the Unknown Knyght or the Tournament. I offered this as a sample, having two more Cento's—The Author Unknown.

(*Works*, 1:23)

The format was unspecific: the poem was "ancient," not dated. The presentation of a jousting match attested to the influence of the *Reliques* again (for instance, "Sir Cauline"). The poem is best seen as a first draft that was later rewritten as "The Tournament. An Interlude." Chatterton employed this strategy many times. It is one of the major ways he experimented with historical points of view.

The editorial subheading to the first version of "The Battle of Hastynges" (*Works*, 1:26–43) set the transmission of history into dynamic operation:

An Ancient poem called the Battle of Hastynges written by Turgot a Saxon Monk in the *Tenth* Century and translated by Thomas Ronlie Parish Preeste St. Johns in the City of Bristol in the year of our Lord

1465 of whom more in Book 1st.—the remayning Part of this Poem I
have not been happy enough to meet with—

(*Works*, 1:26–27)

Note the deliberate errors: "Ronlie" for "Rowley" and tenth for eleventh
century. This date was corrected by Chatterton himself in a footnote,
which suggests he was setting up the subheading as the work of a
previous editor. The poem was a fragment and part of some kind of
pamphlet or anthology series (see Appendix 2). Most important, there
was literary transmission: Chatterton edited Rowley who like Macpherson translated an ancient MS. The precise dating produced a working
model of Hume's "visible gradations": 1066–1465–1768 (and to us).

So Macpherson's position as a translator of ancient epic poetry was
internalized within Chatterton's vision. Chatterton's Saxon epic existed
at second-remove. The epic genre, the conventional voice of war, was
Turgot's not Rowley's. Like Ossian, however, the poem was a native epic,
taking its theme from indigenous history. Turgot's being Saxon gave
added impact to what he was recording: the end of the Saxon age. His
bias, like Rowley's in "Brystowe Tragedie," was made obvious. The
Normans were villains and cowards. The English heroes were the Bristolian Saxons in King Harold's army (Harold was a Dane: though Saxon
rule of England came to an end with the Danish conquest, the two races
united to fight the Normans). Most of the action is tiresome carnage and
slaughter. The major point of interest is the historical digression on
Stonehenge (11.301–20). The seeming irrelevance of this historical information makes the interjection all the more important. Turgot was himself
fascinated by the past:

> Herewald born on Sarims spreddying Playne,
>   Where Thors fam'd Temple manie Ages stood:
> Where Druids auntient preestes did Ryghts ordaine:
>   And in the Middle shed the Victymes Bloude—
> Where auntient Bardi did their Verses syng:
>   Of Caesar conquered and his mightie Host:
> And how Old Tinyan necromancynge Kinge,
>   Wrackd all his Shippynge on the British Coast
>   And made him in his tatter'd Barks to flie
>   Till Tynyans Deathe and Oppurtunitie—
>
> To make it more renomed than before
>   I tho' a Saxon yet the Truth will tell
> The Saxons steinde the Place with British Gore,
>   Where nete but Bloude of Sacrifices fell—
> Tho Christiens, still they reverenced the Pike,
>   And here theie met whan Causes did it need;
> Twas the auntient Elders of the Isle

Did by the Tracherie of Hengist bleed—
O Hengist! han thy Cause bin good and true,
Thou wuldst such murd'rous Acts as these eshew—
(11.301–20)

There was a regression of perspectives here back to Ossianic times. But the transmitter was the most famous historical monument in Britain. The mention of "auntient Bardi" (1.305) can almost be taken as a reference to Ossian. The allusion is a clever one: the Bards sing of native heroism ("Caesar conquered"), just as Turgot is doing. The second stanza of the digression is even more interesting. For the only time in the poem, Turgot's personal voice interposed. The reason is that his historian's instinct for truth was stronger at this point than his racial allegiances: he recounted a shameful deed in Saxon history because the deed happened. Hengist's massacre was particularly criminal, in terms of the values of Chatterton's vision, because the Britons had been converted to Christianity. Turgot like Rowley was a historian with a Christian morality. Truth was always their concern; they made clear when they were transgressing.

The heraldic and genealogical items of the forgery can be the most barren in internal interest. Yet it is important to note that Chatterton had his authors write the older forms of historiography that were reviled in his own time but were respectable in the fifteenth century and earlier. "Extracts from Craishes Herauldry" (*Works*, 1:44–51) was the first non-literary (that is, non-imaginative) work of forgery. Such works can be called antiquarianism. No pejorative overtones are attached to this labelling. Regression was most obviously operating in these works. It is difficult, however, to discriminate between the antiquarian works and the literary or "artistic" pieces in terms of greatest significance or superiority within the vision. One virtue of Donald Taylor's *Works* is that it prints many facsimiles of Chatterton's MSS (see the frontispiece to volume one for part of "Craishes Herauldry"). These plates show that the antiquarian works exhibit better than any other the intimate involvement Chatterton had with the MS. The format of the presentation, the need to supplement the words with sketches and drawings, the fabricated parchment itself, show how much further Chatterton went than Macpherson, who simply claimed the "originals" existed. Chatterton made history *in toto:* the sources and their function. Chatterton's fascination with historical MSS was passed on to Rowley. Rowley's world, it must be stressed, was the MS world, before the appearance of printed texts. This situation meant that Chatterton like Macpherson could have an editorial monopoly over his "discoveries." Logically, there were only likely to be a few extant MS copies of the same text. As Ossian was poised at the end of oral culture, however, so the arrival of the printing press was the topic of "Rowley's Printing Press" (*Works*, 1:60). Rowley was credited with having the idea in England for the invention of a press designed to save "the eyen and handes of poor clerkes" (1.12). The effect of this short piece was to authenticate Rowley's own MS culture, in which *"scrivenyes"* (1.2) and *"amanuenses"* (1.3) were the purveyors of knowledge.

"Craishes Herauldry" enriched Bristol's past by peopling it with aristocratic ancestors. The quoting of extracts from "The Tournament" (11.21–25; 11.194–98) was important in two ways. The poem was cited as history. The first direct inter-allusion of the vision was given. Macpherson used this device skillfully, reinforced by the sequence of the poems. Chatterton was no epigone. He borrowed directly from Macpherson for certain strategies (for instance, the quoting of poems in footnotes),[5] but generally he modified and improved. As Taylor says:

> The tedious cross-referencing of the Rowleyan works makes important points. The Rowleyan imaginary world was thick and rich and interrelated. Places and people occur again and again in different contexts. It was also a world which gradually grew toward this state. (*Works*, 1:xliv)

Chatterton's diversity makes his forgery more readable than Ossian. That diversity arises from the vision's literary status. The next piece was again by Rowley. But he was in a very different role from the poet or translator: "A Brief Account of William Cannings / from the Life of Thomas Rowlie Preeste" (*Works*, 1:51–56). This piece was biography within autobiography. Both genres gained prestige as historiography in the eighteenth century. Counterpointed and mirrored by the fictitious "Lives" of the novel, Boswell's *Life of Johnson* (1791) was a culmination of this brand of historical writing. Rowley's voice from the past was therefore informal, though not spontaneous. For that Ossianic equivalent, readers had to wait for private documents—the letters. Chatterton introduced the relationship between Rowley and Canynge from the inside. The informal, wry, and humorous "Account" was the perfect introductory voice of friendship. The footnote to the title (*Works*, 1:51) gave some essential details about Canynge that the text expanded on. He was a rich Bristol merchant, but he put his wealth to charitable use by founding Chatterton's local church, St. Mary's Redcliff. E. H. W. Meyerstein's *A Life of Chatterton* (1930) gives all the biographical details of Chatterton's involvement with this church.[6] Chatterton's father was sexton there. He found many old deeds and MSS, some of which he brought home. The young Thomas grew up using these MSS as playthings. They were part of his life. So the wheezing Doctor Johnson, who labored up Redcliff church steps to see the famous Rowleyan chest, may have been consoled to know that it did once contain MSS, even if not the ones Chatterton produced.[7]

Canynge was the church's real founder. The text of "Brief Account" immediately contrasted him with his avaricious father and brother. This "Canynge theme," as I would like to call it (the evils of cupidity), was to be rewritten from many different angles as the forgery unfolded and as Chatterton experimented in the modes of access into the past. One result of Canynge's benign temperament was his generosity to his "Fader Confessour" (1.1), Rowley. Rowley was too worldly not to acknowledge his pecuniary debt to his master. But their relationship developed into much more than this. Canynge became the patron and employer of Rowley's literary and antiquarian talents. Chatterton's own title for Canynge in his first letter to Walpole was "Mecenas" (*Works,* 1:259). In a sense, Canynge was Fingal to Rowley's Ossian. We see later how flattering Rowley could be.

Rowley's first commission was a major one. He was ordered to go on an MS-hunting expedition to secure, "at any Price" (l. 16), Saxon plans of church design. Canynge wished to have a Saxon basis for the design of St. Mary's, which he was in the process of planning. Canynge, a true child of the vision, was a Saxonist. So was Rowley. While on this imaginary equivalent of Macpherson's sponsored Highland expedition, Rowley came across the Saxon MS of "Battle of Hastynges." Rowley was too poor to buy the MS. He did not try to cheat Canynge, whose money he was spending. So this poem of great literary and historical value (which we have just read) had to remain neglected for many months. Rowley's antiquarian talents were confirmed when the Saxon architectural plans he had purchased were used and the building of the church began. There is a humorous episode in which Rowley ordained Canynge so he could avoid a marriage arranged for him by King Edward. Chatterton's Christians were also fallible humans. (It is worth pondering that Rowley, being celibate, was like Ossian the last of his race. Being a priest, however, the eschatology did not worry him.) It was only after Rowley had been handsomely rewarded (£20) for "Brystowe Tragedie" and had some free time that he could indulge in his own hobbyhorse and purchase the MS of "Battle of Hastynges." It took him a full year to translate it (ll. 89–94). "Brief Account" ended on a very materialist note, showing Rowley's skill (no doubt learned from Canynge) at negotiating for property. One of the fusions Chatterton's vision sought to achieve was between the material and the spiritual; between the mercantile energy of his native city and the proper aesthetic, civil, and religious harnessing of that energy and wealth. The perfect symbol for such a fusion was a church: a concrete artefact serving God and all who wished to worship in it and built philanthropically by important citizens. There were two major events in the "primary" world of the vision (Rowley and Canynge's fifteenth-century Bristol), and they created a telling juxtaposition: the Roses War and the founding and building of St. Mary Redcliff. Both these events, it must be stressed, were real. They really happened. Chatterton created his own version of how they took place in Bristol. That version was sober, empirical, and brilliant in its operation. A footnote to "Brief Account" (*Works*, 1: 53–54) contained "Onn oure Ladies Chirch," the first example of Rowley's many celebrations of St. Mary Redcliff. Such literature would include his greatest imaginative productions. "Onn oure Ladies Chirch" was, as Chatterton's note pointed out, "much inferior to the generality of Rowlie's Compositions" (*Works*, 1:54). But the poem was interesting in that Rowley presented himself as an eyewitness. He sat on a hill overlooking "this Chapele" (l. 6), and mused on the greatness of its founder.

So within the literary transmission of the vision existed other conduits: monuments, most of them real, through which the past flowed and concretized itself. Chatterton's historical energies flowed through solid reality like the lines of magnetic force of a bar magnet: achieving an area of liberation, but always returning to the visible central core. Churches were such a core. The next piece, "Bridge Narrative" (*Works*, 1: 56–59) used bridges. "Bridge Narrative" was the first item of the forgery to be published, appearing in *Felix Farley's Bristol Journal*, October 1768. The piece was very felicitously placed after "Brief Account," because it also described the erection of an important edifice. The construction this time was secular, but a religious element was very cleverly incorporated. Unlike St. Mary Redcliff, the bridge described was no longer standing. It had in fact been demolished to make way for a new bridge spanning the Avon that was opened in 1769. Chatterton celebrated this opening by indulging in a piece of journalistic typology. He described the equivalent situation five hundred or so years earlier (Taylor (*Works*, 1: 844) notes the earlier bridge was built in 1247), as witnessed by a spectator. The introductory editorial note stated that the piece described "the Mayors first passing over the Old Bridge" (ll. 1–2). That "Old Bridge" contrasted startlingly with the "newe Brydge" of the first line of the account (l. 6). The perspectives of history were vitalized. But the situation was even more sophisticated. The thirteenth-century pageant was itself enacting a typological relationship to its past. The aim of the Bristolians' dress, art, and particularly song was to recall and celebrate the Saxon precedent of their situation. The Saxon bridge was built to commemorate the miracle of St. Warburgh fording the river (ll. 18–19), the act which made him Redcliff's local saint. So in this sense, the Saxon bridge and its eighteenth-century successor were religious constructions. Not content to leave matters there, Chatterton gave in a footnote the actual songs alluded to in the account that celebrated Saxon history. "Songe of Saincte Werburgh" (*Works*, 1:57–59) was sung three times in the procession (l. 21, l. 32, l. 43). The song clarified the legend. Warburgh gave up his earthly belongings (in "Ynn auntient dayes") to become a Bristol saint. The song cleverly stressed the change in building materials: the original Saxon bridge was "All of wood" (l. 23); the new one was " of Stone" (l. 37). The location too stressed the typology: the new bridge was "Standyng where the other stode" (l. 140). The "Songe of Sayncte Baldwyn" (*Works*, 1: 59) (sung in the pageant at line 39) took a very different approach. The bridge was now a military bastion. Baldwyn made a stand there, defeated the Danes, and saved the city. Chatterton's vision did not exclude military glory, but it nearly always existed under certain moral restraints. Baldwyn, like the knight Charles Bawdin in "Brystowe Tragedie," was a Christian warrior. He fought for defense only. After victory, he threw his sword away to become a recluse. The "Songe of Sayncte Baldwyn" was a preparation for the introduction of Bristol's famous soldier, Aella.

The context of Aella's introduction was a Chattertonian equivalent of Ossian's "The Songs of Selma." In two verse letters (*Works*, 1: 60–63) occured a "boutynge matche" or rhyming contest between Rowley and John Ladgate—a deliberate misspelling of Lydgate. He was a precedent, if Chatterton needed one, for a medieval poetical monk. Ladgate and Rowley had an "oulde Freendshyppe" ("To John Ladgate," l. 3). Needless to say, the real poet suffered a resounding defeat. The winning poem was "Songe toe Ella." Rowley's hero was introduced in a concentrated literary context. Ossian, we remember, was first presented in an imaginary poem in the preface to the *Fragments*. Aella was to inspire Rowley's major imaginative work, titled after him. "Song toe Aella" (*Works*, 1:61–62) was a panegyric. Like Baldwyn, Aella defended Bristol from the Danes. He was a local hero. That is as yet all readers were told. In "John Ladgate's Answer" (*Works*, 1:62–63), Ladgate remarked of Rowley's poem "Now Rowlie in these mokie Daies/Sendes owte hys shynynge Lyghte" (ll. 18–19). "Mokie Daies" was deliberately ambiguous ("mokie" means dark, cloudy). If the phrase referred to the Roses Wars, then Rowley became a literary resurrection of Aella: a Bristol hero defending the English tradition. The phrase could also refer to the Dark Ages. In this sense, the meaning was more controversial. The hint was given in the first note to "Brystowe Tragedie": "a Specimen of the Poetry of those Days, being greatly superior to what we have been taught to believe" (*Works*, 1:6). The correction there was to literary history. The Rowley poems proved that the Dark Ages could shine poetically. The hint in Ladgate's words was of a correction of cultural history. When Chatterton sent *Aella* to the publisher James Dodsley in February 1769, he made this facet of the vision explicit:

> The Motive that actuates me to [publish *Aella*] is, to convince the World that the Monks (of whom some have so despicable an Opinion) were not such Blockheads, as generally thought and that good Poetry might be wrote, in the dark days of Superstition as well as in these more inlightened Ages.
>
> (*Works*, 1: 172)

As was shown in chapter 1, the ancient MS was regarded as the source of new, authentic light on the past.

As "Songe toe Ella" was Rowley's first imaginative-historical work, we are now introduced to his antiquarianism. He had already revealed himself as a translator, autobiographer, and poet. Now we must add the historian. Rowley became a prism through which his past could be transmitted. Canynge was now Rowley's patron and was to commission many works. The subheading of "Yellowe Rolle" (*Works*, 1: 63–65) was "Of the Auntiaunt Forme of Monies carefullie gotten for Maystre Wm. Canynge by mee Tho: Rowley." Canynge had commissioned this history of minting because he was fascinated by wealth, its positive and negative aspects. This concern was his "theme." Thus the piece began and ended with his pronouncements on the use of money. " 'Trade is the Soule of the Worlde but Monie the Soule of Trade' " (ll. 4–5) was the voice of the Bristol merchant. "You dyspende Heavenne to gette Goulde but I dyspende Goulde toe gette Heaven" (ll. 69–70) was the voice of the Christian who used wealth in the most charitable way. Canynge balanced the material and the spiritual. He was merchant, mayor, Christian, church-builder. He refused the patent offered by the King to mint money himself. Rowley was present at the refusal, so he could report Canynge's words faithfully. "Yellowe Rolle" continued to build up Bristol fictions. Rowley gave to Bristol mints that never existed (*Works*, 2:853).

Rowley's next antiquarian work ("Englandes Glorye revyved in Maystre Canynge," [*Works*, 1:65–67]) was an obvious sequel. It picked up on the reference to "Maystre Canynge's Cabynet" in line 32 of "Yellowe Rolle" and described some of its contents. This "Cabynet"—a library or "auntyant Reposytorye" as it was called in the first line—was another clever authentication of MS culture. Canynge preserved MSS of the past (Turgot and the Saxons) and the present (Rowley). This particular collection was supposed to be one of the best in the land, as the title confirmed. The title could be seen as Rowley's flattery of a dilettante antiquarian. But the point being made was a serious one. Canynge's library preserved the national heritage. No glorious past was possible without records. They were the building blocks of history.[8] There were also archaeological relics: coins and weapons ("a Syghte moste terryble" (l. 30)). But the most important item was the "Greet Ledger" (l. 15). England's glory was its Saxon past. Rowley's skills as collector and translator of Saxon MSS thus became crucial. The library contained several of Rowley's translations, including "Battle of Hastynges" (l. 16). Rowley only used Latin once in "The Merrie Tricks of Lamyngetowne" and there its usage was burlesqued. The vision was, in Rowley's own words, "Alle thys ynne Englyshe" (ll. 23–24). The recovery of native history was also the establishing of the English language. Chatterton, we can assume, revered Chaucer. Ladgate gave Rowley a supreme accolade when he said "Turgotus and Chaucer live / Inne evry thynge hee wrytes" (*Works*, 1:63). The vision cast off with ease the conventional image of the middle ages as suppressed and dominated by papism and Latin.

The second version of "Battle of Hastynges" (*Works*, 1:68–88) tried to be more impartial than its predecessor in its glorification of native (Saxon) history.[9] The work was in Canynge's "Cabynet" and the title acknowledged this: "translated by Rowlie for W. Canynge Esq.." Chatterton's editorship was absent. But as compensation, Rowley's role as editor as well as translator was established in a footnote to line 48 ("Fierce as a ryver burstynge from the borne"):

> In Turgott's tyme Holenwell braste of erthe so fierce that it threw a stone-mell carrying the same awaie. J. Lydgate ne knowynge this lefte out a line. (l. 70)

Rowley was now the exact counterpart of Macpherson. This note offered historical commentary (Holywell is a river in west England) and contained a red herring in true Macphersonic manner. Rowley attacked a supposedly rival translation by Lydgate. Chatterton's purpose was to show that Rowleyan scholarship was widespread, that a sophisticated literary and historiographical culture existed in a fifteenth century ravaged by civil war. The rewritten epic, however, had little intrinsic interest. The warriors' sense of the historical importance of their actions looked towards *Aella*: "today will Englandes dome / Be fyxt for aie, for gode or evill state" (ll. 131–32). The indication that Turgot was writing, not reciting, the epic was also important. For instance, at line 315: "How shalle a penne like myne then shew it all?" No muse is called on for aid. The Stonehenge digression was revised, reducing the historical information to one stanza only (ll. 531–41) and omitting Turgot's interjection.

The literary culture the vision presented was rich and diverse. So far Rowley had been the major author, with contributions by Craish, Ladgate, Turgot, and various unknowns. Now a new author was introduced: John a Iscam. His appearance made an impact because he wrote the first dramatic work: "The Merrie Tricks of Lamyngetowne" (*Works*, 1:89–93). The piece was really semi-drama, being a series of three "Discoorses" or dialogues. Macpherson experimented with dialogues in the *Fragments*, to little positive effect. "Merrie Tricks" was a satire on greed, ingratitude, arrogance, and doltishness. The topography of Redcliff, Bristol, and the surrounding area was uniquely abandoned for the setting of Cockney London. But only in order to tarnish that setting. Lamyngeton was a bankrupt Bristol merchant, a sort of failed Canynge. He could not get creditors and his London business associates had been the first to seize his property and goods. His resolution was to exact revenge by becoming a pirate (perhaps the influence of "Sir Andrew Barton" from Percy's *Reliques* was present here). Lamyngeton's first plunder was to be the ships of Philpotte and Walworth, which were, ironically, transporting his seized goods to Bristol to be sold. His intentions were to do exactly the same with his plunder: "With Cockneies Bloude Thamysis shall be dyde / Theire Goodes in Brystowe Markette shall be solde" (ll. 15–16). The ascendancy of Bristol over London as a trading center was made. The unfinished piece ended with the words of Lamyngeton's fellow rebel Robynne: "And I to Brystowe Towne wylle haste awaie" (l. 121).

The next antiquarian piece, "A Discorse on Brystowe" (*Works*, 1:93–104) was the first piece of explicit local history writing. It took the form of three treatises by Turgot, which were amended by Rowley at considerable length. Turgot was Rowley's major source of Saxon history, and here he payed scholarly tribute to him by updating and correcting him.[10] Perspectives of regression and transmission were created. It may surprise us to learn that Turgot also had his literary sources. In line 2, he referred to "Algaruses Dome of Somertowne." A "Dome," according to Taylor's glossary (*Works*, 2:1195) was a tax-book. The literary gradations receded in a similar manner to the songs of the past in Ossian. But Chatterton's vision also concretized the perspectives: MSS, churches, bridges. The word "tradition" was very rarely mentioned.

Many key features of the vision were consolidated or mentioned for the first time in "A Discorse on Brystowe." The superiority of Redcliff over Bristol was begun. Despite Turgot's claim to be dealing with his native city of Bristol, the first two treatises dealt with Redcliff and only the third with Bristol proper. But Turgot gave a reason for this procedure. In the first section, the legend of St. Warburgh was retold with significant new details. When Warburgh arrived at Bristol, the whole of the city was pagan. He warned the people to be converted or to risk the consequences. Only the parish of Redcliff heeded him, was converted, and thus saved from the inundation that destroyed most of Bristol. In thanksgiving, the wooden bridge we know of from "Bridge Narrative" was built. So the structure of Turgot's historical account had a religious motive: "Thus I describen the Auntiaunt Monuments of Rudcleve fyrst as theie first receiven the Fayth." (ll. 86–87). The vision was Christian. It was also organic. It is very difficult to deal conclusively with any work of the forgery in isolation. The previous piece dealt with—"Merrie Tricks"—was cleverly incorporated into Rowley's notes to Turgot's account. We learn that Iscam's work was in fact historical literature based on true events. The piece was quoted as history, as biography. From his position of hindsight, Rowley could present the sequel to Iscam's account. Lamyngeton's "evyll corses" (l. 114) were pardoned by the king and the Bristolian became, in terms of the vision, a hero by leading "a godlie Life" (l. 125) and building a church. Rowley's longest note to "A Discorse on Brystowe" was on Canynge's founding of St. Mary Redcliff (*Works*, 1:98–99). More flattery was heaped. The church was "the Glorie and delyght of Brystowe and wonder of Sumerset" (l. 189). Another dull celebratory poem was given, though the opening lines (as did those of "Onn Oure Ladies Chyrche" in "A Brief Account") conjured up Rowley as history's eyewitness: "Stay curyous Traveller and pass not bye / Until this fetive Pile astounde thine Eye" (ll. 191–92). Rowley's panegyric on the church and its builder—"The Pride of Brystowe and the Westerne Lande" (l. 200)—was echoed by Turgot's description of Aella as "the staye of the Weste" (l. 305). We learn more facts about Aella (ll. 300–07): that he was a Mercyan Saxon, keeper of Bristol castle, and that he defeated the Danes in two major battles, in one of which he was mortally wounded. We do not yet know that Aella also founded a church. But this account of Aella in "A discorse on Brystowe" must be remembered, because it was the "factual" data upon which Rowley was to base his major imaginative work, *Aella*.[11] Rowley turned fact into historical fiction.

Before *Aella* however, there was an intermediary dramatic work; an "Entyrlude," which Rowley co-writes with Iscam, called "The Parlyamente of Sprytes" (*Works*, 1:106–16). To avoid any confusion with the Tudor court entertainment, the meaning of an "Entryrlude" was explained in the subheading:

> Plaied bie the Carmelyte Freeres at Mastre Canynges hys greete Howse, before Mastre Canynges and Byshoppe Carpenterre, on dedicatynge the Chyrche of Oure Ladie of Redclefte
>
> (*Works*, 1:106)

The work was actually more akin to a masque. It was performed in a private mansion. Though the occasion was the founding of a church, the "Entyrlude" was not liturgical. It was a formalized, artificial celebration, a pageant of historical builders and founders of churches. The play was yet another blend of the secular and the spiritual: acted at the merchant Canynge's house, but celebrating a church. We learn later that *Aella* too celebrated Canynge's church, having been commissioned by him when the first stone was laid.

Chatterton's editorship flourished in "Parlyamente of Sprytes," grooming this piece for publication. There were ninety-nine footnotes. Most of them were glosses of the Rowleyese diction. Several notes were historical or critical, and in some poems were quoted. Note 19 cited yet another dedicatory poem by Rowley. This one was quoted to prove that Bishop Carpenter blessed the church. The genre of this piece, like several before it, including "Brystowe Tragedie" and "Bridge Narrative," can be called journalism. All three works described a formal procession, as witnessed by a spectator. The tricks Chatterton played with time in "Parlyamente of Sprytes" were elaborate. Rowley's poem, describing the church's dedication, was in the past tense and ended: "Then alle dyd goe to Canynges Howse an Enterlude to playe / And drynk hys Wyne and Ale so Goode and praie for him for aie" (ll. 19–20). The lines referred to that which is occured spontaneously in the text above the footnote. The contrast between the historic reportage of the poem and the immediacy of the drama was striking. Only an editor with hindsight could experiment with the making of history in this way, juxtaposing different literary modes of access into the past, different historical points of view. Chatterton may have picked up the device of quoting poems in footnotes from Macpherson, but he elaborated greatly.

It is useful to compare "Parlyamente of Sprytes" to Ossian. In both works there were voices from the past. But there were major differences. No attempt was made in "Parlyamente of Sprytes" to make us believe we heard the actual voices of the historical characters. Their resurrection was poetic artifice. Their speeches were designated as being the work of either Rowley or Iscam, who also spoke the parts. Each speech was a carefully mannered species of flattery. The builders, beginning with Nimrod, testified that St. Mary's surpassed in beauty their own architectural achievements. Rowley, significantly, took the part of Aella. The most interesting speeches were those of Byrtonnes, Segowen, and Fitz Hardynge, who recited mini-autobiographies. Segowen was the most interesting case. He was a converted usurer. He gave to Canynge a definitive label, "The Prynce of Chyrches Buylders" (1. 174). Ossian, we recall, was a prince and was introduced in Fragment VI as "Prince of men." Chatterton's vision had less exalted values: a more refined notion of heroism.

The nearest Chatterton came to creating the spontaneous voice of the past was in private letters. We have already had formal verse epistles between Rowley and Ladgate. In "Four Letters on Warwyke" (*Works*, 1:121–24) we read private prose correspondence between Rowley, Canynge, and the Earl of Warwyke. The white-hot discussion of contemporary politics in these letters is particularly effective in vivifying and authenticating the turbulent historical events looming over Rowley's Bristol. The letters describe affairs preceding those in "Brystowe Tragedie." Certain noblemen around Bristol, including Warwyke, had declared for the Yorkist, Edward IV. Canynge's first letter to Rowley revealed his dilemma. As mayor of Bristol he was being pressed by his counselors to declare his allegiance, but "wulde not have them doe meane thynges for Gayne" (11. 6–7). He asked Rowley's advice. Canynge's life may have depended on his decision. There is a novelistic deepening of characterization in these letters—quite apt, it might be thought, in the age of the epistolary novel. In Rowley's reply, he is tarnished in our eyes for the first time. He was insensitive to the reality of his friend's situation. He made a half-hearted and impractical suggestion that Canynge resist Henry—"was you of Power and in Possession of Castles" (1. 12)—which of course Canynge was not. Even worse, Rowley switched to some antiquarian chitchat (he was on one of his MS "expeditions"). His letter demonstrated brilliantly an occasion when the present should have assumed precedence over the past. Rowley's priorities were wrong. Canynge's reply to Rowley (*Works*, 1:122–23) was a superb recreation of the way a respected citizen in his situation and at this time may well have thought about politics and religion. His comments also refined some of the values of the vision. He "woulde remayne neutre" (11. 19–20). But he had an obligation to help his country find peace. His criticism of the saintly king Henry was a hint that he would side grudgingly with York and Edward:

> A Kynge shulde bee one who ruleth hys People hymselfe and ne trousteth to untroustie Servantes. Mie Actions shewie mie no Ennemie to Goode, but methynketh a holie Seyncte maketh notte a goode Kynge. From the daies of Saxon Governmente to thys presente Englande haveth been undone by Priest-Kynges. Edgar, Edwarde Confessour, and Henrie 6th. have the mette with Danes, Normannes, and Warwyks. True Englyshmen are lyke untoe Masties never pleased but whan set a-fyghteing. Honours to the Mynster are not allwaie honoures to the Throne.
>
> (11. 23–31)

These sentiments appeared again in the drama "Goddwyn." Canynge revealed here why he, like his church, St. Mary Redcliff, stood for a harmonizing of the civil and religious, the material and spiritual worlds. Chatterton's vision was not uncritical of the Saxons or Christianity. The

Saxons were to blame for establishing the priest-king. It was a misuse of religion for a king to worship God at the expense of the people. Canynge then turned to a more quotidian criticism. He believed Henry was a weak king, dominated and cuckolded by his wife. On an even more worldly scale of values, Canynge owed Henry nothing. He had done the King many favors, such as bringing troops back from France. His conclusion was nationalistic: "Under Henrie we mote have peace but never renome" (11. 52–53). He stressed to the Lancastrian, Rowley, "doe not thynke I am a Yorkeyst" (1. 53). His letter to Warwyck, however, (*Works,* 1:123–24) was a cautious declaration for York. Canynge would not give financial aid himself to the Yorkists, but he would encourage the subscriptions of others. Yet he also wished to smuggle the condemned Charles Bawdin out of Bristol. In "Brystowe Tragedie," Canynge was shown making a final, passionate but unsuccessful plea for Bawdin's life. Our intimacy with Canynge increases beyond that for Rowley.

That intimacy develops further in "Nine Deeds and Proclamations" (*Works,* 1: 124–34). Chatterton manufactured yet another historical "genre": the public or archival record. The documents show Rowley and Canynge administer a Bristol thriving with mercantile and spiritual energy. Rowley, like Ossian, was an important figure in his society.

The first three deeds are wills that Canynge composed at different times of his life, before and after he was ordained. Canynge had a "Cloth Workers" business (1. 11). He appealed to his son William to "support the Trade which my Ancestors have carried on Time out of Mind, in the sd. City of Bristol" (11. 81–82). Canynge was not against the pursuit of wealth, as long as the city felt some of the benefits. The other deeds gave examples of such benefits. The fourth document informs us that not only did Canynge help found Westbury College, but that he had others (including Rowley and Iscam) intended building an annex. The annex will be a school. Iscam will be its master and will form the curriculum: "Grammar, Philosophy and Architecture" (1. 133). At Rowley's expense, he can "purchase MSS relating to the said Sciences" (11. 134–35). The deed was a fake public record, duly endorsed and filed in 1468, exactly three hundred years before its real date of composition. Chatterton was well versed in legal jargon. He was apprenticed to an attorney and did much of his fabricating in spare time at the office. The fifth, sixth, and seventh deeds reported the founding of another building, a chapel. The day-to-day commercial life of Bristol was superbly brought to life:

And also they the sd. Portreves on receipt of 20 Marks so agree to cut away part of the wooden Bridge from Elphege Street to the middle of Corporation Lane and thereby make a Passage for the Boats that bring Stones or other materials for building and also cut away two Pieces of

Timber projecting from the main Arch of the Great Bridge, and that no
Toll shall be taken either by the Greater Portreves of Cattle Horses or
Sleds drawing Stones or the lesser, by Boats Timber or other things
requisite to the buildg.

(ll. 90–98)

In the eighteenth century, only Defoe's *Journal of the Plague Year* could
compare with Chatterton's detailed historical recreation of a living city in
a living past. From ruins arise new edifices, new ruins. The process
continued.

The final two documents are fascinating. They were proclamations
issued by Rowley and Canynge, who were legislating in civil and religious matters. The eighth document concerned a riot caused by "muti-
nous and unholie Friars" (1. 276). The ninth involved a problem of
religious doctrine. The legal voice in both documents was firm, but fair.
Authority was exerted. Some of the rioters were fined and others banished. The heretical preacher was banned. The reasons given for this
decision are important. Chatterton explored behind the scenes of another historical assumption: the tyranny of the Catholic Church. Rowley
and Canynge's concern was for the citizens:

Tho' we Wm Canynge and Thomas Rowley approve not of invalidat-
ing Arguments by violence and Death provided a Man enjoys his
Opinion alone, yet when he goes about to persuade others from the
right way, and speaks openly of the terrestial Being of Christ a bridle
should be laid on his tongue. the weak and ignorant catch at evry
thing they understand not.

(ll. 13–19)

Peace was preserved. The problem preacher was still given a chance to
counter in public a sermon of Rowley's on the Trinity (ll. 323–31).

A considerable contrast was made in the glimpses of the youthful
Rowley presented in "Three Rowley Letters" (*Works*, 1: 135–42): the
private voice of correspondence among friends written at different
times. As might be expected, politics did not figure in Rowley's chatter.
The first letter to Canynge, written in Rowley's youth, shows how far
back their friendship goes. Rowley mourned Canynge's absence from
the Christmas festivities. Canynge's father, who was still alive, was
keeping his son away from the fun. Even at this age, Rowley was
dabbling in antiquarianism. He reported finding the tombs of some of
Canynge's ancestors dating back to the twelfth century. The second
letter to Iscam, written in Rowley's schooldays, contained a good deal of
bawdy humor. It also mentioned that Iscam has sent Rowley a "Hystorie" (1. 32). Rowley's third letter was not really correspondence, but a

piece of antiquarianism requested by Canynge's brother Thomas. Rowley was only too willing to give "anne Accounte of Reddclefte" (1. 53). The account mainly listed churches, giving Redcliff a very rich history of church architecture. In a "Mynsterre" (1. 119) Rowley claimed he had found a Saxon MS, which he had translated. This Saxon chronicle told of new buildings, military, and mercantile events in eleventh-century Bristol and was a preparation for "Chronical 1340–1374." Rowley quoted Turgot as his main source (11. 150–56). Bristol rivaled London (line 205 tells us Bristol had the first mayor) and Redcliff Bristol: "the Brystowe Menne were the fyrst Traders to Ireland and the Radcleft men the fyrst Traders whanne Brystowe han nete botte Souldyers' (11. 160–62).

Rowley's "The Rolle of Seyncte Bartlemeweis Priorie" (*Works*, 1: 143–51) was effectively a guidebook. He described the building with the same relish that would be afforded to a historical account of a church. The MSS that belonged to the priory were described in detail. As with Canynge's "Cabynet," Chatterton created imaginary libraries to store his MSS. The priory's library was larger than Canynge's, containing medical and philosphical treatises, religious dramas (miracle plays and "maumeries"), Saints' Lives, romances, and a "secret History" (as Chatterton informs us in footnote 24). The literary culture of Bristol was made richer than ever. Correspondingly, so was Chatterton's editorial apparatus. He earns the following praise from Taylor:

> In this piece, particularly in his notes, C. emerges as an antiquary of the broadest competence, expert in medicine, books, and plays, and in popular, ecclesiastical, architectural, and artistic antiquities.
>
> (*Works*, 2: 903)

The most memorable footnote is 11, (*Works*, 1: 145–46) which is keyed to "Christmass Maumeries" (1. 29). This footnote was Chatterton's longest and best. It did not involve a display of scholarship. Rather, it established Chatterton's making of a social history. There is little point in quoting the note, because it needs to be read in full for its power to be appreciated.

Chatterton wrote social history in a way that would surely have delighted Percy, Warton, and later Scott. Antiquarian details brought the past vividly to life. More "manners and customs" were presented than in the whole of the *Reliques*. The primitivist attack on fashionable modern society at the opening of the footnote gave way to a marvelous evocation of medieval society participating in religious festivity and Christmas sports. There was no question of the pre-Reformation Church suppressing such activity. "Popery and Old English Hospitality" existed hand-in-hand. Chatterton was shrewd enough, however, to note the political dimensions of the scene he drew. The barons' hospitality secured the loyalty of their inferiors. The hierarchical nature of feudal society was not hidden. But it was subsumed in the general enjoyment. Chatterton rewrote this footnote almost verbatim as "Antiquity of Christmas Games" (*Works*, 1:409–412), which was published in *Town and Country Magazine*, December 1769. Chatterton did more than indulge in his "Hobbyhorse as an Antiquary." He anticipated historiographical practice by several years. Not until the end of the century did Joseph Strutt (who was an influence on Scott) begin to produce historical surveys such as *Sports and Pastimes of the People of England* (1801).

In the short and anonymous "Chronical 1340–1374" (*Works*, 1:154–55), Chatterton's antiquarian skills were transplanted inside the past again. The chronicle form of history writing was generally reviled as being dry, biased, and untruthful: the notorious monkish annal. Yet Chatterton converted this jaded form into a meaningful record of social history. Each entry depicted an important event in the municipal life of Bristol. For instance, an ancestor of Canynge's was buried in 1341. He was an important textile manufacturer, as the entry for 1339 makes clear. The chronicle's author was aware of a prevailing attitude that seemingly minor events were not worth recording. So the entry for 1342 noted: "Tweyen of Howsen brente yn Highe strete The whyche thynge before ne Oulde Manne ne Chronycalle dyd Mynde." The entry for 1346 recorded one of the antiquarian benefits of Bristol's zealous building program: the uncovering of archaeological remains. In this case a section of a bridge and some Norman coins had been discovered. 1352 and 1339 were particularly interesting entries. They recorded technological innovations: primitive street lighting and the manufacture by Canynge's ancestors of a new kind of woollen cloth. The other entries depicted the architectural flux in Bristol. Buildings and their construction were vital to Chatterton's vision. Their making symbolized his own making of history.

The next piece to be written was Rowley's major imaginative work: the drama *Aella* (*Works*, 1:174–228). The full title reads:

> Aella: A Tragycal Enterlude, or Discoorseynge Tragedie, wroten bie Thomas Rowleie; Plaiedd before Mastre Canynge atte hys howse nempte the Rodde Lodge; (also before the Duke of Norfolck, Johan Howard).

Elements of the previous dramas were synthesized. "Merrie Tricks of Lamyngeton" was a series of dialogues or "discoorses." "Parylamente of Sprytes" was an "Enterlude" performed at Canynge's house, and was written to celebrate the completion of St. Mary Redcliff. *Aella*, we learn in "Life of W: Canynge"—the next work—was also authenticated in its relationship to the church, being commissioned by Canynge to celebrate the laying of the foundation stone.

The most interesting part of *Aella*, in relation to this study, is not the text, but Rowley's verse epistles that preceded it. These epistles composed a theoretical preface about historical fiction. Some crucial ideas were foregrounded. For this reason alone, *Aella* is Rowley's major imaginative work. In both epistles, Rowley attacked writing practices of his time. The first epistle lamented the decay in poetry. The second made a more important distinction between poetry and history. The first epistle opened with an evocation of the distant past:

> 'TYS songe bie mynstrelles, thatte yn auntyent tym,
> Whan Reasonn hylt[12] herselfe in cloudes of nyghte,
> The preeste delyvered alle the lege[13] yn rhym;
>
> (ll. 1–3)

Ossianic times were conjured here. No records existed, only minstrels' songs. Rowley styled this period a dark age. By comparison, therefore, his own age was enlightened. The Druidic practice of delivering the law in verse was often condemned in the eighteenth century as pernicious cabbalism. Rowley acknowledged this possibility in line 5 ("The whyche yn yttes felle use do make moke[4] dere[5]"; [4]·much; [5]·hurt, damage), but his point was that, all the same, poetry warranted a very high degree of respect. In his own age, poetry was abused. He catalogued some of these abuses. Monks wrote bawdy verse (Rowley himself had not been exempt). The vernacular was reviled:

> Whoever speketh Englysch ys despysed,
> The Englysch hym to please moste fyrste be latynized.
>
> (ll. 17–18)

Rowley's motives in writing *Aella* were presumably the opposite of those he attacked. He was not writing for mercenary gain, even though Canynge would probably reward him. He was not a literary tradesman or a pedant. The last stanza justified his choice of a historical rather than Biblical theme:

> Playes made from hallie[14] tales I hold unmeete;
> Lette somme great storie of a manne be songe;
> Whanne, as a manne, we Godde and Jesus treate,
> In mie pore mynde, we doe the Godhedde wronge.
>
> (ll. 43–46)

This view suited perfectly Rowley's status as a secular priest. He was a social as well as religious person. Aella was a Christian, who also defended Bristol.

The second epistle also dealt with subject matter, but now the opposition was between history and poetry. It seems that Rowley was casting off his antiquarian garb for the poet's laurels:

> Straunge dome ytte ys, that, yn these daies of oures,
> Nete[15] butte a bare recytalle can have place;
> Nowe shapelie poesie hast loste yttes powers,
> And pynant hystorie ys onlie grace;
> Heie[16] pycke up wolsome weedes, ynstedde of flowers,
> And famylies, ynstedde of wytte, their trace;
> Nowe poesie canne meete wythe ne regrate,[17]
> Whylste prose, and herehaughtrie,[18] ryse yn estate.
>
> (ll. 49–56)

Rowley attacked the predominance of history writing over poetry. History, notably, was in prose. Moreover, history writing was "pynant" or dry, too much concerned with genealogy. Rowley's intention was to bring the past alive. Stanzas 4 and 5 are crucial:

> Pardon, yee Graiebarbes,[19] gyff I saie, onwise
> Yee are, to stycke so close and bysmarelie[20]
> To hystorie; you doe ytte tooe moche pryze,
> Whyche amenused[21] thoughtes of poesie;
> Somme drybblette[22] share you shoulde to yatte[23] alyse,[24]
> Nott makynge everyche thynge bee hystorie;
> Instedde of mountynge onn a wynged horse,
> You onn a rouncy[25] dryve yn dolefull course.
>
> Cannynge and I from common course dyssente;
> We ryde the stede, botte yev to hym the reene;
> Ne wylle betweene crased molterynge bookes be pente,
> Botte soare on hyghe, and yn the sonne-bemes sheene;
> And where wee kenn somme ishad[26] floures besprente,
> We take ytte, and from oulde rouste doe ytte clene;
> Wee wylle ne cheynedd to one pasture bee,
> Botte sometymes soare 'bove trouthe of hystorie.
>
> (ll. 73–88)

Taylor quotes "soare 'bove trouthe of hystorie" to conclude that Rowley was leaving history writing behind, while at the same time apologizing for fiction. (*Works*, 2:924, 929). Neither is in fact the case. Rowley was not casting off the antiquarian's mantle for the laurel crown. In terms of the vision, Aella was a real person about whom certain historical facts were known. Rowley wished to verify these facts. "Hystorie," as used at lines 75 and 78, refers to history writing. The image of "crased molterynge bookes" in line 83 was an attack on "pynant" antiquarianism. Against this mode of access into the past, Rowley was proposing another: the poetical or fictional. This mode would not consist of free invention. It would only "sometymes" indulge in poetical license, and "soare 'bove trouthe of hystorie." The image of Pegasus and airy freedom of movement was used to suggest that a spirited and vivid imagining of the past, based on the known facts, would bring history alive and cleansed of its "oulde rouste" (l. 86) to such an extent that a few factual errors, if they occured, would be more than compensated for.[27] The second epistle can be read as an endorsement of historical fiction: an imagining of the past that had the aim of humanizing and vivifying it to the full. Rowley tried to define a hybrid form that would relate "somme greate storie of a manne" (l. 44) in the spirit of "An onlist[57] lecturn, [58] and a song adygne[59]" (l. 94) ([57.] boundless; [58.] subject; [59.] nervous, worthy of praise). He knew that factual truth was not the only sort of "trouthe." It may be necessary to sacrifice the latter to achieve "sense," "dygne," and "wordie thoughtes" (l. 99, l. 100). Rowley foregrounded his awareness of history as process: a trait of the forgeries.

Aella's uniqueness was that it was an integral part of the overall vision. But the play itself had little historiographical interest. There were few details of social history, and little veneration among the characters for history. The minstrels in the play all sang non-historical pieces: pastorals, epithalamions, dirges. Placed in the context of eighteenth-century British historical drama (see chapter 2), *Aella* was a conventional play, and even included the customary rape scene (*Works*, 1:216–219). My intention is not to tarnish the literary merits of *Aella*. But in the context of this study, the play is less interesting than the means by which it had come to be written.

Rowley's short biography, "Life of W: Canynge" (*Works*, 1:228–35) complemented "A Brief Account," which was biography-in-autobiography. In "Life of W: Canynge," Chatterton conducted a fascinating experiment. He juxtaposed two "genres" of historiography: biography and letters. His aim was to show how different discourses, different historical viewpoints, could illuminate each other. Despite the assurances that "manie notable matteres" (1.3) needed to be related, Rowley's thirty-three lines of biography gave only a bare outline of the main occurrences in Canynge's life. One fact to emerge that we did not know is that Canynge founded a Freemasons' Lodge, of which Rowley was a member. This lodge was a locus of municipal philanthropy:

> Heere dyd the Brodhers arede[28] foree the Goode of the Common
> Wealle and unkevend[29] hyltenne[30] artes and devyces somme amen-
> dynge the Clothe trade odher Somme ybuyldeynge.
>
> (11. 27–29)

At the end of the account, Rowley said: "hys Mynde, knowledge and
Lore hys hylten Epistles wyll shewe and the moe soe as hee dyd ne
entende the same botte forre pryvate Syghte" (11. 40–42). Rowley, like
Chatterton, presented private letters for public view. Canynge's private
voice was juxtaposed against the bare statement of facts in Rowley's text.
Moreover, the letters followed the order of events in the text. In other
words, the "Epistles" acted as footnotes. Canynge's private voice was the
most authentic gloss possibile on his own life.

Most of the letters showed how Canynge used his wealth. The two
letters of 1431 showed Canynge's consistent generosity to his tenants.
The two freemason letters of 1432 composed an exercise in social history
almost comparable to the account of Christmas festivities in Chatterton's
footnote to "Rolle of Seyncte Bartlemeweis Priorie." We go inside
Rowley's account. Canynge recorded what happened inside the Lodge.
The first letter described the opening ceremony. The humor was refresh-
ing—"the Councylmenne felle aslepe" (1. 85). Canynge then quoted his
own speech from a "Paper Rolle" (1. 85), which was later "framed ynn
eguilten Frames" (1. 105). Chatterton rarely lost a chance to incorporate
MSS into the picture. Canynge's turgid oratory set out the Lodge's aims:

> I shall therefore streve to drawe togyderre menne of counynge Witte
> to advaunce the Glorie of thys oure Towne. Whatte wee shalle un-
> keven that wylle benefytte Menne shalle be knowen, whatte wylle
> harme, unknowne, ne will soe despoyle Vice thatte beeynge too eft
> Ken'd shee bee ne moe affrighting botte wee wylle streve to advaunce
> auntyaunt Accountes Glorie and Profytte, with the Helpe of Godde.
>
> (11. 99–105)

Canynge founded an arts and crafts guild to serve Bristol and God. The
guild met every Thursday. The next letter was an unofficial minutes of a
meeting. The assembled included Friars, "Gentylmenn, Maconnes, Car-
penters and deeleres" (1. 110). Note the decor: "Over mie greete Seate
was depycted Architectura in a Saxonne Habytte" (1. 111). The emblem
related to the purpose of the meeting, which was to recommend that
Rowley's Saxon MSS (recovered in "A Brief Account") be used as the
basis for the new church, St. Mary Redcliff. History was white-hot: "The
Londe ys boughte the Maconnes hyred and alle thynges ynne read-
ynesse" (1. 118). Canynge also commissioned *Aella*, to celebrate the
laying of the cornerstone. By the next letter, the play had been per-

formed and Canynge congratulated Iscam's performance as Celmonde and Rowley's as Aella. *Aella* was not mentioned in Rowley's biographical text, and the omission reflected his modesty. Because we have just read *Aella*, Canynge's comments were particularly effective.

The letters for 1435 and 1445 depicted other talents of Canynge: his aesthetic appreciation of painting and his antiquarian interests. He was a man of many gifts. He was an artist as well as art lover. After the remaining letters (which stressed his continuing friendship with Rowley into old age) Rowley remarked: "As a Leorned Wyseager he excelled ynne alle thynges. as a Poette and Peyncter he was greete" (11. 189–90). A specimen of Canynge's poetry, "The Worlde," was given. Canynge joined the ranks of authors. "The Worlde" was the third version of Canynge's life, now changed to autobiographical fantasy. Minstrels sided with the son in his rebellion against the cupidity of his father. The speech of the fourth minstrel would later be rewritten as "The Goulers Requiem" (*Works*, 1:290–91), Canynge's dramatic monologue in which a dying miser was haunted by spectral thieves. The message of "The Worlde" was simple: hoarding wealth leads to misery. Yet wealth, if used properly, could have salutary effects for society, as noted by Rowley: "Wm. Canynge who as a Merchante did emploie alle the Radcleve Syde of Brystowe ynne Trade" (1. 187).

In Rowley's next major work, "Heraldic Account of Bristol Artists and Writers" (*Works*, 1:236–247), Canynge's life was again versified, this time by Rowley. Bristol had already been given a rich and often nationally important past. "Heraldic Account" showed medieval Bristol bristling with artistic energy.

The last of the worthies to be listed was Canynge: "but hee deserveth hys Storie ynn oderwyse than Payncters or Carvellers, and soe shall I gyve yt yn Vearse" (11. 177–78). "The Storie of Wyllyam Canynge" (*Works*, 1:241–47) was very reflexive. It was specifically about the imagining of the past. Until the appearance of the goddess (at line 217), the poem could have been autobiographical. Rowley lay by a stream and wondered what "hardie Champyons" (1. 192) had also been known to the river in the past. He thought of great church builders such as St. Warburgh and Aella. After this imagined roll call of "eche dygne Buylder" (1. 216), he had a vision. The naked goddess Truth arose out of the water, read Rowley's mind and offered to take Rowley back in time:

> Strayt was I carry'd back to Tymes of yore
> Whylst Canynge swathed yet yn fleshlie Bedde
> And saw all Actyons whych han been before
> And all the Scroll of Fate unravelled

(11. 269–72)

Fantasy permitted the acting out of the historical imagination. Before the appearance of the goddess Rowley had mused:

> I see [Warburgh's] Ymage waulkeyng throwe the Coaste
> Fitz Herdynge, Bithrickus, and twentie moe
> Inne Vysyon fore mye Phantasie dyd goe
>
> (11. 212–14)

"Storie of Willyam Canynge" shows how Chatterton differed from those eighteenth-century poets before him who could only enter the past with the aid of the historic muse. In this poem, such an act was conspicuous artifice, from within the past.

A final feature of "Heraldic Account" needs commenting on. Canynge may have been a hero, but he was human and fallible. In the account of Allwarde the Saxon (11. 32–45), a singular incident occured. Allwarde carved statues ("Ymageries") for Aella's chapel. These have descended to the present warden of Bristol castle. Canynge, the patron and collector, tried to purchase them for his "Cabynet." This would have been standard route of transmission. But the warden refused permission, preferring to put the statues on public display "as a goodlie Spectacle for menne to beholde" (11. 40–41). History was given to society at large. Museum ossification was avoided. The warden was no maverick. He knew how to preserve the artefacts, making sure the "depycture of the Faces" (1.44) was retained by facing the statues away from the prevailing winds.

Seven Ossianics: "Ethelgar," "Kenrick," "Cerdick," "Godfred Crovan," "The Hirlas" 1 and 2, "Gorthmund"

Chatterton's Ossianics are an important group of poems. They were the most direct evidence that he had read Macpherson. We can make comparisons between the original and the imitator. The Ossianics were not in Rowleyese. They purported, like Ossian, to be modern translations from Saxon and ancient Welsh. The fact that all the Ossianics were published in *Town and Country Magazine* attested to the great popularity of Macpherson's Ossian. The best way to treat the poems is as Chatterton's modification of the Ossianic voice of war, adapting it to his own vision. There is also a link to the anthologists. "The Hirlas" is a pastiche of the first poem in Evan Evans' *Some Specimens of the Poetry of the Antient Welsh Bards* (1764).

"Ethelgar" (*Works*, 1:253–55) reads at first sight almost like a parody of Macpherson. In Ossian's world, the people were hunters. In "Ethelgar," the hero's son Aelgar was savaged by a wolf he was stalking. Ethelgar's wife was then struck by a bolt of lightning. The incident could have been a skit on the "sublime" Ossianic climate and scenery. The heartbroken Ethelgar tried to commit suicide by throwing himself off a cliff, but he was saved miraculously by St. Cuthbert. As a result, Ethelgar became a monk at the "college of Kenewalcin" (1. 102). The parody tries to make a serious point. "Tis not for thee, O man! to murmur at the will of the Almighty" was the opening moral. The Saxon author of "Ethelgar" was Christian. The poem was a Christian's wry view of the Ossianic world of pagan martial values, deaths, and stormy emotions. There was no attempt, significantly, to authenticate the voice of the author. The only voices in the poem were the hymns of the protagonists and St. Cuthbert's admonishment to Ethelgar that he had forgotten to put his trust in God. There were characteristic Macphersonic inter-allusions however: "noble were his ancestors, as the palace of the great Kenric" (11. 23–24); "his soul was astonished, as the Britons who fled before the sword of Kenric" (11. 33–34). The next Ossianic was "Kenrick." Kenrick was a pagan. The first Christian-Saxon Ossianic, "Ethelgar," was the reference point against which the others were to be judged. There was no warfare in "Ethelgar." Battle and carnage belonged to the pagans.

In "Kenrick. Translated from the Saxon" (*Works*, 1:274–75), the Saxon leader Kenrick routed the Britons. But in "Cerdick. Translated from the Saxon" (*Works*, 1:276–79), the Saxons' treatment of their captive foe was shown to be a barbaric pagan ritual:

> the town of Doranceastre increases the flame, and the great image is red with the blood of the captives: the cries of the burning foe are drowned in the songs of joy; the ashes of the image are scattered in the air, the bones of the foe are broken to dust—Great is the valour of Cerdick, great is the strength of Kenrick.
>
> (ll. 80–85)

A later footnote (to 'Gorthmund') spelt out this 'greatness':

> The Pagan Saxons had a most inhuman custom of burning their captives alive in a wicker image of the god Tewisk. Whilst this horrid sacrifice was performing, they shouted and danced around the flames.
>
> (*Works*, 1: 678)

Chatterton's Ossianics were essentially anti-heroic, and confirmed the Christian values of his vision. His Christian warriors such as Aella fought in defense only. Fingal was a lenient, merciful hero, but Macpherson lauded pagan military values. Chatterton tarnished them. The horrible ritual of the wicker sacrifices occured again in "Godfred Crovan" (*Works*, 1:345–52).

There is little to say about the remaining Ossianics other than that "Gothmund" (*Works*, 1:677–81) used its position as the final Ossianic to great effect by reclaiming the Saxons to Christianity. The Mercians (Aella's tribe) made a stand at Ambroisburgh. A footnote glossed this location:

> Ambresbury, in Wiltshire, where Alfritha, wife to King Edgar, built a nunnery to atone for the murder of her son-in-law, Edward. In this place, Eleanor, queen to Henry the Third, lived a nun.
>
> (*Works*, 1:680)

The site of the Mercians' resistance was to become a Christian building.

Public Dress: The Walpole Affair

Chatterton failed to interest James Dodsley in *Aella* (*Works* 1:157, 171–72). The forger had more success, however, in his application to Horace Walpole. The second edition of Walpole's *Anecdotes of Painting in England* had been published in 1767. An egregious gap in Walpole's account was the state of painting in Saxon times. Chatterton sent to Walpole, on March 25, 1769, a supposed transcript of a "Curious Manuscript" he had discovered (*Works*, 1:258). The MS was "The Ryse of Peynceteynge, yn Englande, wroten bie T. Rowlie. 1469 for Mastre Canynge" (*Works*, 1:259–62). This piece plugged the gap in Walpole's studies by presenting the Saxon origins of painting and heraldry. Chatterton's historical fiction was used quite literally to replenish an historiographical vacuum. "Ryse of Peyncetynge" was heavily annotated, and the first two footnotes introduced Rowley and Canynge in significant terms: Rowley as biographer, historian, and poet; Canynge as church-builder, poet, painter, and, like Rowley, priest. Canynge could easily "blend" his roles (*Works*, 1:259) just as Chatterton's vision blended its factual and fictional elements. Publication of the MS, the first footnote said, would serve "the Englishman, the Antiquary, and the Poet": national historical fiction. Making the date of the piece exactly three hundred years previous was an attempt by Chatterton to enforce a celebratory chronology on Walpole's mind. Publication of Rowley would be a tricentennial commemoration. It would also celebrate Chatterton the "editor." Walpole's initial gullibility, his acceptance of "Ryse of Peyncetynge" as genuine, flattered Chatterton in his dual roles of ancient author and modern editor. Walpole thanked Chatterton for his "learned notes," without which he "should not have been able to comprehend Rowley's text" (*Works*, 1:262).

He also offered to publish Rowley, asking "where Rowley's poems are to be found?" Chatterton responded recklessly and overenthusiastically. He parcelled off immediately another Rowleyan piece of art history: "Historie of Peyncters yn Englande bie T. Rowley" (*Works*, 1: 263–67). He also revealed the location of Rowleyan MSS: "an Iron Chest in Redclift Church" (footnote 31; *Works*, 1:266). The discovery of ancient MSS in obscure recesses was made a device of the Gothic novel by Walpole himself in *The Castle of Otranto* (1765). Little wonder then that disbelief was the reaction stimulated by Chatterton's information. Chatterton's short-lived public triumph was at an end. In an unsent, bitter poem to Walpole, written in July 1769, Chatterton revealed that his brand of historical fiction did bear a relation to Walpole's:

> thou mayst call me Cheat—
> Say, didst thou ne'er indulge in such Deceit?
> Who wrote Otranto?
>
> (*Works*, 1:341)

The essential point to note is that Chatterton could not reveal his creation to be the modern recreation of history that it was. Rather, it had to be the original history, the ancient artefact. Behind the forgeries, lay the judgement of Johnson on Ossian: "As a modern production, it is nothing."

Rowley to Chatterton

In the remaining works of the forgery, there was an ascendancy of imaginative historical pieces over antiquarian treatises. However, Chatterton's editorial apparatus grew in stature until it became, so to speak, the text. "Account of the family of the De Berghams," the longest of all the antiquarian works, was Chatterton's, not Rowley's. But in the work Chatterton did not acknowledge the status of the forgery as historical fiction. He actually abandoned it. Soon after writing "Account of the De Berghams," Chatterton left Bristol for a hack's life in London's Grub Street.

"Englysh Metamorphosis" (*Works*, 1:279–82) revealed its purpose in its title. Rowley began Ovidian mythological history, adapted to English language and history. The poem, which was a fragment, got little further than the colonization of Britain by Brutus. Rowley seemed to have begun to fulfill Pope's projected epic based on this myth.

"The Tournament. An Interlude" (*Works*, 1:282–90) and "Goddwyn. A Tragedie" (*Works*, 1:294–305) were the final two dramatic pieces. Both were unfinished, though they did have substantial glosses provided by

Chatterton. Neither play had very much intrinsic interest. "The Tournament. An Interlude" was a composite rewriting of two earlier works. The
medieval pageantry of "The Tournament" (*Works*, 1:23–26) was combined
with the story of Simon de Burton, who in "Byrtonne" (*Works*, 1:88–89)
declared that if he won a jousting tournament organized by the king at
Bristol in 1285, he would build a church. "Goddwyn" had much historiographical potential that was not realised. In the days prior to the
Norman conquest, the Saxons planned rebellion against King Edward
the Confessor, whom they regarded as too saintly and too pro-French.
Edward's role was played, ironically, by Canynge. We recall his objections to saintly kings such as Edward in "Four Letters on Warwyke." The
theme of "Goddwyn" would be worthy of Scott. Unfortunately we progress no further than oft-uttered nationalist oaths. Chatterton's editorial
notes did not explain the unfinished state of "The Tournament. An
Interlude" and "Goddwyn." So one cannot be sure if the pieces are
deliberate fragments.

Rowley's pastorals also dramatized the past at different levels. "Elinoure and Juga" (*Works*, 1:291–93) dealt with events contemporaneous
with Rowley, though he was inventing a situation and not describing his
own experience. Two wives lamented their husbands' fighting in the
Roses War. At the end of their dialogue, they discovered their husbands
were dead and themselves die of grief. Donald Taylor calls the poem the
"female counterpart" of Collins' fourth eclogue (*Works*, 2:971). Chatterton
could have taken the dramatic situation, however, from some of Macpherson's early *Fragments*, which are dialogues presenting the bereaved
state of those left at home in the Fingalian wars. The major difference is
that Rowley revealed his narration. All the pastorals had a third-person
framework provided by him. In the first eclogue (*Works*, 1:305–08),
Rowley turned from the present to the past, and looked at history
typologically. He presented an earlier civil war in English history: the
"Baronnes Warre" of 1263–1265. The dramatic situation this time could
have been borrowed from Collins' fourth eclogue. Two swains lose their
families, livelihoods, and property. They flee to safety. The poem was
strongly anti-war. Chatterton used English wars in his vision. But rarely
to applaud them. In the second eclogue (*Works*, 1:308–11), there was a
happy ending in that Hygelle's father returned home safe from the
Crusades. Yet Nygelle suffered a great deal.

So the first three pastorals used authentic historical situations to comment on war and its costs. Macpherson was restricted to the imaginary
expeditions of Fingal. Chatterton was much closer to Scott in his method:
blending fictional events with real, often nationally turbulent events in
history. The final eclogue (*Works*, 1:312–15) is of little interest because

Rowley abandoned a specific historical setting for the timeless pastoral landscape in which peasants lead an idyllic existence.

The title of the work in which Chatterton succeeded Rowley and the other authors of the forgery is worth quoting in full. It demonstrates how Chatterton's vision was about the literary transmission of the past and the making of history:

> Account of the Family of the De Berghams from the Norman Conquest to this Time. Collected from Original Records, Turnament Rolls, and the Herald's of March and Garter's Records by—T: Chatterton.
> (*Works*, 1:316)

This work (*Works*, 1:316–38) was anticipated by "Craishes Herauldry," one of the earliest items of the forgery. Now, however, the historiography had become avowedly modern, Chatterton's not Craish's. The sheer lavishness of the piece suggests it was an exercise in authentication for its own sake, a valediction to the processes of history so subtly used in the forgery. There were one hundred and fourteen footnotes. The margin was bursting with the names of historians and antiquaries. One of these, notably, was Rowley. Though he was now relegated to being a mere reference, Chatterton could not resist a chance to authenticate the forgery.

London

Shortly after composing "Account of the Family of the De Berghams," Chatterton left Bristol for London—the city that always figured secondary to Bristol in the vision. After abandoning the historical fiction of Ossian, Macpherson became a historian proper. "Account of the Family of the De Berghams" showed Chatterton also becoming a "legitimate" historian. To this fact can be added certain comments made in letters from London. His post-forgery career would have been very similar indeed to Macpherson's. On May 6, 1770 he planned to "write a history of England and other pieces" (*Works*, 1:560) and on May 30, 1770 recorded "my employment will be writing a voluminous history of London, to appear in numbers the beginning of next winter" (*Works*, 1:587). Neither project, as far as known, saw fruition.

One Rowleyan work remains to be considered: "An Excelente Balade of Charitie. As wroten bie the gode Prieste Thomas Rowley, 1464" (*Works*, 1:645–48). The ballad, which retold the parable of the good Samaritan, adapted it to medieval England. The poem was either written in London in 1770 or selected from the works of the forgery and sent to *Town and Country Magazine* in July 1770, which refused it for publication (*Works*, 2:1114). It is traditionally regarded as Chatterton's comment on the inhospitable conditions of Grub Street, the poverty which eventually drove him to despair and death. For the purposes of this study, "An Excellente Balade of Charitie" completed a circle. We leave the forgery, as we began it in "Brystowe Tragedie," with Rowley's narrative verse: the ballad. The poetical rendering of history. The literary making of the past.

6

"A Higher Species of Antiquarian Research": Imitators and Later Historical Poets

> The Historian has facts ready to hand, so he has no exercise of invention. Imagination is not required in any high degree; only about as much as is used in the lower parts of poetry. . . .
>
> Samuel Johnson, in a conversation reported by Boswell, 1763

In the remaining chapters of this book I want to see if there was a change in the status of historical fiction after the forgeries. I have shown that ancient poetry was given a valid if problematical role as a historical source. The modern poet's version of the past had a much less certain status. In 1756, Joseph Warton saw a great deficiency in imaginative use of national history. Macpherson and Chatterton filled this gap at one remove, masking their historical fiction as original artefacts. But by the time Walter Scott wrote *Waverley* in 1814, the historical novelist was allowed to be the equal of the historian in his ability to bring the past alive. A new confidence had been found, which I believe could first be detected in those "lower parts of poetry" Johnson referred to disparagingly. We need only concern ourselves with the most interesting cases.

Thomas Gray's Welsh Odes, written in 1761, though not published until 1768 (the year Gray became Regius Professor of Modern History at Cambridge), appeared under a borrowed authority. Like Macpherson's poems, the odes were translations, the difference being that Gray's sources were genuine. "The Triumph of Owen" was a translation of a Welsh poem that also appeared in Evan Evans' *Specimens*, and "The Death of Hoel," "Caradoc," and "Conan" were lifted from the *Gododin* (extracts of which appeared in the Latin *De Bardis Dissertatio* Evans showed to Gray in manuscript).[1] Gray complemented the achievements of the anthologists. However, the Welsh Odes were weaker than *The Bard* in their presentation of history. Gray's advertisement to "The Triumph of Owen," added in 1768, said the poem celebrated a battle fought in 1160. Even this task was hardly completed. Gray's decision to translate a "fragment" could easily have been influenced by Macpherson's *Fragments,* which Gray is known to have enthused about. The Welsh odes were short and lightweight. They were Gray's attempts to popularize Welsh poetry, an exercise he was performing at the same time for ancient Norse in "The Descent of Odin" and "The Fatal Sisters."

James Beattie's *The Minstrel* (1768; published 1771) declared its purpose to be

> to trace the progress of a Poetical Genius, born in a rude age, from the first dawnings of fancy and reason, till that period at which he may be supposed capable of appearing in the world as a Minstrel.[2]

There seemed to be some historical potential here. The first footnote acknowledged the influence of the Percyean minstrel. But Percy's chronology was very vague. His minstrel existed at any time from the Dark Ages to the sixteenth century. Lack of historical detail in Beattie's narrative dissipated its historical interest. The poem was set in the dehistoricized pastoral landscape. Beattie had at one time a half-hearted intention of bringing real history into the poem: "the country is invaded by the Danes, or English borderers (I know not which)."[3] The plan was aborted. There was little action of any kind in the poem. Only one incident stood out. Edwin was annoyed that the "Muse of history" devoted too much time to violence. Edwin wished to turn away from history and study the "love, and innocence, and joy" found in poetry. But his mentor checked him, recommending history's "modest truth" to "fiction's gaudy rays."[4] The weighing of the merits of history and fiction within a fictional context had a certain reflexive energy. But that energy would have been boosted by some examples of history's "modest truth." Beattie's interest was not primarily history and its transmission.

The first edition of Chatterton's works appeared in 1777. It seems no coincidence that in the same year appeared a number of important historical poems. One of these was Thomas Warton's "The Grave of King Arthur." The poem presented a scene taken from Camden's *Brittania* in which Henry II was entertained by Welsh bards while on his way to conquer Ireland. Nearly all the bards recited a mythical version of Arthur's death and his being spirited away by fairies. But one bard convinced Henry that Arthur was buried at Glastonbury, something

Henry later confirmed. So "The Grave of King Arthur" was about the debunking of the romantic by the historical. The ageing bard who gave Henry the archaeological truth foregrounded the dichotomy:

> Not from fairy realms I lead
> Bright-rob'd Tradition, to relate
> In forged colours Arthur's fate . . .
> . . . boastful Fiction should be dumb,
> Where Truth the strain might best become.
>
> (ll. 86–92)

Note the key word "forged." Against the imposture of the other bards, the old man pitted his memory. He recalled when the tale was passed on to him:

> Henry, I a tale unfold,
> Never yet in rime enroll'd,
> Nor sung nor harp'd in hall or bower;
> Which, in my youth's full early flower,
> A minstrel, sprung of Cornish line,
> Who spoke of kings from old Locrine,
> Taught me to chant, one vernal dawn,
> Deep in a cliff-encircled lawn,
> What time the glistening vapours fled
> From cloud-enveloped Clyder's head;
> And on its sides the torrents gray
> Shone to the morning's orient ray.
>
> (ll. 95–106)

The transmission was preserved in warm detail. The bard's song had the authority of felt experience. The making of history was an issue within and without Warton's poem, and thus "The Grave of King Arthur" was truly in the spirit of the forgeries. Warton literalized the situation of contemporary anthologists who saw themselves restoring monuments of national antiquity through ancient poetry. Henry thanked the bard for being able to "save/From dark oblivion Arthur's grave" (l. 148).

Forgery was also at the heart of John Home's verse tragedy *Alfred*, which also appeared in 1777. The play centered on Alfred entering the Danish camp in disguise—as an impostor. In a long preface, Home justified his fictional additions to this incident:

preserving these ancient foundations, as the piers of his bridge, the Author may bend his arches, and finish his fabrick, according to his taste and fancy, for the poet is at liberty, and it is the essence of his art, to invent such intermediate circumstances, and incidents, as he thinks will produce the most affecting situations. In this department, the Poet's fancy is controlled by nothing, but probability and consistence of character, the barriers of dramatic truth.[5]

The model allowed for incompatibility between fact and fiction. Authentic history was an armature on which fiction was molded or attached. Chatterton, we remember, made great use of real buildings, including bridges, in his vision. Home's defense of his characterization of Alfred was also fascinatingly angled:

> The dramatic and the real Alfred, are both involved in the charge of imposture; both entered the Danish camp in disguise; the previous events, as narrated in the tragedy, are nearly the same with those mentioned in history.[6]

There were two Alfreds: Home's and the historical one. They existed separately, but they fused in the act of imposture. There could hardly be a more telling irony: "the feigned incidents of the piece are altogether consistent with the true."[7]

The increased confidence in the value of historical fiction could be seen in the apparatus of several minor poems of the late eighteenth century. Though the verse was negligible, the stated aims of the poets were often important. The subtitle of John Ogilvie's *Fane of the Druids* (1789) was "Comprehending an account of the origin, progress, and establishment of society in North Britain." The poem intended to present a large slice of the social history of Scotland, "a subject so new to Poetry."[8]

In *Songs of the Original Bards of Britain* (1792), George Richards foregrounded the preliminary spadework that must be undertaken by the writer of historical fiction:

> with an enthusiasm of research, he must convey himself back among our primitive ancestors, and enter into the genius of the times in which they lived. With a judicious selection he must collect the monuments and narratives, which illustrate their dispositions, their military prowess, their domestic economy, their religious rites and sentiments, the characters of their Bards and Priests, and the spirit displayed in their edifices, songs, and public institutions.[9]

The model of a "judicious selection" from a plethora of antiquarian detail seemed on course for the nineteenth-century historical novel. Far from regarding historical fiction as a second-rate form of historiography, Richards called it "a higher species of antiquarian research."[10] That accolade was a telling counterblast to Johnson's formula quoted earlier. Walter Scott's friend Richard Polwhele certainly supported this new-found confidence. The task of Polwhele's poem *The Old English Gentleman* (1797) was specifically to preserve details of social history against the rapidly advancing encroachments of historical oblivion:

> The idea of a character now almost extinct in this island, gave rise to the following Poem; in which I conceived the design of exhibiting the manners of the last century in a country gentleman. . . . So great a revolution in the little moralities of life, has lately taken place, that we are anxious to catch a few traits of the last age whilst yet they remain visible, and to preserve these, at least, as curiosities.[11]

The use of literature as a bulwark against evanescence fuelled Walter Scott's creative powers for the early Waverley novels. Little wonder then that Scott praised *The Old English Gentleman* for its "topographical labours conducted at once with the accuracy of the antiquarian and the elegance of the man of general literature."[12]

So it could not be coincidence that in the decades in which the controversy surrounding the authenticity of the forgeries of Macpherson and Chatterton raged there was a growing awareness among historical poets of the value of imaginative use of the past. This movement achieved fruition in the historical novels of Walter Scott. The minor poets we have looked at in this chapter acted as a bridge between the forgeries and the Waverley novels.

7

"A Second M'pherson"?—Walter Scott and the Forgeries

In the dedicatory epistle to *Ivanhoe* (1819), Scott's surrogate narrator Laurence Templeton reminded the revered and equally fictional antiquarian Jonas Dryasdust of the latter's view of historical novels, and specifically, of the reasons for the success of the Waverley novels:

> It seemed then to be your opinion, that the charm lay entirely in the art with which the unknown author availed himself, like a second M'pherson, of the antiquarian stores which lay scattered around him, supplying his own indolence or poverty of invention, by the incidents which had actually taken place in his country at no distant period, by introducing real characters, and scarcely suppressing real names.[1]

However wry or ironical the connection, Scott equated himself with Macpherson. Dryasdust viewed both "unknown authors" as mercenary plunderers of history, using the past as a glossy veneer masking a hollow artifact. Templeton refuted the allegation and went on to defend the integrity of his methods. Regarding archaic language, he noted

> he would act very injudiciously if he were to select from the Glossary the obsolete words which it contains, and employ these exclusively of all the phrases and vocables retained in modern days. This was the error of the unfortunate Chatterton.[2]

The equivalence here was a negative one. Scott attempted to avoid an artificially indiscriminate historicizing of the language of the text. These comments and their application will be returned to later. What is important to note at the outset is that Macpherson and Chatterton are brought under the same canopy as Scott. Their aims were the same: the literary making of the past. Scott fashioned the dedicatory epistle to *Ivanhoe* as 'expressing the author's purpose and opinions in undertaking this species of composition."[3] So the forgeries had a role to play in determining what this "species of composition"—historical fiction—entailed.

In this final chapter, it will be shown that in his making of history, Scott consummated and consolidated many of the issues dealt with in this study. This chapter will serve as a conclusion in two ways. First, the development of historical fiction after the forgeries (looked at in chapter 6) is continued to the Waverley novels—or what is traditionally regarded as the foundation of historical fiction (the historical novel). Second, the focus is on the Scott-forgeries relationship, and in the main, Scott-Macpherson. As a Scotsman, one would expect Scott to have been more interested in what he called the "great national question" of Ossian, rather than the Rowley poems.[4] As a boy Scott had been introduced by Blacklock to Ossian and Spenser simultaneously.[5] Scott soon came to regard Ossian as a "tissue of forgeries."[6] But that did not mean he was any the less fascinated. As he said to Miss Seward in 1805:

> I should be no Scottishman if I had not very attentively considered [Ossian] at some period of my studies; and, indeed, I have gone some lengths in my researches.[7]

The holdings of books in Scott's library related to the forgeries reflected his interest.[8] Here is then an apt point at which to close this study, in the absorption of Ossian into Scott's historical novels.

Scott came to the Waverley novels through historical poetry. Initially he collected and edited border ballads, which he valued in true eighteenth-century manner for their display of the customs of the past. Then he began interpolation and imitation, culminating in the long verse narratives. Scott's pre-Waverley apprenticeship was in the poetical rendering of history. When young, he had been tremendously influenced by Percy's *Reliques:*

> it may be imagined, but cannot be described, with what delight I saw pieces of the same kind which had amused my childhood, and still continued in secret in the Delilah of my imagination, considered as the subject of sober research, grave commentary, and apt illustration, by an editor who showed his poetical genius was capable of emulating the best qualities of what his pious labour preserved.[9]

A continuum was created. Scott admired and later imitated (first in *Minstrelsy of the Scottish Border* (1802) and then throughout his imaginative career) Percy's dualism: scholarly authentication (revealed formally in annotation) and "emulation" or invention. Percy's dualism was anticipated by Macpherson. Ritson had censured Percy's method of interpolation as imposture. Scott followed this perilous path also. In the cited celebration of the *Reliques*, he saw "poetical genius" rather than forgery. But the original prefaces to the Waverley novels reveal Scott's persistent misgivings that he could not run the gauntlet of imposture unscathed. *The Monastery* (1820) was prefaced by an exchange between the phantom narrator, Captain Clutterbuck, and the "author of Waverley." Clutterbuck revealed how he had obtained a MS that he sent to the "author of Waverley" to prepare for the press. "Waverley," however, exploded Clutterbuck's mask, and identified him as a novelist. Clutterbuck was a denizen of the novelists' nation:

> Having told you your country, I must next, my dear Captain Clutterbuck, make free to mention your own immediate descent. You are not to suppose your land of prodigies so little known to us as the careful concealment of your origin would seem to imply. But you have it in common with many of your country, studiously and anxiously to hide any connection with it. There is this difference, indeed, betwixt your countrymen and those of our more material world, that many of the most estimable of them, such as an old Highland gentleman called Ossian, a monk of Bristol called Rowley and others, are inclined to pass themselves off as denizens of the land of reality, whereas most of our fellow citizens who deny their country are such as that country would be very willing to disclaim. The especial circumstances you mention relating to your life and services, impose not upon us.[10]

Scott was playing reflexive games with persona and fictionality. Many of the original prefaces to the Waverley novels were of this kind, replete with wry self-regard and teasing mockery. It is significant then that the forgeries should in this instance have been cited as precedents for the creation of an authenticating persona. The forgeries were an implicit presence behind much of Scott's theorizing, especially when the debate resolved into questions of history and fiction. In Jediah Cleishbotham's *Prolegomenon to The Heart of Mid-Lothian* (1818), he was affronted by critics impugning his works as "forgeries":

> These cavillers have not only doubted mine identity, although thus plainly proved, but they have impeached my veracity and the authenticity of my historical narratives! Verily, I can only say in answer, that I have been cautelous in quoting mine authorities.[11]

Clearly Scott did have such worries. He never abandoned his fictional surrogates (not even after admitting publicly his authorship in 1827). A large part of his "endless prefaces and colossal introductions"[12] was designed to ground the fiction in authenticated fact. For the "Magnum Opus" edition of the novels (1829), Scott added lengthy introductions (retaining also the original packaging) whose job was to present

> obscure historical facts, which have formed the groundwork of these Novels, and to give some account of the places where the scenes are laid, when these are altogether or in part real; as well as a statement of particular incidents founded on fact; together with a more copious Glossary, and Notes explanatory of the ancient customs and popular superstitions referred to in the romances.[13]

If "novels" is changed to "poems," that statement could read as Macpherson's or Percy's, or many late eighteenth-century anthologists' and historical poets.' Scott's central concern was the one that underpins this thesis: how to resolve the hybrid and apparently paradoxical nature of historical fiction. His theory seemed sometimes to oscillate between the poles of the argument without being able to settle at any point. Hence the various tussles between phantom narrators and the "author of Waverley." In the prefatory letter to *Peveril of the Peak* (1822), Dryasdust met "Waverley." The latter had just been admitted to the Roxburghe Club of London. Dryasdust wondered that "Waverley" did not fear the club's antiquarian scrutiny of the novels:

> Author. You mean to say these learned persons will have but little toleration for a romance, or a fictitious narrative, founded upon history?
> D. Why, sir, I do rather apprehend, that their respect for the foundation will be such, that they may be apt to quarrel with the inconsistent nature of the superstructure. . . . you stand much censured for adulterating the pure sources of historical knowledge.[14]

"Waverley's" ultimate retort was to borrow Prior's maxim: "Odzooks, must one swear to the truth of a song."[15] But in the introduction added in 1831, Scott recanted, calling Prior's witticism an "excellent joke," but a "bad palliation."[16] The novel's characters would "fail in their moral aim, if fiction were placed at variance with truth." Fiction, truth; foundation, superstructure. The perennial issues. Scott shared with the forgeries an historiographical reflexiveness. The rest of this chapter will trace this awareness in the texts as well as the notes, specifically to see if the forgeries had a part to play.

The title of Scott's first major imaginative success showed an immediate influence of Ossian. *The Lay of the Last Minstrel* (1805) was designed

to illustrate the customs and manners, which anciently prevailed on
the borders of England and Scotland. . . . As the description of scenery and manners was more the object of the Author, than a combined
and regular narrative . . . the poem was put into the mouth of an
ancient Minstrel, the last of the race.[17]

The device heightened the presentation of social history, the minstrel
being a mode of regression: "The date of the tale itself is about the
middle of the sixteenth century, when most of the personages actually
flourished." The voice of the minstrel, who died in the eighteenth
century, recuperated an earlier century. The syndrome was very like that
in the forgeries, except that the minstrel's making of history existed
within the modern poet's omniscient third person framework: "A wandering Harper, scorned and poor,/He begged his bread from door to
door."[18] Scott made history from the inside only to a limited extent. His
primary concern was not to create an imaginative version of empirically
rendered historical situations: an authentic memoir. Nonetheless, the
eschatology of *The Lay of the Last Minstrel* was more than poetic glitter.
For Scott, the extinction of minstrelsy in the eighteenth century was an
index of the death of traditional Scottish culture. The transformation of
the Highlands under British rule after the 1745 rebellion was almost
complete by the time Scott was born.[19] Macpherson, who unlike Scott
lived through the catastrophic changes, invented his own millenial situation in the distant past, where history and the bardic voice were one.
Scott was not so exclusive. But he did share with Ossian the combating of
evanescence by historical fiction. The divergence from Macpherson was
that Scott admitted the fiction was his own. He built on the foundations
established by poets at the end of the eighteenth century (as was shown
in chapter 6). Evanescence impelled Scott into imaginative action. In
Minstrelsy of the Scottish Border (1802), he included "Modern Imitations"
(some by himself) and annotations to "contribute somewhat to the
history of my native country; the peculiar features of whose manners
and character are daily melting and dissolving into those of her sister
and ally."[20] "The task of tracing the evanescent manners of his own
country" was how Scott described his purpose in the postscript to
Waverley (1814).[21] Scott's task was of national importance. His first three
novels *Waverley*, *Guy Mannering* (1815), and *The Antiquary* (1816) were
designed specifically to encapsulate the social history of Scotland in the
last half of the eighteenth century.[22] Scott replicated imaginatively the
stance of anthologists like Percey. He fused literature and history. Scott's
narratives were social history. Nearly all of them paralleled the omniscient presentation of the orthodox historian: third person, past tense,
continuous narration. (The exceptions are *Rob Roy* (1818)—in the first

person past tense, like Defoe's *Plague Year,*—and *Redgauntlet* (1824), which is partially in the epistolary and journal form, though relapsing into third person omniscience just over halfway). This did not mean, however, that the forgeries had no bearing on the texts of the novels.

It is worth pointing out a piece of "external" information about *Waverley* (1814). It was noted in the last chapter that the discovery of a literary MS had become a conventional device in novels by Scott's time. Scott indulged in the creation of imaginary authentic sources for his novels as late as *Woodstock* (1826). Typically (and often infuriatingly), he also mocked the device. In *The Monastery*, for instance, the "author of Waverley" mocked Clutterbuck's

> happy combination of fortuitous circumstances which usually put you in possession of the works which you have the goodness to bring into public notice.[23]

The fictional precedents for those "fortuitous circumstances" included of course the forgeries. By Scott's own testimony, the actual composition of *Waverley* concurred remarkably well with such fictional counterparts. The first seven chapters were written in 1805 (hence the subtitle "Tis Sixty Years Since"). The story was abandoned, and, on moving to Abbotsford in 1811, "was placed in a lumber garret, and entirely forgotten."[24] The location may remind one of Chatterton's famous trunk in Redcliff church.[25] Scott's discovery of the "mislaid manuscript"[26] was a classic piece of serendipity:

> I happened to want some fishing tackle for the use of a guest, when it occurred to me to search the old writing-desk already mentioned, in which I used to keep articles of that nature. I got access to it with some difficulty, and in looking for lines and flies the long-lost manuscript presented itself. I immediately set to work to complete it according to my original purpose.[27]

In chapter 11 of *The Antiquary* (1816), we find Jonathan Oldbuck in his drawer, "rummaging among a quantity of miscellaneous papers, ancient and modern."[28] Oldbuck's MS prey was "the controversy upon Ossian's poems between Mac-Cribb and me." The real and fictional dovetailed again here. In 1792, roughly the time in which *The Antiquary* was set, Scott delivered a paper on the authenticity of Ossian's poems to the Speculative Society of Edinburgh.[29]

Even on a superficial level, there was a satisfying irony in the use of Ossian as an authenticating reference in an historical novel. Ossian was itself dominated by history and authentication. The significance of Ossian for Scott went deeper than this footnoting level, however. In *Waverley* and *The Antiquary*, Ossian was a touchstone for the treatment of indigenous poetry and bardic history.

A measure of the importance of Ossian to *Waverley* was the way Scott managed to have one of his characters prophesy Ossian's appearance. The action of *Waverley* took place some fifteen years before Ossian burst on the world. The narrator could of course refer to Ossian (as he did),[30] but a protagonist could not. Chapter 22 is entitled "Highland Minstrelsy." Traditional songs were always a living presence in Scott's narratives, and more than one of his characters had an interest in collecting such songs. Such a person was the Highland princess, Flora Mac-Ivor. She extolled the virtues of Celtic poetry to Waverley:

> The recitation of poems, recording the feats of heroes, the complaints of lovers, and the wars of contending tribes, forms the chief amusement of a winter fireside in the Highlands. Some of these are said to be very ancient, and if they are ever translated into any of the languages of civilised Europe, cannot fail to produce a deep and general sensation.[31]

There is no doubt the reference was to Ossian, and to Ossian as genuine, not fake poetry. Flora uttered a cunning self-fulfilling prophecy. Waverley's initial experiences in the Highlands were suffused with Ossianic atmosphere. In chapter 20 ("A Highland Feast"), Fergus the clan leader ordered his *bhaird* Mac-Murrough to entertain the company. The incident could almost have been from Ossian. Fergus believed Mac-Murrough to be "a far greater poet than Homer."[32] Hugh Blair and many others conferred that status on Ossian. Mac-Murrough chanted "a profusion of Celtic verses, which were received by the audience with all the applause of enthusiasm."[33] Waverley, of course, did not understand Celtic. So Flora became a kind of proto-Macpherson in offering a translation. We know Flora was a budding anthologist, delighting in her spare time "researches" into "the music and poetical traditions of the Highlanders."[34] Flora fashioned the clan bards as "the poets and historians of their tribes."[35] The song in question was

> little more than a catalogue of names of the Highland clans under their distinctive peculiarities, and an exhortation to them to remember and to emulate the actions of their forefathers.[36]

The atmosphere was truly Ossianic. But Flora was concealing essential information. The history in the poem was absolutely contemporary, being nothing less than a coded war cry for the coming rebellion. The poem was hardly "historical," though its kinetic quality was again Ossianic. Waverley had heard his own name mentioned in the original, because he was being encouraged to join the Jacobite cause. He failed to understand this, even in the translation which had been artfully engineered by Flora to have a sublime accompaniment of harps and mountainous waterfalls. The initiation offered to Waverley was presented in Ossianic terms. The martial verse of the bard stood as a symbol for Jacobite ideals at their purest—that is, represented by Flora. A dark irony pervaded all, of course. Martial times were past, and the rebellion was in many ways a swansong. Fergus knew that the destruction of the Highlands, hereditary clans and their bards, was imminent.[37] Flora's editorial labors were themselves an indication of the evanescence. Bardism was being replaced by literary history.

Waverley was also a dilettante editor of ballads. Earlier in the novel, at the home of Baron Bradwardine, the lowland equivalent of the above events occured. Rose Bradwardine sang a minstrel song, the text of which, as the editor-narrator of *Waverley* had obtained it, had been "corrected by Waverley, to suit the taste of those who might not relish pure antiquity."[38] Waverley was a Percyean interpolator. We are told a debate ensued about whether such ballads had a basis in fact. Scott used four lines from *The Faerie Queene* to characterize the topics of discussion. Note in particular the final line:

> All those idle thoughts and fantasies,
> Devices, dreams, opinions unsound,
> Shows, visions, soothsays, and prophecies,
> And all that feigned is, as leasings, tales, and lies.[39]

We might suspect a novel entitled *The Antiquary* (1816) to have had much to say about history. That promise was fulfilled. The solemnity of *Waverley* was replaced by comic self-scrutiny and good humored irony. As with all good comedy, however, serious issues were at stake.

A historical novel about a historian involves regression. Oldbuck, the antiquarian, was a transmitter of the past, but not the sole transmitter. There was a tussle between his pedagogical approach to history and the bardic knowledge of the beggar, Eddie Ochiltree. The mendicant Blue Gowns were believed "to be descended from the ancient bards."[40] Early in the novel, we see that Oldbuck had been duped into buying land where he believed once stood the Roman "Praetorium at the Kaim of Kimprunes."[41] A battle was supposed to have been fought here between the Romans and Caledonians: "a national concern."[42] But the only conflict we see is historiographical. Ochiltree interrupted Oldbuck with the news that he saw the site being prepared by the person who sold the land. His empirical knowledge exploded the hoax and Oldbuck's theory.

Such deflations were common in the novel. The demoralized Oldbuck described Ochiltree as

> one of the last specimens of the old-fashioned Scottish mendicant, who kept his rounds within a particular space, and was the news-carrier, the minstrel, and sometimes the historian of the district.[43]

Scott, unlike Macpherson, did not give the bardic figure a monopoly on the making of the past. Ochiltree's empirical and folk knowledge provided him with many secrets, but the resolution of the tale—the identity of the hero Lovel—was not his work alone. The moribund Elspeth Mucklebackit had vital first-hand information about the Glenallen family, to which Lovel belonged. Oldbuck, Ochiltree, and the Highlander Hector went to her cottage to obtain a recorded statement. They heard her singing a ballad. Oldbuck was electrified. We know of his bibliomania, his "bundle of ballads" (p. 34) and his love of the "original broadside" (p. 35). Being

> a diligent collector of these legendary scraps of ancient poetry, his foot refused to cross the threshold when his ear was thus arrested, and his hand instinctively took pencil and memorandum book. (P. 357)

Another anthologist. But, as in *Waverley*, traditional poetry was kinetic. Oldbuck quickly realized that Elspeth's song was dramatizing the very information he was seeking:

> It's a historical ballad . . . a genuine and undoubted fragment of minstrelsy!—Percy would admire its simplicity—Ritson could not impugn its authenticity. (P. 357)

Elspeth sang poetry-history. Oldbuck's nephew Hector was only interested in nationalist sentiment:

> I hear . . . a silly old woman sing a silly old song. I am surprised, sir, that you, who will not listen to Ossian's songs of Selma, can be pleased with such trash. (P. 359)

Hector was an avid supporter of Ossian. He was the fictional equivalent of those Highlanders who claimed they had heard Ossian recited to them in their youth. Scott would not allow the nationalist fetishizing of indigenous poetry to be uncritically endorsed. *The Antiquary* scrutinized issues that were clearly close to Scott's heart. In chapter 30, Hector and Oldbuck came to verbal blows over Ossian. Whatever songs Hector heard all those years ago, said Oldbuck, they could not be "the same as

Macpherson's English Ossian—you're not absurd enough to say that, I hope?" (p. 280). Scott's own view, following Johnson, was that Macpherson had ensured a credulous reaction like Hector's by making use of every scrap of Ossianic verse that existed in the Highlands.[44] Hector was bullied into attempting recitation of a sample of the verse, with hilarious results. The extract was "a dialogue between the poet Oisin, or Ossian, and Patrick, the tutelar Saint of Ireland."[45] Such a dialogue from the Irish Fenian poems was the basis of that ingenious exchange between Ossian and the Culdee in the preface to Macpherson's *Fragments*. Oldbuck retorted "It is a pity there should not be a word of this in Macpherson's translation."[46] Hector's translation burlesqued his boorish and ignorant nationalism:

> Patrick the palm-singer,
> Since you will not listen to one of my stories,
> Though you never heard it before,
> I am sorry to tell you
> You are little better than an ass—[47]

Hector's passions were deflated when he attempted to prove his prowess immediately after by wrestling with a seal and was defeated—"a single combat, worthy to be commemorated by Ossian himself."[48]

Scott was doing more than simply poking fun at the Ossianic controversy. He saw the Ossianic making of history as a dangerous lure, an unreasonable extreme. As he said in a letter to Miss Seward in 1805:

> When once the Highlanders had adopted the poems of Ossian as an article of national faith, you would far sooner have got them to disavow the Scripture than to abandon a line of the contested tales.[49]

Oldbuck represented the complementary flawed relationship with the past. He was far too fastidious about points of fact. His energies were dissipated in fruitless controversies. He lacked the powers of judicious selection. He and his fellow antiquarian, Arthur Wardour, were gullible to "receiving legends as current and authentic coin" (p. 50). Imposture was a theme in the novel. Wardour was being milked by the charlatan Dousterswivel, and Lovel's identity turned on a "counterfeit marriage" (p. 311). Oldbuck and Wardour wrangled over the derivation of the word "Pict" (in which Oldbuck pitched Pinkerton, Gordon, and Innes against Wardour's Chalmers, Sibbald, and Ritson) and the ancient constitution. Typically, Oldbuck's objections to Ossian resolved into a pedantic battle with Macpherson's notes. Misguided antiquarianism was thus equated with the authenticating apparatus of Ossian. Scott needed such machinery, but was constantly worried by the dangers of having it loom too large over the text. Oldbuck represented the factual aspect of historical fiction. His flaw was that he could not appreciate the role of fiction in the making of the past. This was shown beautifully when he prodded the hero Lovel into thinking about writing a "real epic":

> the grand old-fashioned historical poem which moved through twelve or twenty-four books. We'll have it so—I'll supply you with a subject—The battle between the Caledonians and Romans—The Caledoniad. (P. 127)

The Caledoniad would be a historical poem, but Oldbuck's historical hobby horse would be the focal point: "I will write the critical and historical notes on each canto. . . . I'll annihilate Ossian, Macpherson and Mac-Cribb." (Pp. 128–29). The notes and text were separate entities. Lovel never even began his task, but at the end of the novel, Oldbuck "has completed his notes, which, we believe, will be at the service of any one who chooses to make them public" (p. 409).

The underlying issue could not be more central. Macpherson was made to represent an imbalance in the dualism of historical fiction. On the one hand, flagrant invention and liberties with fact; on the other, top-heavy authentication. Yet Scott could not dispense with this dualism. He would have agreed with George Richards that historical fiction was a rarefied form of antiquarian research. But he frowned on making that research an unintegrated part of the story. In his *Journal* he remarked that his rivals

> have to read old books and consult antiquarian collections to get their information—I write because I have long since read such works and possess thanks to a strong memory the information which they have to seek for. This leads to dragging in historical details by head and shoulders. . . . Perhaps I have sinned in this way myself . . . but I have repented of it, and in my better efforts while I conducted my story through the agency of historical personages and by connecting it with historical incidents I have endeavoured to weave them pretty closely together.[50]

Compare now that final statement with Scott's censure of Macpherson as "weaving a web in which truth and falsehood should be warped and blended together in inseperable union."[51] Scott was ambivalent. His anti-research method of composition was not to be followed by later historical novelists, and in fact he made acknowledged use of sources in several novels.

This point brings us to *Ivanhoe*. Scott's innovation in this novel in relation to the Waverley novels was not only to take a topic from English rather than Scottish history, but also to deal with very distant times—in this case the late twelfth century. In other words, Scott was wholly reliant on literary sources (historians and MSS) for his information. The major problems were two. First, the ability of "musty records and chronicles" to yield "hints concerning the private life of our ancestors."[52] Scott believed that the information could be gleaned by diligent research—reading widely and collecting judiciously.[53] It was not a case of recalling to mind long-remembered facts. Such delving into the "dust of antiquity" was not required in the previous Waverley novels, we are told. Unlike England, Scotland had a "mine so plentiful"[54] of oral history extant, particularly in its evanescent phase, when there was a flurry of activity to preserve tradition. Such historical information had been used in the previous novels. It was in this context then that Scott was a "second M'pherson," mining a rich and readily available vein. Macpherson was not seen as a pedant. When compared to Scott's reliance on literary sources for *Ivanhoe*, Macpherson was viewed as being at history's fountainhead. This led into the second problem. Because Scott's historical foundation in *Ivanhoe* was so clearly defined, his methods were more accountable:

> the severer antiquary may think, that, by thus intermingling fiction with truth, I am polluting the well of history with modern inventions, and impressing upon the rising generation false ideas of the age which I describe.[55]

We are back to the virtues or transgressions of "mingling fiction with truth." The professed job of the introductions and some of the notes to the novels was to delineate fact from fiction. Some did this. For instance, the death of Balfour Burley in *Old Mortality*[56] was admitted to be fiction. But such scrutiny was very limited. Scott could not refute satisfactorily the charge that he was "polluting" history. Rather, he "traverses"[57] the issue by saying that his invention was always within "legitimate bounds."[58] (We are reminded here of John Home's comments in *Alfred*.) Scott had not gone to the extreme of historicizing everything, as "the unfortunate Chatterton" did with language. His ultimate aim was accurate social history: there had to be "nothing inconsistent with the manners of the age."[59]

If the forgeries had to be absorbed into acknowledged historical fiction, then Scott's novels could hardly have been a more satisfying recipient. In 1805 Scott began *Waverley*. He also reviewed Malcolm Laing's edition of Ossian, together with the Highland Committee Report on Ossian's authenticity. There was an ending and a beginning. Scott's review began "This celebrated controversy seems now to be finally at issue"[60] and it was "not likely again to be argued."[61] But the forgeries had a role to play in the birth of modern historical fiction. Scott concluded that Macpherson had taken unjustifiable liberties with his sources. Scott clearly saw some of himself in the forgers. The nature and extent of the liberties taken with authentic sources is the eternal thorn in the side of the creator of historical fiction. So it may be the case that Scott's evaluation of Chatterton's success—"the ambiguous reputation of an ingenious impostor"[62]—may have applied uncomfortably to himself.

If he could not answer with certainty the charge that he was a falsifier of history, Scott made the issue, as the forgers did, part of his enterprise. Foregrounding the issues involved in his making of history, Scott consolidated those concerns about history and fiction that gave birth to the forgeries. The forgeries also, as has been shown, had an important role to play in that foregrounding. The historical novel became quickly an accepted literary genre, and has enjoyed a chequered career since. One wonders if an historical vision such as Chatterton's, manifested in such a unique diversity of form, will ever be created again.

Appendix 1

The Continuation of Keating's Account of the Assembly at Tarah

One end of the Table was appointed for the Antiquarians and the Historians, who understood and were perfectly skill'd in the Records and ancient Monuments of the Kingdom; the other End was filled by the chief Officers of the Court: and Care was particularly taken that their Debates should be kept secret, for which Reason no Woman was ever to be admitted.

When Dinner was ended and everything removed, they ordered the Antiquities of the Kingdom to be brought before them, and read over them, and examined them strictly, least any Falshoods or Interpolations should have crept in; and if they found any Mistakes or false Representations of Facts occasioned either by the Prejudice or the Ignorance of the Historians, they were scratch'd out after they had been censured by a select Committee of the greatest Learning, appointed to inspect into those old Records. The Histories and Relations that were surveyed and found true and perfect, were ordered to be transcribed after they had past the Approbation of the Assembly, and inserted in the authentick Chronicles that were always preserved in the King's Palace, and the Book wherein they were written was called the Psalter of *Tara*: This ancient Record is an invaluable Treasure, and a most faithful Collection of the Irish Antiquities; and whatever Account is delivered in any other Writing repugnant to this, is to be esteemed of no Authority, and a direct Imposition upon Posterity.

In this solemn Manner did the Milesians (a learned and generous People) preserve from the most early Times the Monuments of every memorable Transaction that deserved to be transmitted to the World;

and in the Interval between every Session of this Triennial Parliament not only the professed Antiquaries, but the Gentry, and Persons of Abilities in all Professions and Capacities, did with all Diligence and Fidelity, collect what was worthy to be observed in their several Districts and Provinces, and laid their Remarks before the next Assembly to be examined, and if they were approved, to be transcribed in the Royal Records for the Benefit and Information of their Descendents. If the same Care had been taken by other Nations, we should not see so many fabulous Histories abroad, that are founded upon no Authority, but supported only by the Effrontery of the Relators; but this Method it seems was peculiar to the ancient Irish, whose Policy and Civil Government have been the Wonder, and ought to have been the Example and Standard of After-Ages. And this Form of Assembling, and bringing their Antiquities to a publick Scrutiny, was followed till the Time of *St. Patrick,* and continued with some Alterations, but rather with more Care and Exactness than to any Disadvantage, as will be observed in the Course of this History in its proper Place.

I am obliged to mention it as the singular Glory of the Irish Nation, that their *Milesian* Ancestors had so great a Veneration, and valued themselves so much upon the Nobility of their Extract, that they preserved their Pedigrees and Genealogies with the strictest Care; and it is evident, that in former Times there were above two hundred principal Annalists and Historians in that Kingdom, who had a handsome Revenue and a large Estate in Land assigned to them, to support themselves in the Study of Heraldry and Chronology, and to gain a perfect Knowledge in those useful Professions. Every Nobleman of any Quality retained a Number of these learned Men, on purpose to record the Actions of himself and his Family, and to transmit them to Posterity, besides such as were in constant Pay and Attendance for the Service of the Publick. But these private Antiquaries had no Liberty of themselves to enter any Thing upon Record, unless it had been first approved by the great Triennial Assembly, whose Confirmation gave Authority to all the private as well as the publick Records of the Kingdom.[1]

Appendix 2
Chatterton's Plans for the Publication of the Forgery

I use the term "forgery" and not "Rowley" in the title of this appendix quite deliberately.[1] The latter has often been used as shorthand for the former, but Thomas Rowley was only one of several authors invented by Chatterton. The scope and versatility of Chatterton's forgery are one of his greatest advances on his predecessor Macpherson. Macpherson's forgery was Ossian's Erse poetry, translated and edited by Macpherson. There were few obstacles to publication in such a format, and between 1760 and 1763 Ossian appeared in print for the first time with great success.[2] The popularity of Thomas Percy's *Reliques of Ancient English Poetry,* which appeared in 1765, can be seen as a literary "legitimization" of Macpherson's stance as a scholarly editor of ancient poetry (which of course he had invented). Chatterton borrowed from Macpherson the device of creating ("discovering") and editing an ancient author, enabling the past to be recreated from the inside. But Chatterton also rendered affairs considerably more sophisticated. By bringing his "vision" of the past forward from the oral culture of the Caledonian bard Ossian to the literate world, Chatterton was able to experiment with varieties of authorship. The Ossianic bard's monopolistic hold over history—the sole spokesman for early society—had gone. Multifarious genres of historiography and literature evolved and reacted to form Chatterton's vision of the past and its transmission to the present. The obstacles in the way of publication of such a literary phenomenon, particularly in the 1760s, can well be imagined. I refer here to publication on the terms Macpherson obtained them: with the publishers giving him a free hand. If Chatterton had been able to produce an "edition" of his

forgery, what would the format, or even the title have been? The difficulty of labelling or classifying the vision in literary terms can be seen by
looking at the titles of the earliest editions. They were helped, it must be
added, by the general consensus that Chatterton was the creator of the
supposed ancient works, ie. that they were forgeries. Thomas Tyrwhitt's
pioneering edition of 1777 was titled: *Poems, Supposed to have been written
at Bristol, by Thomas Rowley, and Others, in the Fifteenth Century.*[3] By no
means all of the forgery was poetry, but Tyrwhitt did make reference to
these "Other" authors, albeit unnamed. Tyrwhitt admitted he had been
selective. He had extracted poems of value from "as many compositions,
in prose and verse, under the names of Rowley and Canynge, etc as
would nearly fill such another volume."[4] Tyrwhitt's conduct strengthens
the point about how difficult a publishable product the forgery was. The
next edition, edited by John Broughton, chose a title that can be seen as
the eighteenth-century version of most modern editions: *Miscellanies in
Prose and Verse; by Thomas Chatterton, the Supposed Author of the Poems
Published under the Names of Rowley, Canning etc* (1778).[5] That "etc" first
used by Tyrwhitt in the comment cited above had become a very expedi-
ent tag, and it occured again in the title of the 1782 reprint of the 1777
edition.[6] Broughton had relied on the disproving of the forgery's authenticity, and his title was really as bland and unrevealing as possible. A
further consideration entered the picture here, for the option of publishing the works of Thomas Chatterton meant that many pieces that were
not part of the forgery or vision had also to be included. The identity of
the forgery thus began to blur, its existence as an imaginative artifact
suffered diminution. This question bore directly on the arrangement of
the bicentennial Oxford *Works*, published in 1971. The editor, Donald
Taylor, arranged Chatterton's works in strict chronological order to show
that Chatterton was not a literary split-personality, a forger and a hack.
To see that Chatterton wrote "authentic" poems both before and during
and not only after the forged works was designed to make the point. As
Taylor says: "Suffice it to say here that if less than a year was devoted to
Rowley" (Taylor is using the shorthand description of the forgery referred to earlier) "out of a creative span of over six years, we can no
longer divide C's writings and character into more or less simultaneous
Rowleyan and anti-Rowleyan halves."[7] Actually the statement shows
that we can. Taylor's edition proves that the forged works teemed from
Chatterton's brain in a sustained imaginative output of around six
months (October 1768–March 1769). All other work in this period—
mainly love poems for his friends—was by comparison of any kind,
insignificant. Returning to the question of contemporaneous publication, then, it is highly unlikely Chatterton believed his vision would ever
be published in any complete form. The product he had to sell, so to

speak, was simply too eccentric and unmanageable. Reading the Oxford *Works* can lull one into assuming that if Chatterton had edited or produced his own edition of the forgery, as Macpherson had done, the works would have appeared in chronological order. Donald Taylor has gone a great service in giving us this sequence, enabling us to see how the vision grew and authenticated itself and to chart the fascinating directions the evolution took. We can treat the forgery as an imaginative unity. But my aim here is to consider what publishable shape Chatterton himself imposed upon the forgery. That he was not thinking in terms of totality is suggested by the biographical details that have been recounted many times. At various stages in the growth of the vision, attempts were made to sell bits of it to various patrons, Bristolian and other. To some extent, these imagined recipients influenced the next forged item—for instance the MS on Saxon painting sent to Horace Walpole. But this influencing can be overrated, and the tendency is once again to detract from the autonomy of the historical vision. Chatterton's greatest biographer, E. H. W. Meyerstein, declared "the Rowley cycle was evolved, and for the most part ready, before [patrons] appeared on Chatterton's horizon."[8] Patrons of whatever kind gave Chatterton very limited success in terms of being published in his own lifetime. The only works of the forgery he saw in print were "Bridge Narrative" (*Felix Farley's Bristol Journal*, October 1, 1768), "Elinoure and Juga" (*Town and Country Magazine*, May 1769), six of the seven Ossianics (*Town and Country Magazine*, March to December 1769—the last Ossianic, "Gorthmund," was published in the same magazine in September 1770, only a few weeks after Chatterton's death), "Antiquity of Christmas Games" (*Town and Country Magazine*, December 1769), and "The Court Mantle" (*Town and Country Magazine*, March 1769). Many short prose pieces were accepted by William Barrett for inclusion in his *The History and Antiquities of the City of Bristol*, but the book did not appear until 1789. Barrett was the main retainer of Chatterton MSS until the end of the eighteenth century, and it has yet to be determined how many works were taken from Chatterton while he was alive and for which the forger might feel he had achieved some publication success. Considering then that the individual items of the forgery number well into three figures, this *ad hoc* procedure of approaching patrons did not produce very good results.

It is in this context that I want to discuss certain extant evidence that Chatterton had been devising a more calculated and, for the literary historian, more illuminating approach to the whole question. Publication was not actually achieved, but that does not deter investigation of and speculation upon the data. The materials in question are several copybooks in Chatterton's own hand. These volumes are in fact anthologies: arrangements and groupings of works by the editorially minded Chatterton. These anthologies are the clearest indication that Chatterton was thinking about a partial though controlled publication of the forgery—a translation or transformation, in his own terms, of a highly involuted art form into an acceptable literary format. Chatterton had begun to edit the vision.

But before I move on to the anthologies themselves, I need to say something about Chatterton's working methods. It has not been sufficiently pointed out by editors and commentators that the term "Chatterton MS" can be misleading when dealing with the forged works. There are in fact two kinds of MS: the "original" or fabricated parchment on which the works in antiquated spelling were composed; and the transcript or copy made by Chatterton from this original "ancient" MS. The situation is problematical, because the original of a copy need not, logically, exist. Indeed, many do not. Chatterton could compose straight onto a copybook or modern paper and claim he was transcribing. The precedent here again is Macpherson, who for most of his life claimed that the Erse MSS of Ossian were in his possession but never produced them. It was only after his death that the Gallic sources (though not MSS) appeared, probably (though this has yet to be proven) concocted by himself in his later years.[9] Chatterton stood in the same position of being the exclusive owner of his literary discovery: Chatterton's fifteenth-century Bristol ended very carefully at the invention of the printing press, ie. before the termination of the MS world and thus of editorial monopoly by later anthologists. But Chatterton was not to follow in Macpherson's footsteps exactly. Consistency was lacking. Beyond the evidence I mean to consider, no coherent editorial policy can be grasped. (Macpherson's format, with its historical introductions and notes to each poem anticipated Percy's method in the *Reliques*.) It is impossible to ascertain, often, why some pieces are annotated and others not. This uncertainty increases even further the importance of the MSS I now turn to.

The three extant anthologies are "Antiquities—Book Third," "Poems, by Thomas Rowley Priest of St. Johns In the City of Bristol Containing The Tournament an Interlude and a Piece by Canynge—called the Goulers Requiem," and "Eclogues and Other Poems, by Thomas Rowley, with A Glossary, and Annotations by Thomas Chatterton."[10] All are in Chatterton's hand, and "originals" for all the works contained in the volumes have not been traced. It is known that other, now lost, anthologies existed, and I shall refer to those also. I have listed the surviving volumes in chronological order, because there is an important progression embodied in them. However, before I proceed to look at each anthology in detail, I must deal with an irony. I have used the Oxford *Works* for all my dating. But Taylor's method of tabulating the sequence of works relies in part on the anthologies. As the chart on page xxxix of the introduction to *Works* shows, the works linked by dotted lines are "groupings in manuscripts" (p. xxxviii). I sidestep the irony somewhat by trusting in Taylor's morphology (he used several other methods for dating, including old words' proportions), but I want to draw attention to that term "manuscript" again. Of the seven "groupings," only the "Yellowe Rolle" ("Of the Auntient Forme of Monies," "Englandes Glorye Revyved in Maystre Canynge") and "Purple Rolle" ("Explayneals of the Annexed Yellowe Rolle," "Discorse on Brystowe," parts 2 and 3) are original fabricated parchments. Taylor acknowledges that status in his textual notes (*Works*, 2:851, 865),[11] but it would have been useful to have noted the distinction in the introduction. The arrangement of works in the Yellowe and Purple Rolles, then, was Thomas Rowley's. The arrangement on the other MSS was Thomas Chatterton's. I am not being pedantic here. The two rolles cannot, by their nature, be in an edited state, unless the editor was Rowley himself. The rolles were purely Rowleyan material, and I want to stress the difference between this level and that of Chatterton's editorial machinations. I have noted that the latter are not always easy to confirm. A copy or transcript can exist in an unedited state—no notes, often no title (many titles in *Works* are printed in parentheses to show they have been invented by Taylor), no indication of what Chatterton meant to do. It is a pity, therefore, that the remaining MS groupings in a "copied" state—excluding the anthologies—are in this unedited condition. The coupling of "Mass Book Inscription" and "Discourse on Brystowe," part 1, and the combination of "Painter's Bill," "Heraudyn," and "Chronical of Brystowe" seems arbitrary, giving these MSS the status of "jotters" or rough books into which Chatterton was either directly creating or transcribing, with possible later rearrangement in mind. That category would seem to fit "Nine Deeds and Proclamations," "Abstracts from Letters," and "Three Rowley Letters," a grouping which makes a fine historical portfolio.

A copy of the title page of "Antiquities—Book Third" can be seen in Meyerstein's *Life* (p. 85). The full title runs: "ANTIQUITIES—BOOK 3rd. / TO ALEXANDER MACKINTOSH ESQUIRE / This Book is most humbly Dedicated / By his obedient Servant / THE EDITOR—/ CONTENTS of this BOOK / Page 3—An Ancient poem called the Battle of the Hastynges written by / Turgot a Saxon Monk in the Tenth Century and translated by / Thomas Rowley parish preeste St. Johns in the City of Bristol in / the year of our Lord 1465 of whom, more in Book 1st—the remayning / Part of this Poem I have not been happy enough to meet with/ Page 21— Extracts from Craishes Herauldry—author of Famous / Legend of Beevis of Southampton—/ Page 27—One Cento of an ancient Poem called the Unknown Knight or the / Tournament, I offered this as a sample, having two more / Cento's—The Author Unknown / *The Battle of Hastynges was fought / on the 14th of Octr; 1066. / N.B. The Ode to Lais is a Modern production—." In *Works*, Donald Taylor prints these headings before each piece, but there is no indication that the titles were originally devised as a contents table to this anthology. So we have an epic poem translated by Rowley, an ancient antiquarian work by one Craish, and an anonymous romance: a mixed bag. All three pieces were unfinished: "Battle of Hastynges I" (actually the first of two versions Chatterton wrote, and so given the suffix "I") posed as a genuine fragment; the other two were teasing morsels of longer works. With no pretense to completeness, therefore, and with a medley of literary and historical works, what kind of an anthology had Chatterton put together? He was obviously planning an anthological series under the general heading "Antiquities." So the aim was primarily historical. Yet only one piece in "Book 3rd" was an antiquarian relic—the other two were poems. An important deduction can be made here, I believe, about Chatterton's sensitivity to the historiographical climate of his time. The growth of an unprecedented interest in social and cultural history by the eighteenth century led to a theory that ancient literature was an invaluable source of the manners and customs of our ancestors. Old poetry in particular was aggrandized as historical documentary. The staunchest defenders of the view were those formulating literary history: Thomas Warton, Thomas Percy, and the many anthologists inspired by Percy's *Reliques*. The old ballad or romance need not simply illustrate or support history, it could be history *per se*. Chatterton understood this potential, and chose for "Book 3rd" apparently unrelated works that stood as "antiquities" by themselves. The view of literature as social history valued those "minute circumstances" (to quote Percy)[12] that were revealed independently of narrative events. Thus a fragment of a work could still be of great value.

It is unfortunate that I cannot refer to any annotation in "Book 3rd" to secure my point, for the anthology is unedited, apart from those comments on the title page. But if we turn to the poem "Bristowe Tragedie," the poem that could easily have been in "Book 2nd,"[13] we find a note on the title:

> As the following Transaction happen'd in Bristol the 2nd year of King Edward 4th it deserves to be commemorated as one Instance of the severe Treatmnt. that Prince showed those who oppos'd his coming to the Crown; and as the Story is told in a very affecting mannr. in the following little Poem wrote by Thomas Rowlie Priest, I shall insert the whole. . . .[14]

Chatterton set the poem up as a historical document, and though he appeared to be referring to public events rather than to social history, one has only to read the poem to see that it is replete with—to use a Percyean phrase again—"peculiar manners and customs of former ages."[15]

But Percy was a literary editor. Chatterton mixed ancient literature with ancient antiquarianism. Is the only bond between these works the shared canopy of historical value I have just outlined? I believe not. The clue lies in lines 16 to 23 of Craish's heraldic account:

> 1369   Johannes Adderlie Knyghte wedded a Ladie of
> Boheme of greete Familie who did bear the
> Armes of Hongarie something like this did
> Syr John bear, witness the following Lines
> from the Tournament
>
>> Next rode in Syr John of Adderleigh Lord
>> Who over his Back his thick Sheeld did flyng
>> In Checkee of Red and Silver shining[16]

Craish produced an inter-allusion of the forgery. Such a reference to another forged work served to authenticate that work and also to bind the imagined world of the vision together. Craish's reference was actually very important, because he quoted "The Tournament" (ll. 73–76) for its historical information. Craish is like a surrogate Chatterton, performing the exercise described above. So the "Antiquities" series may have begun to build up the interconnected world of Chatterton's historical vision. There is fairly firm evidence that "Book 1st" contained "A Brief Account," which is an extract from Rowley's autobiography: hence the reference in the contents title to "Battle of Hastynges I": "Thomas Rowley parish preeste St. Johns in the City of Bristol . . . of whom, more in Book 1st." "A Brief Account" is a superb exercise in social history, a fascinating recreation of a developing relationship between Rowley, the "Fader Confessour" and antiquarian, and his patron, the merchant and mayor of Bristol, William Canynge. The detail and humor, the portrayal of history from the inside, would surely have delighted Percy and Warton. (It will be appreciated now how the MS grouping of "Nine Deeds and Proclamations," "Abstracts from Letters" and "Three Rowley Letters" formed a similar historical picture.)[17] One of the incidents described was an expedition Rowley was commissioned to undertake by Canynge to recover any Saxon MSS relating to architecture (Canynge was planning the new Redcliff church and wished to have Saxon designs as the basis). Rowley did his job well, but also found, and later procured and translated, a Saxon-Latin MS poem he titled "Battle of Hastynges." So just as Craish authenticated "The Tournament," so "A Brief Account" authenticated the epic of Turgot. The tightly knit vision began to be generated.

So when we consider the speed with which the forgery was produced, we can regard the vision as an autonomous imaginative product. The idea of an "Antiquities" series enabled an imaginative level of authentication to operate, because any work could be included in each anthology—the only requirement being venerable age (note Chatterton's audacity in saying "The Ode to Lais is a Modern production" at the end of the contents of "Book 3rd." The poem is lost, but the idea was to enforce the supposed antiquity of the other works). Yet Chatterton was not happy with the format, and no "Book 4th" has been found. One can detect a noncommittal or uncertain feeling in "Book 3rd": not only in the dedication to an obscure patron, who has not yet been identified, but also in the anonymity of "The Editor." The final importance of the anthology is that it placed the right emphasis on the forgery as an historiographical rather than literary phenomenon. The forgery was an example of that hybrid, historical fiction.

Before I leave "Antiquities," however, I want to disagree with Taylor about the identity of "Book 1st." Chatterton's only reference to its existence is in the title to "Battle of Hastynges I," cited above. Taylor tries to be more positive and declares "Book 1st" was a certain copybook Chatterton gave to the Bristol antiquarians. Taylor says:

> The first book must have contained "A Brief Account" (see C's introductory note to "Battle of Hastynges I"), the lost manuscript of which was a "thin quarto copy book" containing also extracts from "Battle of Hastynges I," "Brystowe Tragedie," and two shorter poems.[18]

Taylor's sources is Meyerstein's *A Life of Chatterton,* and the relevant passage there describes:

> A thin quarto copy book containing, in Chatterton's hand, Rowley's Memoirs of himself (first published in *Town and Country Magazine* Nov., 1775), in which were included about thirty lines of "Battle of Hastynges 1," beginning "Where Thor's fam'd temple manie ages stood," a few stanzas from *Brystowe Tragedy,* the *Songe to Aella,* and "some other little pieces," ie, the two poems *On our Ladies Chyrche.*[19]

It is obvious that this volume could hardly be "Antiquities—Book 1st." Why is it not titled such? There seems little point in "Battle of Hastynges I" appearing in Books 1st and 3rd. I believe this lost copybook can be viewed as a kind of Ur-"Antiquities," a prototype grouping. I conclude this because the extract from "Battle of Hastynges I" is the digression on Stonehenge, a purely historical passage in which the author Turgot described the monument's history and events surrounding it.[20] The emphasis was on history, and almost any passage from "Brystowe Tragedy" would have retained the emphasis, for that poem was written with Rowley as poetical eyewitness to an event in Bristol's past. So if we add to this grouping "A Brief Account" (of which the poem "On our Ladies Chyrche" is a part, being quoted in a footnote by Chatterton), it seems that the seeds of the ill-fated "Antiquities" series were sown in this lost "quarto copy book."

The titles of the two remaining extant anthologies show a striking reversal of emphasis. Their titles, in order of composition, are: "Poems, by / Thomas Rowley / Priest of St. Johns / In the City of Bristol / Containing / The Tournament an Interlude / and a Piece by Canynge— / called / Goulers Requiem" and "Eclogues, and / other Poems / by / Thomas Rowley— / with / A Glossary, and Annotations / by / Thomas Chatterton." The anthologies are wholly literary, but it is important not to see any aspect of the forgery in isolation. If we knew only of these two anthologies, we might conclude that Chatterton's only desire was to emulate Macpherson: to produce an edition of fake ancient poetry. But as I have stressed, Chatterton's vision was different from Macpherson's, and within it the bard or poet was not the sole creator of the past. The real significance of "Antiquities" becomes apparent. Those volumes, had they been successful, would have given to the public the authenticated, richly populated world of Chatterton's vision. Only after this base had been formed could Rowley the poet assume precedence (Chatterton seemed to have understood the merit of Rowley's verse; as I noted earlier, Rowleyan poetry soon became a kind of shorthand term for the whole forgery). Rowley would then be a believable entity, fully formed and on intimate terms with the reader. He would not be a literary "find." In other words, Chatterton the editor would have judiciously selected the literary masterpieces from many "ancient" MSS.

There was in fact a satisfying progression, a process of fruition, between the two poetry anthologies. Despite the indication of the title of "Poems, by Thomas Rowley," Rowley shared the volume with his friend and patron Canynge. There is only one poem each, so the anthology was probably incomplete, or, more likely, an aborted venture, succeeded by the second anthology. "The Tournament. An Interlude" was unfinished and is a lesser work than Canynge's "Gouler's Requiem." Both pieces were annotated, but this was restricted to a word-for-word gloss. So there is an air of incompletion about this anthology, as if Chatterton could not decide between making a memorial to Bristol poets or a sole celebration of Rowley. Note that the anthology was still anonymously edited, as was "Antiquities—Book 3rd."

The title of the later anthology shows that any lack of confidence had been swept away: "Eclogues, and other Poems by Thomas Rowley—with a Glossary and Annotations by Thomas Chatterton." Both Rowley and

Chatterton the editor—acknowledged for the first time—achieved a prominent position. There was no mention of Bristol, no obvious tie to the overall historical vision. Several of the notes were more than mere glosses, expanding into pockets of information. For instance, note 19 to "Eclogue the Third" explained "aumeres" as "Borders of Gold and Silver on which was laid thin Plates of either Metal counterchanged—not unlike the present spangled Laces—."[21] Apart from the three eclogues (whose subject matters were historical in relation to Rowley), the anthology contained an unfinished historical play of Rowley's called "Goddwyn." Despite that fact, the amount of verse in the volume was considerable: some four hundred and sixty-six lines compared to two hundred in "Poems by Thomas Rowley." So in every way this anthology represented something of a triumph for Chatterton the editor. The volume was in a particularly apt chronological position in relation to the forgery, for it marked effectively the end of the enterprise. After its composition, according to Taylor, only the Ossianics and "An Excelente Balade of Charitie" remained to be written before Chatterton's death.

Seen in isolation, "Poems, by Thomas Rowley" and "Eclogues and other Poems" stand as weak versions of what had been done so well by Macpherson and (legitimately) by Percy. But I have shown that behind the two anthologies lies a process of development that gives us a valuable if inconclusive insight into the attitude Chatterton bore to the publishability of his forgery, and the relation of this to the forgery's making of history.

Appendix 3

The Shakespeare Forgeries and Sharon Turner's *Vindication*

After the detection of Chatterton, and the demolition of the chest with six keys, I did not expect to have heard again, for some time at least, of such a repository for ancient manuscripts.

Edmond Malone

No study of literary forgery in the eighteenth century can fail to take account of William Henry Ireland's Shakespeare fabrications. Nor can this study ignore Sharon Turner's *Vindication of the Genuineness of the Ancient British Poems of Aneurin, Taliesin, Lywarch Hen, and Modlin* (1803), which attempted to provide once and for all a method of detecting fake ancient poetry. At the heart of the work of Ireland and Turner was the ancient literary document, so it is appropriate to deal with these two writers in the same appendix.

Macpherson and Chatterton were not the only eighteenth-century writers to present their literary creations as edited documents. Defoe's *Memoirs of a Cavalier* appeared as historical manuscripts, and Samuel Richardson went as far as to make use of forged letters in *Clarissa*. With the appearance of Horace Walpole's Gothic novel *The Castle of Otranto* in 1764, the discovery of a sensational old manuscript also became a feature of the plot. Thomas Rowley rode around England collecting Saxon manuscripts in Chatterton's vision. But there is a vast difference between the way Rowley did this and the way a similar activity took place in a novel. Macpherson and Chatterton broke with the need for a conventionalized homogeneous literary narrative. The function of the manuscript in the novel all too quickly became a matter of convention. By the time the second edition of *Castle of Otranto* was issued in 1765, Horace

Walpole was ready to explode the pretense that the novel was a translation of a black letter manuscript dated 1529 and discovered in "the library of an ancient Catholic family in the north of England."[1] The Gothic novel may actually have tarnished Chatterton's achievement by encouraging the view that the role of MSS in his vision is also harmless chicanery. In fact, Chatterton's concern was always history and its transmission. The famous chest in Redcliff church should not be used as a weapon against Chatterton—no more than Macpherson's Highland expedition and Percy's rescue of the folio MS. These accounts, whether true or false, are of peripheral interest and importance. W. H. Ireland's machinations should also be viewed in this impartial light, though he too has probably done much to sully the gains made by the forgers. Edmond Malone, who opposed vigorously both Chatterton and Ireland, clearly thought the forging of MSS had become a risible, but pernicious joke by the end of the century. Malone's views were perhaps understandable when one considers how the novel popularized and vulgarized the status of the ancient MS. Henry Mackenzie's *The Man of Feeling* (1771) had one of the more interesting introductions. The narrator and his friend the curate were out shooting when they came across a ruin. The original house used to belong to a man whose memoirs the curate possessed. Asked to produce the MS, he confessed he was at that moment using it for guncotton—"'Tis excellent wadding."[2] Mackenzie both captured and burlesqued the evanescence of the MS and its salvaging from oblivion. Needless to say, the fact that the main narrative was a MS had no intrinsic or informed part to play in the text, unlike Thomas Rowley's discovery of "The Battle of Hastynges." There the discovery was an integral part of a system of authentication and transmission. Even Scott's use of the pretense was conventional. Little is added to our reading of *Old Mortality* by its supposedly having been written by Robert Pattieson. As chapter 7 showed, however, Scott did question such conventions.

The fabrications of W. H. Ireland combined the old practice of counterfeiting another's work with a Chattertonian creation of social history through diversity of documents. His "new" Shakespeare plays, *Vortigern* and *Henry II*, were not taken seriously for very long.[3] *Vortigern* ran for one night only in 1796 at Drury Lane. The modern reader of the play would agree with David Garrick, who was an unwilling member of the cast, and who had the audience in hysterics by his accentuation of the lines "And when this solemn mockery is ended."[4] *Vortigern* went the way of Lewis Theobald's *Double Falsehood* (1728), an earlier Shakespearian counterfeit. Theobald anticipated the central impulse behind Ireland's enterprise:

if you shall think fit to pronounce this Piece genuine, it will silence the Censures of those *Unbelievers*, who think it impossible a Manuscript of *Shakespeare* could so long have lain dormant.[5]

Ireland attempted to replenish the greatest vacuum in all literary studies: Shakespeare MSS. *Vortigern* was a failure as Shakespearian pastiche, but it is important to see that Ireland claimed he had discovered a MS and not a printed text. In fact *Vortigern* and *Henry II* were only two of many "new" documents. In Chattertonian manner, the imaginative works existed within a larger authenticating system of literary and non-literary relics. Seventeen of these MSS were published in facsimile by Ireland's bardolatrous father, Samuel Ireland. The forbidding tome appeared in 1796 as *Miscellaneous Papers and Legal Instruments under the Hand and Seal of William Shakespeare: Including the Tragedy of King Lear and a small fragment of Hamlet, from the original MSS in the possession of Samuel Ireland of Norfolk Street*. One can see in this title the potential for a radical revision of the received textual status of Shakespeare, the equivalent of the forgeries shedding new light on history. Ireland provided Shakespeare scholars and lovers with ardently desired artefacts. Boswell is said to have gone on his knees before some of the MSS and cried "I now kiss the valuable relics of our bard: and thanks to God that I have lived to see them!"[6] All the fake documents were in antiquated orthography. Ireland like Chatterton managed to obtain some genuinely old parchment from a bookseller. The seventeen MSS in *Miscellaneous Papers* included letters to and from Shakespeare, receipts of payments to actors, contracts of employment, deeds of trust, deeds of gift and a billet-doux. The presence of the bard was the unifying factor. The wealth of public and private detail did make for interesting reading, and the evocation of history began to take on a Chattertonian vitality. The dearth of Shakespeare MSS was matched of course by the lack of knowledge about his life. Ireland's recreation of such information had limited success, although items 10, 11, and 12 were counterproductive. These three documents were the only ones to be closely interrelated. What they formed was a brazen fiction. A close friendship was concocted between Shakespeare and one of Ireland's (imaginary) ancestors. This began when Ireland rescued the bard from drowning. Ireland was immediately bestowed with gifts (item 10). Other byproducts of the friendship were tributary lines to Ireland from Shakespeare (item 11) and a sketch by the same of Ireland's house (item 12). Chatterton would never have been so self-indulgent and wish-fulfilling. Shakespeare's account of the drowning incident must be quoted for its hilarity:

onne or abowte the thyrde daye of the laste monethe beyng the
monethe of Auguste havynge withe mye goode freynde Masterre
William Henrye Irelande and otherres taene boate neare untowe myne
house afowresayde wee dydd purpose goynge upp Thames butt those
thatte were soe toe conducte us beynnge muche toe merrye throughe
Lyquorre theye dydd upsette oure fowresayde boate baynge alle butte
myeselfe savedde themselves bie swimmyng for thought the Waterre
was deepe yette owre beynge close nygh toe shore made itt lyttel
diffyculte for themm knowinge the fowresayde Arte Masterre William
henrye Irelande notte seeynge mee dydd aske for mee butte oune of
the Companye dydd answerre thatte I was drownynge onn the
whyche hee pulled off hys Jerrekyne and jumpedd inn afterre mee
withe muche paynes he draggedd mee forthe I beynge then nearlye
deade and soe he dydd save mye life and for the whyche Service I doe
herebye give hym as followithe!!! fyrste mye written Playe of Henrye
fourthe Henrye fyfthe King John King Leare as allsoe mye written
Playe never yett impryntedd whych I have named Kyng henrye thyrde of England.[7]

Malone called the incident "a very pretty story, and almost as interesting
as some of our modern novels."[8] Ireland's attempt to blend the real and
fictional did not (in Wilkie's term) "unite." Ireland wished to give the
Ireland family legal rights of possession of the newly discovered relics.
Nothing could be more authoritative than Shakespeare's own voice declaring this very information.

Note that one of the plays presented to Ireland was a new one entitled
"Henry III." W. H. Ireland never wrote this play, but the manner in
which it was given birth and authenticated was very Chattertonian. The
same ploy was repeated in the final document of *Miscellaneous Papers.*
The MS was a "Deed of Trust" (duly witnessed) in which Shakespeare
distributed some of his plays to friends. The plays were all in MS form,
and were kept in "the Oakenn Cheste att owre Globe Theatre."[9] The
significant references were to new plays: an interlude called *The Virgin
Queen, Henry VII,* and *Vortygerne.* It is another Chattertonian feature that
Vortigern and *Henry II* (the new plays that were written) were both
historical. Ireland's plan was to supplement Shakespeare's English history plays by filling in the chronological gaps. Ireland wished to make
the past through Shakespeare, as Chatterton and Macpherson had made
it through their imaginary authors:

Had the play of Vortigern succeeded with the public, and the manuscripts been acknowledged as genuine, it was my intention to have
completed a series of plays from the reign of William the Conqueror to
that of Queen Elizabeth; that is to say, I should have planned a drama

on every reign the subject of which had not been treated of by Shakespeare.[10]

Ireland himself admitted that he was following in Chatterton's footsteps. In his *Confessions* (1805) he declared the major literary influences on his career to have been, first, Percy's *Reliques,* and then Chatterton: "I used to envy his fate, and desire nothing so ardently as the termination of my existence in a similar cause."[11] Ireland did not go that far. But he visited Bristol, haunted Chatterton's haunts, and spoke to Mrs. Newton, Chatterton's sister.[12] Yet he lacked his mentor's genius. *Aella* was not a great play, but its power was generated by its function within Chatterton's vision—we witness Rowley dramatizing, relative to the vision, historical fact. The dullness of *Vortigern* and *Henry II* is not rescued by the documents. Neither are those vital "revisions" that Ireland made to *King Lear* and *Hamlet*. Ireland's alterations were supposed to restore the authentic version of the text—that is, the MS version he actually confected. The revision of Kent's lines at the end of *Lear*—"I have a journey, sir, shortly to go:/My master calls, and I must not say no"—can be cited to show Ireland's success. The "restored" reading is:

> Thanks, sir: but I go to that unknown land
> That chains each pilgrim fast within its soil;
> By living men most shunn'd, most dreaded.
> Still my good master this same journey took:
> He calls me; I am content, and straight obey:
> Then farewell world! the busy scene is done:
> Kent liv'd most true, Kent dies most like a man.[13]

If only some of the documents had given us Shakespeare's views on history or literature. Nevertheless, the documents were the best part of the exercise, and they did evoke a historical Shakespeare, living and working, writing letters and receiving replies. Had he gone on, Ireland might have produced Shakespeare's laundry list. Yet the unscholarly of the time saw nothing but triviality and banality in the parade of antiquarian minutiae. A burlesque of this aspect of the forgery (and the admittedly absurd orthography) appeared in *The Telegraph:*

Tooo Misteerree Benjaamminnee Joohnnssonn
DEEREE SIREE,
            Wille youe doee meee theee favvouree too dinnee wythee meee onnn Friddaye nexte att twoo off theee clockee to eatee sommee muttonne choppes andd somme poottaattooeesse.[14]

In fact, domestic details were seen to be of vital importance in the making of the past. As was shown in the last chapter, the writer of historical fiction needed theoretically to be a skillful selector of such information. Chatterton had been. Ireland only showed promise.

Ireland's *Confessions* appeared in 1805. That same year saw the publication of the "Highland Committee Report on the Authenticity of Ossian." The report concluded that though Macpherson may have had access to genuine ancient Gallic poetry, he had duplicitously interpolated his sources. The official verdict on Ossian had been given (Macpherson's "originals"—a probable Gallic translation from his English—appeared in 1807). One might think therefore that the forgeries had been laid to rest, especially when the detection of Ireland's fabrications is included in the picture. Forgery should no longer have been a problem. The historian Sharon Turner believed he could seal the fate of forgeries of ancient poetry. In 1803 appeared his pamphlet *A Vindication of the Genuineness of the Ancient British Poems of Aneurin, Taliesin, Llywarch Hen, and Modlin.* Turner had cited poems by these poets in his *History of the Anglo-Saxons* (1799), saying they were "contemporary with some of the Saxon Invasions."[15] Accusations were leveled that the poems were his own inventions—that is, forgeries. To refute this charge, Turner wrote the *Vindication,* for which word can be read "authentication." The posture of his defense was to prove that the poems he had used were ancient and could not be modern. By systematic analysis, he provided rules for distinguishing the "genuine" (ancient) product from the "fake" (modern). His main concern was to delineate the former: the latter then existed by negation and did not necessarily have to be stated. We have come full circle to the drawing up of authenticating rules that began with Locke, Hume, and Du Fresnoy. The difference is that they were discussing history. Turner was discussing poetry. He wrote in the wake of three major literary forgeries, all of which recreated the situation of the "ancient" writer. It remains to be seen whether Turner could exorcize Macpherson's and Chatterton's achievements.

Thus the *Vindication* was as much an attack on forgery as it was a defense of ancient Welsh poetry. Indeed, the one was used to prove the other. Note the first volley to have been fired:

> These poems have not become known to us under the circumstances which attended those of Chatterton and Macpherson, or the Pseudo Shakespeare. They are not works now starting up suddenly for the first time to our knowledge. They do not own their discovery to any individual. No friendly chest—no ruinous turret—no auspicious accident—has given them to us. No man's interest or reputation is connected with their discovery. Their supporters are therefore, at least, disinterested.[16]

As was remarked at the opening of this chapter, the purported discovery of old MSS was an easy target and was already by the end of the century something of a joke. In any case, Turner was in immediate trouble. Whether or not he knew of the attitudes of the anthologists, Turner could hardly pin his case on a communal or national indifference to ancient poetry:

> Such indifference as this, about documents so curious, never yet attended any forgery. Nothing can be more favourable to their cause,—nothing can more strongly mark the difference which subsists between these poems and all those writings which are known to have been fabricated.
>
> (P. 6)

Yet he was forced to admit immediately that "the spirit of literary patriotism has begun" (p. 11), and he was clearly one such patriot. He was also far from indifferent about the "documents so curious" under consideration. Leaving behind the picturesque aspects of the matter, he provided a lengthy analysis, conventionally divided into the external and internal categories.

Each category had eight subdivisions. Turner's argument will be followed step by step, beginning with the external points. The first topic was, once again, the MS. But Turner had no actual "original" MSS to talk about. He was forced to speculate about later records:

> My object is to authenticate the genuineness of such of them as I think beyond all dispute. . . . I am satisfied that some are not genuine, and that some have been interpolated.
>
> (Pp. 33–34)

In other words Turner realized, like Locke, Toland, and Innes before him, that forgery was an inextricable attribute of ancient literary records. This led on to a second assertion, which was that the poetry of Taliesin and the others was alluded to by twelfth-century bards, whose works did survive:

> These facts will show that they are at least no modern forgery, and that they were in existence in the twelfth century. The question will then become this—Were these poems existing genuinely in the twelfth century, or were they then forged?
>
> (P. 17)

The parameters had already been substantially revised. Turner had to prove his poems were "at least no modern forgery." Note that he had created a regression, a gradation, of exactly the kind that Chatterton exploited so brilliantly: one age recuperating another, one MS referring to an earlier one. Turner's subsequent six external points tried to prove that his poems were transmitted unsullied from the sixth century through the twelfth to the present. Points three, five, and six used Latin and early Christian sources to show that sixth-century Britons were (in part) literate, and so MSS must have been in existence. But the existence of Turner's poets and their writings was again dependent on that later gradation: twelfth-century allusions (points four and eight): "in the twelfth century there were writings of old British Bards extant, which were *then* called *ancient*." (p. 18) So far, then, Turner had described the forgeries' use of regression perspicuously. The *Vindication* begins to function as a gloss of Macpherson's and Chatterton's historical visions, the opposite of its intention. There could hardly be a more potent irony.

Turner had no better success with the internal evidence—textual considerations. His remarks were potentially more interesting, because he had to show how the literary characteristics of a poem defined that poem's position in history. He first pointed out that all his poems, particularly the *Gododin*, had martial themes. Such a topic would not be conducive to poetry of later, more refined times. Shaky as this notion was, Turner was aware that it hardly excluded Ossian. So his second point was that the type of martial action his poems described was usually tragic. In the depicted battles, the natives were usually the losers. A forger would never be so unpatriotic:

> We can perceive at once, why such poems as those of Ossian should be fabricated, even independent of individual advantage. In making a Fingal, an irresistable warrier—an Alexander of the third century who only moves to conquer—whose presence is so decisive of conflict, that in comparison to the fame of other warriors he keeps awhile out of it. In forming such a character there is an obvious gratification of national vanity.
>
> (P. 153)

Ossian did gratify Scottish vanity. But Turner was clearly misrepresenting Macpherson. Nothing was more tragic than Fingal's glorious action, because it was recalled by Ossian, the bard who was the last of his race. Also Turner's basic point was very suspect. He had already admitted that "literary patriotism" was rife in Wales, as much as in the rest of Britain (Welsh scholars, as was shown in chapter 4, rated the *Gododin* as a Welsh *Iliad*).

The third point was totally inapplicable as a weapon with which to attack the forgeries. Turner noted that Arthur was never alluded to in his poems, which showed they were not of the twelfth century. Those times could not have resisted such an embellishment. Yet neither did Arthur appear in Macpherson's or Chatterton's works. They created their own heroes. The illogicality of Turner's arguing by negation was rather like Percy's remark that Ossian's poems could not be genuine because no mention was made in them of the wolf.[17] The point was pressed no further.

The fourth point looked at subject matter in a positive way again. Turner reckoned the topics in his poems were "natural topics for such bards to have chosen—too natural—too artless, for fraud to have selected" (p. 165). Breaking this down further, there were five poetical markers or "allusions" (p. 165) of this naturalness. The first "allusion" was the poet's mentioning of himself in the poem. That device was of course central to Macpherson's creation of Ossian's voice. Turner struggled to keep forgery on the "unnatural" side of the fence:

> to find the name of the author in any poem is to find a circumstance which has often accompanied genuineness, though it does not prove it. . . . But we certainly gain a material point by having the author's name inserted in a composition. It rescues us from the doubt which must always attend anonymous poetry, whether it may not belong to some other century than that to which we ascribe it. The author's name in a poem narrows the question into this alternative. The poem, then, either must be the genuine work of the author named, or an express forgery made for the purpose of passing to the world as that author's composition.
>
> (Pp. 165–6; P. 169)

Turner's observations could easily have been a positive appraisal of how well Macpherson understood the authentic making of the past by poetry. Turner's resolution was mere guesswork:

> The chances of such a direct wilful forgery, are much fewer than the chances of that possible mistake to which anonymous poetry is liable. But I think that the supposition of a wilful forgery of these poems cannot be supported.
>
> (P. 169)

The second kind of "allusion" was any reference in the poem to a contemporary author. Chatterton's elaborate use of the device need only be mentioned. The third type of "allusion" was that the poets "speak of events which happened in the age in which they lived, as passing under their own eyesight" (pp. 171–72). The *Vindication* acted as a detailed gloss on the forgeries, a marvelous celebration of their "traits of genuineness" (p. 171). The last "allusion" referred to the poem as the poet's empirical experience, his eyewitnessing of history. The forgeries recreated this situation brilliantly. The fourth kind of "allusion" was that

> many passages may be noticed in these poems which seem to have been taken from objects and incidents then really existing, and which could hardly have occurred to the mind of a fraudulent imposter.
>
> (P. 177)

Turner argued that "the topics of a forger are more general than these, and more remote from individual reality" (p. 181). Turner ignored Chatterton. The final type of "allusion"

> relates to the personal feelings of the bard. Fictitious poems seldom touch on this topic, because it is not easy to counterfeit true feeling.
>
> (P. 186)

Turner could not appreciate or allow for the power of fiction, and historical fiction in particular. A surfeit of contemporary opinions testified to Ossian's containing more "true feeling" (especially the qualities of sensibility or compassion) than any previous epic poet.

So much for the "allusions." The fifth general point concerned ancient Welsh language, irrelevant as regards the forgeries. The sixth and seventh points returned to subject matter and its authenticity: "the historical allusions are true" (p. 20), and "the manners . . . are consistent" (p. 20). Turner described basic attributes of historical fiction that Chatterton helped to establish. Moreover, Turner's statements were prone to a circular logic, because he gave no idea how the authenticity he refered to was checked. Turner had already used rhetoric of supposition and speculation, wherein poems "seem to" be genuine (p. 177; the fourth "allusion"). From purporting to be a scientific analysis of literary authentication, Turner's *Vindication* had fallen off into a Humean "feeling." The reason for this was that all his observations had applied equally well to the forgeries, and had certainly not distinguished between them and the "genuine" article. His final point was very lame. Stylistically, his poems were "such compositions as such bards, in such an age, would be expected to write" (p. 212).

Turner was particularly out of touch with the developments looked at in the previous chapter. The thoroughly "researched" historical poem was being mooted, if not yet successfully practiced. Turner was simply blind to the skill and awareness of Macpherson and Chatterton in the making of history. This awareness was shown so strikingly in the fact that he celebrated the forgeries, while attempting to outlaw them. Turner was a historian admired by Scott, and he was cited in *Ivanhoe*. The *Vindication* was not a conclusion, but an indicator of a transformation. If historical fiction of the kind Macpherson, Chatterton, and Ireland wrote was no more, the reason was not that Turner had banished it. Rather, the imaginative making of history had found its stable and most successful manifestation in homogeneous narrative: the novel.

Appendix 4

A "Prolific Age" of Forgery

In 1797 William Mason wrote the following verses commemorating W. H. Ireland:

> Four forgers born in one prolific age
> Much critical acumen did engage
> The first was soon by doughty Douglas scar'd
> Tho' Johnson would have screen'd him had he dar'd
> The next had all the cunning of a Scot
> The third, invention, genius,—nay, what not?
> Fraud, now exhausted, only could dispense
> To her fourth Son, their threefold impudence.[1]

The identities of the forgers referred to, just in case anyone was in doubt, were revealed in footnotes: William Lauder, Macpherson, Chatterton, Ireland. It seems then I must justify the omission in this book of Lauder's forgery, which opened Mason's roll call of infamy. My defense is simple: Lauder's work is not relevant to my approach. In 1750 he published *An Essay on Milton's Use and Imitation of the Moderns, in his Paradise Lost.* This treatise attempted to prove that Milton had plagiarized several modern Latin poets, including Grotius and Masenius. In fact, Lauder had interpolated into their work passages and lines from William Hog's Latin translation of *Paradise Lost* (1690). The fraud was exposed almost immediately by John Douglas in *Milton Vindicated from the Charge of Plagiarism* (1751). Lauder publicly acknowledged his transgression, but his forgery had been convincing enough to persuade Johnson to write a preface. There is much of interest in all this, but no application to the issues dealt with in this study. Indeed, I have attempted to counter the

195

oft-used view that Macpherson and Chatterton were simply creatures of their time, turning to forgery as seekers of overnight fame. More importantly, I have avoided treating forgery as some kind of autonomous, unified endeavor. The inevitable result of such a view is that Macpherson's and Chatterton's work would not be taken seriously as literature.

Other writers involved in the controversy over the forgeries of Macpherson, Chatterton, and Ireland produced lists of precedents. What these lists showed was a lack of any definable critical angle on the part of the compilers. Herbert Croft, in *Love and Madness* (1780), suggested as influences on Chatterton, Psalmanazar, *Castle of Otranto,* Lauder, Ossian, "The Concubine," "Hardyknute," and the Junius letters.[2] All these may have had their place in Chatterton's imagination. My point is that an indiscriminate grouping of forgeries—the term itself remained undefined by Croft—has a very limited use, and certainly goes little way to a proper critical understanding of Macpherson and Chatterton. Most of the items in Croft's list have in fact received some treatment in this study. Of those that have not, "The Concubine" (1767) was simply a Spenserian pastiche, and "Junius" was the pseudonym of a writer of subversive political letters that appeared in the *Public Advertiser* from 1769 to 1772. Chatterton imitated Junius in his Grub Street months, but those letters were no part of the forgery.

A little later in the century, Joseph Riston summoned up an infernal legion:

> the forgeries of Hector Boethius, David Chalmers, George Buchanan, Thomas Dempster, Sir John Bruce, William Lauder, Archibald Bower, James Macpherson and John Pinkerton, stamp a disgrace upon the national character.[3]

Ritson's list is closer to my purposes. Boethius, Chalmers, Buchanan, Dempster, and Bower were all Scottish historians, and all were involved in nationalist mythologizing and the confecting of roots for the Scottish nation. They have not been studied because only Bower belonged to the eighteenth century, and his *History of the Popes* (1748–66) was a forgery in the sense of being a plagiarism of the French historian Tillemont.[4] Plagiarism is not a relevant issue in this study. The other figures in Ritson's list have all been looked at in this book. Sir John Bruce was regarded as the likely author, aided by Elizabeth Wardlaw, of "Hardyknute" (see chapter 4).

Finally, there is Edmond Malone. He noted of Ireland's fabrications in 1796: "IMPOSTURES of this kind are no novelties in the History of Letters."[5] Malone did not say what "this kind" referred to. His list included several foreign instances of the supposed discovery of a manuscript by a famous author. He then mentioned Psalmanazar, Ossian, Rowley (Chatterton), and William Rufus Chetwood. Chetwood had suggested in *The British Theatre* (1750) that in a 1634 folio of Shakespeare, several previously unknown plays could be found: "The London Prodigal," "Sir Thomas Cromwell," "Sir John Old-Castle," "The Puritan," "The Yorkshire Tragedy," and "The Tragedy of Locrine." Chetwood did say, however (as Malone did not), that "we make a Doubt if any of them were wrote by our Author."[6] Malone eventually contradicted himself, saying that Ireland's forgery was actually different from the previous ones in having the audacity to put the "new" MSS on display.

Forgery is a fascinating concept, particularly in relation to art. Forgery is also a multifaceted enterprise, which needs to be pinned down if any meaningful critical observations are to be made. I have tried to do that. My approach has been consistent: I have looked at eighteenth-century ideas of history and fiction, and how these came alive in the forgeries of Macpherson and Chatterton. A study that encompasses the many other ramifications of literary forgery in the eighteenth century would make a valuable study. But that study is not this book.

Notes

Introduction

1. The term "Ossian" is used throughout this book to refer to the poetry of Ossian and to the poet himself. The context should make clear which meaning is appropriate.

2. Eric Rothstein, *Restoration and Eighteenth Century Poetry,* (London: Routledge and Kegan Paul, 1981), 116.

Chapter 1. The Influence of Historiography

1. David Hume, *Letters to William Strahan* (Oxford: Clarendon Press, 1888), 155.

2. Edward Gibbon, *Autobiography of Edward Gibbon* (London: Oxford Univ. Press, 1959), 179.

3. Ibid., 180.

4. Quoted in Paul J. Korshin, *Studies in Change and Revolution* (Menstone: Scolar Press, 1972), 73.

5. Herbert Weisinger, "The Middle Ages and the Late Eighteenth Century Historians," *Philological Quarterly* 27 (1948): 63–79, 79.

6. Lawrence Lipking, *The Ordering of the Arts in Eighteenth Century England* (Princeton: Princeton University Press, 1970), 142–43.

7. John Butt, *The Mid Eighteenth Century* (Oxford: Clarendon Press, 1979), 5.

8. Edward Gibbon, *Memoirs of My Life and Writings* (London: Macmillan, 1930), 145.

9. Joseph Addison, *The Spectator,* 4 vols. (London: Everyman, 1951), 3:302.

10. Richard Steele, *The Spectator,* 4 vols (London: Everyman, 1951), 1:412.

11. James Moor, *Essays, read to a Literary Society at their weekly meetings within the College at Glasgow* (Glasgow: Robert and Andrew Foulis, 1759), 128–78, 138. The *Essay on Historical Composition* was read February 6, 1752.

12. James Boswell, *Life of Johnson* (London: Oxford Univ. Press, 1970), 527–28.

13. Gilbert Stuart, *Critical Observations concerning the Scottish Historians Hume, Stuart, and Robertson* (London: T. Evans, 1782), 7.

14. Ibid., 37.

15. See also Peter Whalley, *An Essay on the Manner of Writing History* (London: M. Cooper, 1746), 5: "The Characters, in [romance], are represented as they *ought* to be; whereas History exhibits them as they really are"; Joseph Priestley, *Lectures on History and General Policy* (Dublin: P. Byrne, 1788), 6: "independent of any further use, we have many well-written histories, which, I think, are calculated to give as much pure entertainment . . . as the generality of novels and romances."

16. Hugh Blair, *Lectures on Rhetoric and Belles Lettres,* 2 vols., (London: W. Strahan; T. Cadell, 1783), 2:303. The lectures were originally delivered in the 1760s.

17. Clara Reeve, *The Progress of Romance,* 2 vols. (London: Printed for the Author, 1785), 1:111; Gilbert Stuart, *A View of Society in Europe* (London: J. Murray, 1788), v.

18. Boswell, *Life of Johnson,* 24.

19. John Locke, *An Essay Concerning Human Understanding* (London: Fontana, 1968), 412.

20. Henry Saint John, Viscount Bolingbroke, *Letters on the Study and Use of History* (London: A. Miller, 1752), 64.

21. William Warburton, *A Critical and Philosophical Enquiry into the Causes of Prodigies and Miracles as related by Historians* (London: Thomas Corbett, 1727), 63–64.

22. Ibid., 64.

23. The word "literary" as used by eighteenth-century writers and myself refers both to written records in general and, more specifically, ancient imaginative literature. The context of usage should make clear which sense is meant.

24. Pierre Nicolas Lenglet Du Fresnoy, *A New Method of Studying History,* 2 vols. (London: W. Burton, 1728), 1:225.

25. Ibid., 261.

26. Thomas Innes, *A Critical Essay on the Ancient Inhabitants of the Northern Parts of Britain, or Scotland,* 2 vols. (London: William Innys, 1729), 1:xv.

27. Ibid., 1:iv–v.

28. Ibid., 2:500.

29. James Macpherson, *Original Papers,* 2 vols. (London: W. Strahan; T. Cadell, 1775), 1:6–7.

30. Carte, *A General History,* 2 (1750):iii.

31. Ibid., 1 (1747): x.

32. John Toland, *A Critical History of the Celtic Religion and Learning* (London: Lackington & Co; 1740), 81–82.

33. Ibid., 83.

34. William Robertson, *The History of America,* 2 vols. (London: W. Strahan; T. Cadell, 1777), 1:xv.

35. William Robertson, *The History of the Reign of Emperor Charles V,* 3 vols. (London: W. Strahan; T. Cadell, 1769), 1:xii–xiii.

36. Carte, *A General History,* 1 (1747): x.

37. Ibid.

38. James Macpherson, *The History of Great Britain,* 2 vols. (London: W. Strahan; T. Cadell, 1775), 1:iv.

39. Locke, *Essay,* 405.

40. Ibid.

41. Ibid., 410.

42. Ibid.

43. Ibid.

44. Ibid., 411–412

45. Ibid.

46. Ibid.

47. David Hume, *A Treatise of Human Nature,* Book One. (London: Fontana, 1962), 1:128–29.

48. Ibid.

49. Ibid.

50. Ibid., 195.

51. Ibid.

52. Ibid., 196.

53. Bolingbroke, *Letters,* 96–97.

54. Edward Gibbon, *An Essay on the Study of Literature* (London: T. Becket; P. A. De Hondt, 1764), 47.

55. Ibid.

56. Ibid.

57. Ibid., 99–100.

58. David Hume, *Treatise*, 146.

59. Ibid., 325.

60. Keith Stewart, "History, Poetry, and the Terms of Fiction in the Eighteenth Century," *Modern Philology* 66 (1968–69): 110–120, 114–15.

61. Adam Smith,. *Lectures on Rhetoric and Belles-Lettres* (London: Thomas Nelson and Sons Ltd., 1963), 86.

62. Ibid.

63. Bolingbroke, *Letters*, 98–99.

64. Robert Wood, *An Essay on the Original Genius of Homer* (London: Privately printed, 1769), xxxvi.

65. Hume, *Treatise*, 169.

66. Keith Stewart, "Ancient Poetry as History in the 18th Century," *Journal of the History of Ideas*, 19 (1958): 335–47, 339, 340.

67. Gibbon, *Essay*, 115.

68. John Lewis, *The History of Great Britain* (London: F. Gyles, 1729), 3.

69. T. P. Peardon, *The Transition in English Historical Writing 1760–1830* (Columbia: Columbia Univ. Press, 1933), 111.

70. Boswell, *Life of Johnson*, 628.

71. Peardon, *The Transition*, 117.

72. Innes, *A Critical Essay*, 1:xiv.

73. Innes, *Critical Essay*, 1:iii–iv.

74. Ibid, 2:467.

75. Ibid., 2:469.

76. Ibid., 2:476.

77. Ibid., 2:473.

78. Ibid., 2:501.

79. Roderic O'Flaherty, *Ogygia*, 2 vols. (Dublin: W. M'Kenzie, 1793), 1:lxiv–v.

80. O'Flaherty, *Ogygia*, 1:lxvi.

81. O'Flaherty, *Ogygia*, 1:lxix.

82. John Toland, *A Critical History*, 81–82.

83. Ibid.

84. Ibid., 86.

85. Geoffry Keating, *The General History of Ireland*, 2 vols. (Dublin: James Carson, 1723), 1:iv.

86. Ibid., xvii.

87. Ibid., xvii–xviii.

88. Ibid., xviii.

89. Ibid.

90. Ibid., 67.

91. Ibid.

92. Charles O'Conor, *Dissertations on the Ancient History of Ireland* (Dublin: James Hoey, 1753), 57.

93. Keating, *History of Ireland*, 1:67.

94. Blair, *Lectures*, 2:317.

95. Ibid.

96. Smith, *Lectures*, 100.

97. David Hume, *The History of England* (London: A. Millar, 1763), 1:24.

98. G. Sale, A. Bower, G. Shelvocke, J. Swinton, *An Universal History* (London: J. Batley), 1 (1736): xxix.

99. Ibid.

100. William Robertson, *The History of Scotland*, 2 vols. (London: A. Millar, 1759), 1:1–2.

101. Blair, *Lectures*, 2:288.

102. Ibid.

103. Quoted in J. W. Thomson, *A History of Historical Writing* (New York: Macmillan, 1942), 94.

104. Thomas Percy, *Reliques of Ancient English Poetry*, 3 vols. (London: J. Dodsley, 1765), 2:179.

105. Thomas Pownall, *A Treatise on the Study of Antiquities* (London: J. Dodsley, 1782), 76.

106. Quoted in René Wellek, *The Rise of English Literary History* (Chapel Hill: University of North Carolina Press, 1941), 33.

107. Priestley, *Lectures on History*, 69.

Chapter 2. The Literary Impetus

1. Quoted in J. R. Hale, *The Evolution of British Historiography* (Cleveland, New York: World Publishing Co. Ltd. 1964), 36.

2. Quoted in James Boswell, *The Journal of a Tour to the Hebrides*, ed. R. W. Chapman (1924; reprint, London: Oxford Univ. Press, 1979), 320.

3. Joseph Warton, *An Essay on the Writings and Genius of Pope*, 2 vols. (London: M. Cooper, 1756), 1:253–54.

4. Ibid.

5. Samuel Johnson, *Lives of the English Poets* (London: Everyman, 1975), 394.

6. Ibid., 394: "a book which teaches how the brow of Criticism may be smoothed, and how she may be enabled, with all her severity, to attract and to delight."

7. Warton, *Essay on Pope*, 1:253.

8. E. M. W. Tillyard, *Milton* (Harmondsworth: Penguin, 1968), 79.

9. *The Works of John Milton* (New York: Columbia Univ. Press, 1938), 18:243.

10. John Dryden, *Selected Criticism*, ed. James Kinsley and George Parfitt (London: Oxford Univ. Press, 1970): 224.

11. Dryden, *Selected Criticism*, 302.

12. Sir Richard Blackmore, *Alfred* (London: James Knapton, 1723), vii–viii.

13. From Henry Pemberton, *Observations on Poetry* (1738); quoted in H. T. Swedenberg, *Theory of the Epic*, 182.

14. Blackmore, from *Essays Upon Several Subjects* (1716), quoted in Swedenberg, *Theory of the Epic*, 174.

15. Aristotle, *The Poetics*, in *Classical Literary Criticism* trans. T. S. Dorsch (Harmondsworth: Penguin, 1975), 43.

16. Quoted in H. T. Swedenberg, *The Theory of the Epic in England 1650–1800* (Berkeley and Los Angeles: Univ. of California Press, 1944), 180.

17. Ibid.

18. See Owen Ruffhead, *The Life of Alexander Pope Esq* (London: C. Bathurst, 1769), 409–23.

19. Warton, *Essay on Pope*, 1:276.

20. Ibid., 277–278.

21. Ibid., 279.

22. William Wilkie, *The Epigoniad*, in *The Works of the English Poets*, ed. Alexander Chalmers (London: J. Johnson, 1810), 16:124. To confirm that fact that national history was felt to have been neglected by poets in the mid-eighteenth century, we find Thomas Percy in 1759 remarking about *The Epigoniad:* "I wish it had been employed on some domestic subject." See *The Correspondence of Thomas Percy and William Sherstone* (New Haven and London: Yale Univ. Press, 1977), 33.

23. Wilkie, *The Epigoniad*, 124.

24. Ibid.

25. Ibid.

26. Ibid., 125.

27. Ibid.

28. Ibid., 126.

29. Ibid., 130.

30. Ibid., 130.

31. Ibid.

32. Hugh Blair, *A Dissertation on Ossian* (London: T. Becket; P. A. De Hondt, 1763), 29.

33. *The Poems of Alexander Pope*, ed. John Butt (London: Methuen & Co Ltd., 1975), 147.

34. Thomas Blackwell, *An Enquiry into the Life and Writings of Homer* (1735; reprint, Menstone: Scolar Press, 1972), 34–35.

35. Thomas Rymer, *Edgar, or the English Monarch* (London: Richard Tonson, 1678), A_4 recto.

36. John Dryden, *King Arthur, or, The British Worthy* (London: Jacob Tonson, 1691), A_3 recto.

37. John Bancroft, *King Edward the Third* (London: J. Hindmarsh, 1691), A_2 verso.

38. Ibid., prologue.

39. Charles Hopkins, *Boadicea Queen of Britain* (London: Jacob Tonson, 1697), 12–13.

40. William Shakespeare, *Antony and Cleopatra*, IV, 6, 1.5.

41. Charles Gildon, *Love's Victim; Or, the Queen of Wales* (London: M. Benet, 1701), A_4 recto.

42. Nicholas Rowe, *The Royal Convert* (London: Jacob Tonson, 1708), A_4 verso.

43. Ambrose Philips, *The Briton* (London: B. Lintot, 1722), 35–36.

44. *Burlesque Plays of the Eighteenth Century*, ed. Simon Trussler, (London: Oxford Univ. Press, 1969), 151.

45. Robert Dodsley, *The King and the Miller of Mansfield* (London: Printed for the Author, 1737), 36.

46. Ibid., 44.

47. William Mason, *Elfrida* (London: T. and P. Knapton, 1752), 17.

48. Ibid., 55–56.

49. William Mason, *Caractacus* (London: J. Knapton; R & J Dodsley, 1759), 6.

50. Ibid., 93.

51. Blair, *Lectures* 2:303.

52. Bolingbroke, *Letters*, 16.

53. Daniel Defoe, *A Journal of the Plague Year* (Harmondsworth: Penguin, 1972), 13.

54. Ian Watt, "Defoe as Novelist," in *From Dryden to Johnson*, vol 4 of the *New Pelican Guide to English Literature*, ed. Boris Ford, (Harmondsworth: Penguin, 1982), 151–164, 153.

55. Quoted in A. D. McKillop, *The Early Masters of English Fiction* (Lawrence: Kansas Univ. Press, 1956), 42.

56. Ibid., 9.

57. N. M. Penzer, *The Library of Impostors*, 2 vols. (London: Robert Holden and Co Ltd, 1926), 1:v–vi.

58. Defoe, quoted in Watt, in "Defoe as Novelist," *From Dryden to Johnson*, 152.

59. Daniel Defoe, *Moll Flanders* (London: Mayflower-Dell, 1965), 7–8.

60. Daniel Defoe, *Roxana* (London: Oxford Univ. Press, 1976), 1.

61. Ibid.

62. Ibid., 1–2.

63. Daniel Defoe, *Memoirs of a Cavalier* (Oxford: Basil Blackwell, 1927) ix.

64. Ibid., x.

65. Lucaks may be right in seeing historical fiction as commenting on its own times, but that view does not exclude the work also having a serious historical purpose.

66. Defoe, *Memoirs of a Cavalier*, 274.

67. Daniel Defoe, *A Journal of the Plague year* (Harmondsworth: Penguin, 1972), 21.

68. Ibid., 57–66.

69. Ibid., 110.

70. Ibid. 23.

71. Ibid. 27, 215.

72. Ibid.

73. Ibid., 71.

74. Ibid., 102.

75. Ibid., 167.

76. Ibid., 168.

77. Ibid.

78. Ibid., 111.

79. Ibid., 169.

80. Ibid., 56.

81. Ibid. 51.

82. Ibid., 144, 153n.

83. Ibid., 94.

84. See Frank Edgar Farley, *Scandanavian Influences in the English Romantic Movement* (Boston: Ginn and Company, 1903), 76–78n, for a list of imitations and editions of the poem.

85. Thomas Warton (Elder), *Poems on Several Occasions* (London: R. Manby; H. S. Cox, 1748), 157.

86. James Thomson, *The Complete Poetical Works of James Thomson*, ed. J. Logie Robertson (1908; reprint, London: Oxford Univ. Press, 1951), 48. The lines were excised by Thomson from the edition of 1744, the last he supervised.

87. Ibid., 118.

88. Ibid., 207.

89. Ibid., 290, 294.

90. Ibid.

91. Gray reckoned Macpherson had "lighted on a treasure hid for ages." See the *Correspondence of Thomas Gray*, ed. Paget Toynbee and Leonard Whibley, 3 vols. (London: Oxford Univ. Press, 1935), 2:680.

92. Thomas Gray and William Collins, *Gray and Collins Poetical Works*, ed. Austin Lane Poole (1937; reprint, London: Oxford Univ. Press, 1974), 212.

93. The extent of the mid-eighteenth-century fascination with the extinction of bardism can be seen in a short piece written by Goldsmith for the *British Magazine*, July 1760, called "The History of Carolan, the Last Irish Bard." (See *Collected Works of Oliver Goldsmith*, ed. Arthur Friedman (London: Oxford Univ. Press, 1966), 3:118–20.) The bard, who died in 1738, was blind (like Homer and Ossian). There is no mention of his having been a historian, nor are reasons given for his decline other than old age. But the appearance of this work in the year Ossian appeared is surely no coincidence.

94. Gray and Collins, *Gray and Collins*, 304.

95. Pat Rogers, *The Augustan Vision* (London: Methuen and Co Ltd, 1974), 142.

Chapter 3. Ossian: The Voice of the Past

1. All references, unless otherwise specified, are to first editions: *Fragments of Ancient Poetry, Collected in the Highlands of Scotland, and Translated from the Galic or Erse Language* (Edinburgh: G. Hamilton; J. Balfour, 1760); *Fingal, an Ancient Epic Poem, in Six Books.*

Together with several other Poems, composed by Ossian the son of Fingal. Translated from the Galic Language, by James Macpherson (London: T. Becket; P. A. De Hondt, 1762); *Temora, An Ancient Epic Poem, in Eight Books. Together with several other Poems, composed by Ossian the son of Fingal. Translated from the Galic Language, by James Macpherson.* (London: T. Becket; P. A. De Hondt, 1763). Page references are given in parentheses after quotation. I refer to the last two anthologies as *Fingal* and *Temora*, and the context of usage should make clear when I refer to the anthologies or to the epic poems contained in them of the same name. The second edition of the *Fragments* (1760) is not used, and Macpherson's revisions, including the inclusion of a new fragment, did nothing to change the way the anthology operated.

2. Patrick Graham, *An Essay on the Authenticity of the Poems of Ossian* (London: J. Murray, 1807), 49.

3. Henry Home, Lord Kames, *Sketches of the History of Man*, 2 vols. (London: W. Strahan; T. Cadell, 1774), 1:283–84.

4. Graham, *An Essay*, 48–49.

5. For Johnson's opinion that Macpherson "may have translated some wandering ballads," see *A Journey to the Western Islands of Scotland* (1930; reprint, Oxford Univ. Press, 1979), 107. See also Derick S. Thomson, *The Gaelic Sources of Macpherson's Ossian* (London: Oliver and Boyd, 1951).

6. Alfred Nutt, *Ossian and the Ossianic Literature*, Popular Studies in Mythology, Romance and Folklore 3 (London: David Nutt, 1899), 24.

7. The poem was shown to John Home at Moffat in 1759. See Bailey Saunders, *The Life and Letters of James Macpherson* (London: Swann Sonnenschein & Co., 1894), 65–68.

8. See Sir John Sinclair: *The Poems of Ossian, in the Original Gaelic; with a Literal Translation into Latin, By the Late Robert Macfarlan, A.M.* 3 vols. (London: G. and W. Nicol, 1807).

9. Malcolm Laing, *The Poems of Ossian*, 2 vols. (London: Longman, 1805), 1:231.

10. See *The Poems of Ossian*, 2 vols. (London: A. Strahan, T. Cadell, 1796). Macpherson's preface is dated August 15, 1773 (a copy of the 1773 edition has not been available). The new order of the poems was "Cath-Loda," "Comala," "Carric-Thura," "Carthon," "Oina-Morul," "Colna-Dona," "Oithona," "Croma," "Calthon and Colnal," "The War of Caros," "Cathlin of Clutha," "Sul-Malla of Lumon," "The War of Inis-Thona," "The Songs of Selma," *Fingal*, "Lathmon," "Dar-Thula," "The Death of Cuthullin," "The Battle of Lora" (Volume 1); *Temora*, "Conlath and Cuthora," "Berrathon" (Volume 2). Macpherson's motives for a rearrangement were, significantly, for the better making of history: "One of the chief improvements, on this edition, is the care taken in arranging the Poems, in the order of time; so as to form a kind of regular history of the age to which they relate" (pp. ix–x).

11. Johann Wolfgang von Goethe, *The Sorrows of Young Werther* (London: New English Library Limited, 1962), 118.

12. Percy, *Reliques* 3:xii.

Chapter 4. Literary Archaeology: Macpherson, Percy, and the Anthologists

1. See the appendix to *The Correspondence of Thomas Percy and William Shenstone*, ed. Cleanth Brooks (New Haven and London: Yale Univ. Press, 1977), 175–193.

2. Ambrose Philips, *A Collection of Old Ballads*, 3 vols. (London: J. Roberts; D. Leach, 1723–1725), 1 (1723):vi–vii.

3. Ibid., 1:vii.

4. Ibid., 1:138.

5. Ibid., 1:181.

6. Ibid., 2:79–89. The introduction occupies pages 79–85.

7. Ibid., 1:28.

8. Ibid., 1:91.

9. Ibid., 1:120.

10. Ibid., 1:19.

11. Ibid., 3 (1725): iii–iv, 17.

12. John W. Hales and Frederick J. Furnivall, *Bishop Percy's Folio Manuscript,* 4 vols. (London: Trubner & Co., 1867–1868), 1 (1867): 12.

13. Joseph Ritson, *Ancient Songs* (London: J. Johnson, 1792), xii.

14. Hales and Furnivall, *Bishop Percy's Folio Manuscript,* 1:xii.

15. Percy, *Reliques* 1:ix.

16. Derrick S. Thomson, *The Gaelic Sources of Macpherson's Ossian* (London: Oliver & Boyd, 1951).

17. See letters 44, 46, 52 in *The Correspondence of Thomas Percy and William Shenstone,* 118, 124, 142.

18. Percy, *Reliques* (1765), 1:ix.

19. Ibid., 3:ix.

20. Ibid., 1:vi.

21. Macpherson, *Fingal* (1762), A_2 recto.

22. Quoted by Aneirin Lewis in *The Correspondence of Thomas Percy and Evan Evans,* ed. Aneirin Lewis (Baton Rouge, La.: Louisiana State Univ. Press, 1957), vi.

23. Ibid., 9.

24. Ibid. 1.

25. Ibid., 17–18.

26. Evan Evans, *Some Specimens of the Poetry of the Ancient Welsh Bards* (London: R. & J. Dodsley, 1764), 158.

27. *The Correspondence of Thomas Percy and George Paton,* ed. A. F. Falconer (New Haven: Yale Univ. Press, 1961), 13.

28. *Correspondence of Percy and Evan Evans,* 18–19.

29. Extracts from *The Gododin* appeared in Evans' Latin dissertation on bardism in *Specimens,* 59–93, passim.

30. *Correspondence of Percy and Evans,* 18n.

31. *Correspondence of Percy and Shenstone,* 177.

32. *Hau Kiou Choaan, or the Pleasing History,* 4 vols. (London: R. & J. Dodsley, 1761), 1:xvii.

33. *The Correspondence of Thomas Percy and David Dalrymple, Lord Hailes,* ed. A. F. Falconer (Baton Rouge, La.: Louisiana State Univ. Press, 1954), 99.

34. Thomas Warton, *The History of English Poetry,* 4 vols. (London: J. Dodsley etc., 1774–81), 1 (1774): ii–iii.

35. Percy, *Reliques* (1765), 1:3.

36. Ibid., 1:71.

37. Ibid., 1:99.

38. Ibid., 3:225.

39. Ibid., 2:179.

40. See the attack by Walter Jackson Bate in "Percy's Use of his Folio MS," *Journal of English and Germanic Philology* 43 (1944): 337–48. Percy is defended by Albert Friedman, *The Ballad Revival* (Chicago and London: University of Chicago Press, 1961), Chapter 7.

41. *Reliques,* ed. H. B. Wheatley, 3 vols. (1886; reprint, New York: Dover Publication, 1966), 1:66. Wheatley printed the folio and Percy versions of the ballads concurrently.

42. *Reliques,* ed. Wheatley, 3:91.

43. Ibid., 3:91.

44. Percy, *Reliques* (1765), 1:xxii.

45. Ibid., 1:258.

46. *Correspondence of Percy and Paton*, 21.

47. *Correspondence of Percy and Paton*, 21.

48. Evans, *Specimens*, A₁ recto.

49.

> Vos quoque, qui fortes animas, belloque peremptas
> Laudibus in longum, Vates, dimittibus acurum,
> Plurima securi sudistis carmina Bardi.

50. Evans, *Specimens*, 153.

51. David Herd, *The Ancient and Modern Scots Songs*, 2 vols. (Edinburgh: Martin and Witherspoon, 1769), 1:ii.

52. David Dalrymple, Lord Hailes, *Ancient Scottish Poems* (Edinburgh: John Balfour, 1770), vii.

53. Quoted by A. D. McKillop, "A Critic of 1741 on Early Poetry," *Studies in Philology* 30 (1933): 504–521, 507.

54. John Smith, *Galic Antiquities* (London: T. Cadell, 1780).

55. Edward Jones, *Musical and Poetical Relicks of the Welsh Bards* (London: Printed for the Author, 1784), 14.

56. Joseph Cooper Walker, *Historical Memoirs of the Irish Bards* (London: T. Payne and Son, 1786), 8.

57. Charlotte Brooke, *Reliques of Irish Poetry* (Dublin: George Bonham, 1789), 119.

58. William Owen, *The Heroic Elegies and Other Pieces of Llyswarch Hen* (London: J. Owen, 1792), v–vi. n.

59. Walker, *Historical Memoirs*, 8.

60. Smith, *Galic Antiquities*, 124.

61. John Pinkerton, *Ancient Scottish Poems*, 2 vols (London: C. Dilly, 1786), 1:lii.

62. John Pinkerton, *Scottish Tragic Ballads* (London: J. Nichols, 1781), xvii; *Select Scottish Ballads*, 2 vols. (London: J. Nichols, 1783), 1:xxiii.

63. Pinkerton, *Ancient Scottish Poems*, 1:xv.

64. Pinkerton, *Scottish Poems*, 3 vols. (London: John Nichols, 1792), 1:viii.

65. John Pinkerton, *The Bruce*, 3 vols. (London: G. Nicol, 1790), 1:ix–x.

66. Pinkerton, *Scottish Tragic Ballads*, xxxv.

67. Joseph Ritson, *Gentleman's Magazine*, 54, pt. 2 (Nov. 1784): 812–814.

68. Joseph Ritson, *Scottish Songs*, 2 vols. (London: J. Johnson, 1794), 1:lxii, lxxvi.

69. Ibid., 1:lxx.

70. Samuel Johnson, *A Journey to the Western Islands* (1930; reprint, London: Oxford Univ. Press, 1979), 108.

71. Ritson, *Scottish Songs*, 1:lxii.

72. Joseph Ritson, *Ancient Songs* (London: J. Johnson, 1792), xix.

73. Bertrand Bronson, *Joseph Ritson. Scholar-at-Arms*, 2 vols. (Berkeley and Los Angeles: University of California Press, 1938), 2:546.

74. Joseph Ritson, *Ancient English Metrical Romances*, 3 vols. (G. and W. Nicol, 1802), 1:cix.

75. Percy, *Reliques* 3:350.

76. Ritson, *Ancient English Metrical Romances*, 1:cxli.

Chapter 5. Chatterton: Literary Transmission

1. *The Complete Works of Thomas Chatterton*, ed. Donald S. Taylor, 2 vols. (Oxford: Oxford Univ. Press, 1971). All page references are to this edition and are given in parentheses after citation.

2. Thomas Warton, *Specimen of a History of Oxfordshire* (London: J. Nichols, 1783), iii.

3. Chatterton's source as revealed in his final footnote (*Works*, 1:20) was the Elizabethan chronicler, Stowe. Bawdin, a Lancastrian supporter, had vowed to assassinate the Yorkist Earl of Warwick or, as was the case, forfeit his own life. Donald Taylor has discovered likely literary sources for most of the works of the forgery.

4. In the best biography of Chatterton, E. H. W. Meyerstein (*A Life of Chatterton* [London: Inpen and Grant, 1930]), says of "Brystowe Tragedie":

> This virile, direct, and fiery piece of 392 lines can be regarded as a case of Chatterton having "exerted all his might" to produce a ballad that could vie with some of those in Percy's *Reliques*. (p. 211)

Yet Percy, I believe, gave to Chatterton the ability to use poetical genres such as the ballad as viable history, rather than being merely a rival.

5. Meyestein was the first to notice this borrowing. See "The Influence of Macpherson," *English* 7 (1948–49):95–98, 96.

6. Meyerstein, *Life of Chatterton*, chapters 1–10.

7. See Boswell, *Life of Johnson*, 751–52. One of the most entertaining works of the controversy surrounding Chatterton's forgery was W. J. Mickle's *The Prophecy of Queen Emma* (London: J. Bew, 1782), which was supposedly, as the subtitle says:

> An Ancient Ballad lately discovered written by Johannes Tourgotus, Prior of *Durham*, in the Reign of William Rufus. To which is added, by the Editor, An Account of the Discovery, and Hints towards a Vindication of the Poems of Ossian and Rowley.

Mickle parodied the serendipitous "poetical Resurrection" of "long lost poetical MSS" (p. 16). His own piece, we are told, was discovered in an old chest in Durham cathedral by an antiquarian friend. Enraged at finding no MS inside the chest, the friend

> seized the carpenter's ax, and so violently struck the lid, using indeed some rash words, that he fairly split it in two. And now the treasure appeared!—a fair MS in good preservation. (p. 21)

8. In "The Chyrche Oratorie of the Calendaryes" (*Works*, 1:155), Chatterton exploited the catastrophic element inherent in library collections of MSS: conflagration. Donald Taylor informs us that "the Guild of Calendaryes was a lay-clerical society founded for religious purposes and for preserving civil records" and that a fire destroyed the Bristol library in 1466 (*Works*, 2:912). In Chatterton's version of the fire "was brente 8 hondreth bookes, in the bochorde meint Saxonne Hystorie and Lege" (ll. 3–4; "bochorde" means library; "Lege" means law books).

9. For the biographical details behind the two versions of "Battle of Hastynges," see Meyerstein, *A Life of Chatterton*, chapter 10.

10. Chatterton could have learned this technique from Gibson's edition of Camden's *Brittania*, a source Chatterton used frequently.

11. In "Elle's Coffin" (*Works*, 1:235–36), Aella's bones were exhumed: he was literally brought back from the dead. This work showed the antiquarian zeal that existed in Rowley's Bristol, and the awe for Aella. Various bones were allotted as relics. Rowley crowned his staff with an armbone. Canynge got the skull, complete with its wound.

12. hid, concealed (C)

13. law (C)

14. holy (C)

15. naught (C)

16. they (C)

17. esteem (C)

18. heraldry (C)
19. greybeards (C)
20. curiously (C)
21. lessened (C)
22. small (C)
23. that (C)
24. allow (C)
25. carthorse (C)
26. broken (C)
27. The significant deviation from the facts of Aella's life in *Aella* was his death by suicide, rather than by combat in battle.
28. counsel (T)
29. uncovered (T)
30. hidden (T)

Chapter 6. "A Higher Species of Antiquarian Research": Imitators and Later Historical Poets

1. See *The Poems of Gray, Collins and Goldsmith*, ed.Roger Lonsdale (London: Longmans, 1976), 229–31, 234.
2. James Beattie, *The Poetical Works of James Beattie*, 2 vols. (London: Bell and Daldy, 1871), 1:3.
3. Ibid., 1:xxii.
4. Ibid., 1:51.
5. John Home, *Alfred* (Dublin: Byrn and Son, 1777), iii–iv.
6. Ibid., iv.
7. Ibid.
8. John Ogilvie, *The Fane of the Druids* (London: J. Murray, 1789), Advertisement.
9. George Richards, *Songs of the Aboriginal Bards of Britain* (London: G. G. J. and J. Robinson, 1792), iii.
10. Ibid., iv.
11. Richard Polwhele, *The Old English Gentleman* (London: Cadell and Davies, 1797), 1–11.
12. Walter Scott, *Letters of Sir Walter Scott* (London: J. B. Nichols and Son, 1832), 32.

Chapter 7. "A Second M'pherson"?—Walter Scott and the Forgeries

1. Walter Scott, *Ivanhoe* (London: Everyman's Library, 1980), 13–14.
2. Ibid., 18–19.
3. Ibid., 5–6.
4. J. G. Lockhart, *Memoirs of the Life of Sir Walter Scott, Bart* (Edinburgh: Robert Cadell, 1837–38), 2 (1838): 58.
5. Ibid., 1:36, II:54.
6. Ibid., 2:55.
7. Ibid., II:54.
8. Scott had the following Ossianic material: *Fragments of Ancient Poetry* (1760); *Fingal* (1762); Malcolm Laing, *The Poems of Ossian* (1805); Hugh Blair, *A Dissertation on Ossian* (1763); John Smith, *Galic Antiquities* (1780); Sir John Sinclair, *Dissertation on the authenticity of Ossian's Poems* (1806); Patrick Graham, *Essay on the authenticity of Ossian's Poems* (1807);

Henry Mackenzie, *Report of the Committee of the Highland Society on Ossian's Poems* (1805). In contrast, the library contained only Southey and Cottle's *Works of Chatterton* (1803) and John Britton, *Essay on the Life of Chatterton* (1813). See *Catalogue of the Library at Abbotsford* (Edinburgh: T. Constable, 1838), 10, 14, 19, 186, 64, 19, 20, 19, 198, 32.

    9. Lockhart, *Memoirs*, 1:38.

    10. Walter Scott, *Waverley Novels*, 5 vols. (Edinburgh: Robert Cadell, 1845–48), 2:654–55.

    11. Walter Scott, *The Heart of Mid-Lothian* (London: Everyman's Library, 1970), 10.

    12. G. K. Chesterton, *Essays and Poems* (Harmondsworth: Penguin, 1958), 72.

    13. Walter Scott, *Waverley* (Harmondsworth: Penguin, 1980), 518.

    14. Scott, *Waverley Novels*, 3:694.

    15. Ibid.

    16. Ibid., 2:682.

    17. *The Poetical Works of Walter Scott, Esq.* (London: John Murray, 1820), 1:5.

    18. Ibid., 1:10.

    19. See Scott, *Waverley*, 492.

    20. Walter Scott, *Minstrelsy of the Scottish Border*, 3 vols. (Kelso: James Ballantyne, 1802–03), 1 (1802):cix–cx.

    21. Scott, *Waverley*, 494.

    22. Walter Scott, *The Antiquary* (London: Everyman's Library, 1969), 1.

    23. Scott, *Waverley Novels*, 2:655.

    24. Scott, *Waverley*, 523.

    25. A manuscript has to turn up somewhere, of course. The Boswell papers are perhaps the most striking modern instance of "fortuitous circumstances" leading to a discovery in a stately home.

    26. Scott, *Waverley*, 523.

    27. Ibid., 525.

    28. Scott, *The Antiquary*, 102.

    29. Lockhart, *Memoirs*, 1:176.

    30. "the joys of the shell, as Ossian has it," Scott, *Waverley*, 188.

    31. Ibid., 173.

    32. Ibid. 172.

    33. Ibid., 165.

    34. Ibid., 169.

    35. Ibid., 173.

    36. Ibid.

    37. Ibid., 405.

    38. Ibid., 112.

    39. Ibid., 115. The quoted lines are from *The Fairy Queen*, 2:ix, 51.

    40. Scott, *The Antiquary*, 3.

    41. Ibid., 50.

    42. Ibid., 39.

    43. Ibid., 45.

    44. See *Edinburgh Review*, 6 (1805): 436; Lockhart, *Memoirs*, 2:55.

    45. Scott, *The Antiquary*, 281–82.

    46. Ibid., 282.

    47. Ibid.

    48. Ibid., 283–84.

    49. Lockhart, *Memoirs*, 2:56.

    50. Walter Scott, *The Journal of Sir Walter Scott*, ed. W. E. K. Anderson (Oxford: Oxford Univ. Press, 1972), 214–15.

51. *Edinburgh Review,* 6 (1805):445.

52. Scott, *Ivanhoe,* 15, 16.

53. Ibid.

54. Ibid., 14.

55. Ibid., 17.

56. Walter Scott, *Old Mortality* (Hardmondsworth: Penguin, 1980), 588: "The return of John Balfour of Kinloch, called Burley, to Scotland, as well as his violent death in the manner described, is entirely fictitious."

57. Scott, *Ivanhoe,* p. 17.

58. Ibid., 20.

59. Ibid.

60. *Edinburgh Review,* 6 (1805), 429.

61. Ibid., 433.

62. *The Miscellaneous Prose Works of Sir Walter Scott, Bart* (Edinburgh: Robert Cadell, 1834–71), 17:241.

Appendix 1. The Continuation of Keating's Account of the Assembly at Tarah

1. Geoffry Keating, *The General history of Ireland,* 2:68–69.

Appendix 2. Chatterton's Plans for the Publication of the Forgery

1. An earlier version of this appendix appeared in *Review of English Studies,* 141 (February, 1985): 58–68.

2. Macpherson, *Fragments of Ancient Poetry* (1760); *Fingal* (1762); *Temora* (1763).

3. *Poems, Supposed to have been Written at Bristol, in the Fifteenth Century; the Greatest Part now First Published from the Most Authentic Copies, with an Engraved Specimen of One of the MSS.*

4. Ibid., xii.

5. *Miscellanies in Prose and Verse; by Thomas Chatterton, the Supposed Author of the Poems Published under the Names of Rowley, Canning, etc.*

6. *Poems, Supposed to have been Written at Bristol, in the Fifteenth Century, by Thomas Rowley, priest, etc.*

7. Chatterton, *Works,* 1:xl.

8. Meyerstein, *Life of Chatterton,* 134.

9. Macpherson, *The Poems of Ossian.*

10. The manuscripts are located at Bristol Public Library B21040 and B20927, and British Museum Add. 24890.

11. See also the description in *The Works of Thomas Chatterton,* ed. Southey and Cottle, 3 vols. (London: T. N. Longman and O. Rees, 1803), 3:501.

12. *Correspondence of Percy and Evans,* 14.

13. *Works,* 2:813–14. All further references are to this edition.

14. Ibid., 1:6.

15. Percy, *Reliques of Ancient English Poetry,* 1:ix.

16. *Works,* 1:44.

17. Ibid., 1:124–42. For a detailed study of each work referred to in this Appendix, see chapter 5.

18. Ibid., 2:820.

19. Meyerstein, *A Life of Chatterton*, 132–33.

20. *Works*, 1:36, ll. 301–20.

21. Ibid., 1:313.

Appendix 3. *The Shakespeare Forgeries and Sharon Turner's* Vindication

1. Horace Walpole, *The Castle of Otranto,* in *Three Gothic Novels,* ed. Peter Fairclough (Harmondsworth: Penguin, 1968), 39.

2. Henry Mackenzie, *The Man of Feeling* (London: Oxford Univ. Press, 1970), 5.

3. The most concise account of Ireland's career is "Shakespeare Fabricated," chapter 7 of Frank E. Halliday's *The Cult of Shakespeare,* (London: Gerald Duckworth & Co Ltd., 1957). Some interesting contemporary reactions are given in John Mair, *The Fourth Forger* (London: Cobden-Sanderson, 1938), Chapter 5.

4. Ireland, *Vortigern* 64. The incident was recalled by Ireland in the preface to *Vortigern, An Historical Play* (London: Joseph Thomas, 1832), vi.

5. Lewis Theobald, *Double Falsehood; or, The Distrest Lovers* (London: J. Watts, 1728), A_3 recto–A_4 verso.

6. *The Confessions of William Henry Ireland* (Thomas Godard, 1805), 96.

7. W. H. Ireland, *Miscellaneous Papers and Legal Instruments* (London: Cooper and Graham, 1796), q^2 verso.

8. Edmond Malone, *An Inquiry into the Authenticity of Certain Miscellaneous Papers and Legal Instruments* (London: H. Baldwin, 1796), 213.

9. Ireland, *Miscellaneous Papers*, y^2 recto.

10. Ireland, *Confessions*, 177.

11. Ibid., 11.

12. Ibid., 11–15.

13. Ibid., 117–18.

14. Quoted in Mair, *The Fourth Forger*, 62.

15. Sharon Turner, *The History of the Anglo-Saxons*, 4 vols. (London: T. Cadell, 1799–1805), 1 (1799):191.

16. Sharon Turner, *A Vindication of the Genuineness of the Ancient British Poems of Aneurin, Taliesin, Llywarch Hen and Modlin* (London: E. Williams, 1803), 5–6. All further references are given in parentheses after quotation.

17. Boswell, *Life of Johnson*, 615.

Appendix 4. *A "Prolific Age" of Forgery*

1. See Mair, *The Fourth Forger*, v.

2. Herbert Croft, *Love and Madness* (London: G. Kearsley, 1780), 211–12.

3. Ritson, *Scottish Songs* 1:lxiii.

4. See *Dictionary of National Biography,* ed. Leslie Stephen (London: Smith, Elder, & Co., 1886) 6:48–51.

5. Malone, *Inquiry*, 347–52.

6. William Rufus Chetwood, *The British Theatre* (Dublin: Peter Wilson, 1750), 16.

Bibliography

The best general bibliographies on Macpherson and Chatterton are the relevant entries in the *New Cambridge Bibliography* and MLA annual bibliography. For Chatterton alone, see also Murray Warren, *A Descriptive and Annotated Bibliography of Thomas Chatterton* (London: Garland Publishing Inc., 1977).

Primary Sources

Bancroft, John. *Henry the Second*. London: Jacob Tonson, 1693.

————. *King Edward the Third*. London: J. Hindmarsh, 1691.

Beattie, James. *The Poetical Works of James Beattie*. 2 vols. London: Bell and Daldy, 1871.

Blackmore, Sir Richard. *Alfred*. London: James Knapton, 1723.

————. *King Arthur*. London: A. and J. Churchill, 1697.

————. *Prince Arthur*. London: A. and J. Churchill, 1695.

Blackwell, Thomas. *An Enquiry into the Life and Writings of Homer*. 1735. Reprint. Menstone: Scolar Press, 1972.

Blair, Hugh. *A Dissertation on Ossian*. London: T. Becket: P. A. De Hondt, 1763.

————. *Lectures on Rhetoric and Belles Lettres*. 2 vols. London: W. Strahan; T. Cadell, 1783.

Boswell, James. *Boswell's London Journal 1762–1763*. Edited by Frederick A. Pottle. London: Book Club Associates, 1974.

————. *The Journal of a Tour to the Hebrides*. Edited by R. W. Chapman, 1924. Reprint. London: Oxford University Press, 1979.

————. *Life of Johnson*. Edited by R. W. Chapman. London: Oxford University Press, 1970.

Brooke, Charlotte. *Reliques of Irish Poetry.* Dublin: George Bonham, 1789.

Bruce, Sir John. *Hardyknute. A Fragment.* Edinburgh: James S. Watson, 1719.

————. *Hardyknute. A Fragment. Being the First Canto of an Epick Poem.* London: R. Dodsley, 1740.

Carte, Thomas. *A General History of England.* 4 vols. London: Printed for the Author, 1747–55.

Chatterton, Thomas. *The Complete Works of Thomas Chatterton.* Edited by Donald S. Taylor. 2 vols. Oxford: Oxford University Press, 1971.

————. *Miscellanies in Prose and Verse; by Thomas Chatterton the Supposed Author of the Poems Published under the Names of Rowley, Canning, etc.* Edited by John Broughton. London: Fielding and Walker, 1778.

————. *Poems, Supposed to have been Written at Bristol, in the Fifteenth Century; the Greatest Part now First Published from the Most Authentic Copies, with an Engraved Specimen of One of the MSS.* Edited by Thomas Tyrwhitt. London: T. Payne and Son, 1777.

————. *Poems, Supposed to have been Written at Bristol, in the Fifteenth Century, by Thomas Rowley, Priest, etc.* London: T. Payne and Son, 1782.

————. *The Works of Thomas Chatterton.* 3 vols. Edited by Robert Southey and Joseph Cottle. London: T. N. Longman and O. Rees, 1803.

Chetwood, William Rufus. *The British Theatre.* Dublin: Peter Wilson, 1750.

Collins, William. *Gray and Collins. Poetical Works.* Edited by Austin Lane Poole, 1937. Reprint. London: Oxford University Press, 1974.

Cottle, A. S. *Icelandic Poetry.* Bristol: Joseph Cottle, 1797.

Croft, Herbert. *Love and Madness.* London: G. Kearsley, 1780.

Dalrymple, David, Lord Hailes. *Ancient Scottish Poems.* Edinburgh: John Balfour, 1770.

Defoe, Daniel. *A Journal of the Plague Year.* Harmondsworth: Penguin Books, 1972.

————. *Memoirs of a Cavalier.* Oxford: Basil Blackwell, 1927.

————. *Moll Flanders.* London: Mayflower-Dell, 1965.

————. *Robinson Crusoe.* Harmondsworth: Penguin Books, 1965.

————. *Roxana.* London: Oxford University Press, 1976.

Dodsley, Robert. *The Blind Beggar of Bethnal Green.* London: R. Dodsley, 1741.

————. *The King and the Miller of Manfield.* London: Printed for the Author, 1737.

————. *Sir John Cockle at Court.* London: R. Dodsley, 1738.

Douglas, John. *Milton Vindicated from the Charge of Plagiarism.* London: A. Millar, 1751.

Downman, Hugh. *Editha*. In *Tragedies*. Exeter: G. G. J. and J. Robinson, 1792.

Dryden, John. *King Arthur: or The British Worthy*. London: Jacob Tonson, 1691.

———. *Selected Criticism*. Edited by James Kinsley and George Parfit. London: Oxford University Press, 1970.

Edinburgh Review 6, 1805.

Evans, Evan. *Some Specimens of the Poetry of the Antient Welsh Bards*. London: R. and J. Dodsley, 1764.

Fielding, Henry. *Tom Jones*. Harmondsworth: Penguin Books, 1975.

———. *Tom Thumb*. In *Burlesque Plays of the Eighteenth Century*. Edited by Simon Trussler. London: Oxford University Press, 1969.

Francklin, Thomas. *The Earl of Warwick*. London: T. Davies, 1766.

Gentleman's Magazine 54, 1784.

Gibbon, Edward. *Autobiography of Edward Gibbon*. London: Oxford University Press, 1959.

———. *An Essay on the Study of Literature*. London: T. Becket; P. A. De Hondt, 1764.

———. *Memoirs of My Life and Writings*. London: Macmillan and Co., 1930.

Gildon, Charles. *Love's Victim; Or, The Queen of Wales*. London: M. Benet, 1701.

Goethe, Johann Wolfgang von. *The Sorrows of Young Werther*. Translated by Catherine Hutter. London: New American Library, 1962.

Goldsmith, Oliver. *Collected Works of Oliver Goldsmith*. Vol. 3. Edited by Arthur Friedman. Oxford: Oxford University Press, 1966.

Graham, Patrick. *An Essay on the Authenticity of the Poems of Ossian*. London: J. Murray, 1807.

Gray, Thomas. *Correspondence of Thomas Gray*. 3 vols. Edited by Paget Toynbee and Leonard Whibley. London: Oxford University Press, 1935.

———. *Gray and Collins. Poetical Works*. Edited by Austin Lane Poole, 1937. Reprint. London: Oxford University Press, 1974.

———. *The Poems of Gray, Collins and Goldsmith*. Edited by Roger Lonsdale. London: Longman, 1976.

Hales, J. W. and Frederick J. Furnivall. *Bishop Percy's Folio Manuscript*. 4 vols. London: Trubner and Co., 1867–68.

Hayley, William. *An Essay on History*. London: J. Dodsley, 1780.

Herd, David. *The Ancient and Modern Scots Songs*. 2 vols. Edinburgh: Martin and Witherspoon, 1769.

Hill, Aaron. *Elfrid: or, the Fair Inconstant*. London: Bernard Lintott, 1710.

Hole, Richard. *Arthur, or the Northern Enchantment.* London: G. G. J. and J. Robinson, 1789.

Home, John. *Alfred.* Dublin: Byrn and Son, 1777.

———. *Douglas.* London: A. Millar, 1757.

———. *The Fatal Discovery.* London: T. Becket, P. A. De Hondt, 1769.

Home, Henry, Lord Kames. *Sketches of the History of Man.* 2 vols. London: W. Strahan; T. Cadell, 1774.

Homer. *The Odyssey.* Translated by E. V. Rieu. Harmondsworth: Penguin Books, 1976.

Hopkins, Charles. *Boadicea Queen of Britain.* London: Jacob Tonson, 1697.

Howard, George Edmond. *The Seige of Tamor.* Dublin: Elizabeth Lynch, 1773.

Hume, David. *The History of England.* Vol 1. London: A. Millar, 1763.

———. *Letters to William Strahan.* Oxford: Clarendon Press, 1888.

———. *A Treatise of Human Nature.* Book One. Edited by D. C. Macnabb. London: Fontana, 1962.

Innes, Thomas. *A Critical Essay on the Ancient Inhabitants of the Northern Parts of Britain, or Scotland.* 2 vols. London: William Innys, 1729.

Ireland, William Henry. *The Confessions of William Henry Ireland.* London: Thomas Godard, 1805.

———. *Henry II.* In *Vortigern.* London: Frank Cass and Co. Ltd., 1971.

———. *Miscellaneous Papers and Legal Instruments under the Hand and Seal of William Shakespeare: Including the Tragedy of King Lear and a small fragment of Hamlet, from the original MSS in the possession of Samuel Ireland of Norfolk Street.* London: Cooper and Graham, 1796.

———. *Vortigern.* 1799. Reprint. London: Frank Cass and Co. Ltd., 1971.

———. *Vortigern. An Historical Play.* London: Joseph Thomas, 1832.

Johnson, Samuel. *The Adventurer.* Vol. 3 of *The Yale Edition of the Works of Johnson.* Edited by W. J. Bate, M. Bullitt, L. F. Powell. New Haven and London: Yale University Press, 1963.

———. *A Journey to the Western Islands.* Edited by R. W. Chapman, 1930. Reprint. London: Oxford University Press, 1979.

———. *Lives of the English Poets.* London: Everyman's Library, 1975.

Jones, Edward. *Musical and Poetical Relicks of the Welsh Bards.* London: Printed for the Author, 1784.

Keating, Geoffry. *The General History of Ireland.* 2 vols. Dublin: James Carson, 1723.

Lauder, William. *An Essay on Milton's Use and Imitation of the Moderns, in his Paradise Lost.* London: J. Payne and J. Bouquet, 1750.

Lenglet Du Fresnoy, Pierre Nicholas. *A New Method of Studying History.* 2 vols. Translated by Richard Rawlinson. London: W. Barton, 1728.

Lewis, John. *The History of Great Britain*. London: F. Gyles, 1729.

Locke, John. *An Essay Concerning Human Understanding*. Edited by A. D. Woolsey. London: Fontana, 1968.

Lockhart, J. G. *Memoirs of the Life of Sir Walter Scott, Bart*. 7 vols. Edinburgh: Robert Cadell, 1837–38.

Mackenzie, Henry. *The Man of Feeling*. London: Oxford University Press, 1970.

Macpherson, James. *Fingal, an Ancient Epic Poem, in Six Books. Together with several other Poems, composed by Ossian the son of Fingal. Translated from the Galic Language, by James Macpherson*. London: T. Becket; P. A. De Hondt, 1762.

———. *Fragments of Ancient Poetry, Collected in the Highlands of Scotland, and Translated from the Galic or Erse Language*. Edinburgh: G. Hamilton; J. Balfour, 1760.

———. *The History of Great Britain*. 2 vols. London: W. Strahan; T. Cadell, 1775.

———. *Original Papers*. 2 vols. London: W. Strahan; T. Cadell, 1775.

———. *The Poems of Ossian*. 2 vols. London: A. Strahan; T. Cadell, 1796.

———. *The Poems of Ossian*. 2 vols. Edited by Malcolm Laing. London: Longman, 1805.

———. *The Poems of Ossian, in the original Gaelic, with a Literal Translation into Latin, by the Late Robert Macfarlan*. London: W. Bulmer and Co., 1807.

———. *Temora, an Ancient Epic Poem, in Eight Books. Together with several other Poems, composed by Ossian the son of Fingal. Translated from the Galic Language, by James Macpherson*. London: T. Becket; P. A. De Hondt, 1763.

Malone, Edmond. *An Inquiry into the Authenticity of Certain Miscellaneous Papers and Legal Instruments*. London: H. Baldwin, 1796.

Manley, Mrs. *Lucius, the First Christian King of Britain*. London: John Barber, 1717.

Mason, William. *Caractacus*. London: J. Knapton; R. Dodsley, 1759.

———. *Elfrida*. London: T. and P. Knapton, 1752.

Mickle, William Julius. *The Prophecy of Queen Emma*. London: J. Bew, 1782.

Milton, John. *The Works of John Milton*. Vol. 18. New York: Columbia University Press, 1938.

Moor, James. *Essays read to a Literary Society at their weekly meetings within the College at Glasgow*. Glasgow: Robert and Andrew Foulis, 1759.

Myln, James. *The British Kings; Darthula*. In *Poems*. Edinburgh: William Creech, 1790.

O'Conor, Charles. *Dissertations on the Ancient History of Ireland*. Dublin: James Hoey, 1753.

O'Flaherty, Roderic. *Ogygia*. 2 vols. Dublin: W. M'Kenzie, 1793.

Ogilvie, John. *The Fane of the Druids*. London: J. Murray, 1787.

————. *The Fane of the Druids. A Poem. Book the Second*. London: J. Murray, 1789.

————. *Rona, A Poem in Seven Books*. London: J. Murray, 1777.

Owen, William. *The Heroic Elegies and Other Pieces of Llywarch Hen*. London: J. Owen, 1792.

Percy, Thomas. *The Correspondence of Thomas Percy and David Dalrymple, Lord Hailes*. Edited by A. F. Falconer. Baton Rouge, La.: Louisiana State University Press, 1954.

————. *The Correspondence of Thomas Percy and Evan Evans*. Edited by Aneirin Lewis. Baton Rouge, La.: Louisiana State University Press, 1957.

————. *The Correspondence of Thomas Percy and George Paton*. Edited by A. F. Falconer. New Haven: Yale University Press, 1961.

————. *The Correspondence of Thomas Percy and William Shenstone*. Edited by Cleanth Brooks. New Haven and London: Yale University Press, 1977.

————. *The Earl of Northumberland's Household Book*. 1770.

————. *Five Pieces of Runic Poetry. Translated from the Islandic Language*. London: R. and J. Dodsley, 1763.

————. *Hau Kiou Choaan, or the Pleasing History*. 4 vols. London: R. and J. Dodsley, 1761.

————. *Reliques of Ancient English Poetry*. 3 vols. London: J. Dodsley, 1765.

————. *Reliques of Ancient English Poetry*. 3 vols. London: F. and C. Rivington, 1794.

————. *Reliques of Ancient Poetry*. 3 vols. Edited by H. B. Wheatley, 1886. Reprint. New York: Dover Publications, 1966.

Philips, Ambrose. *The Briton*. London: B. Lintot, 1722.

————. *A Collection of Old Ballads*. 3 vols. London: J. Roberts; D. Leach, 1723–25.

Pinkerton, John. *Ancient Scottish Poems*. 2 vols. London: J. Nichols, 1783.

————. *The Bruce*. 3 vols. London: G. Nichol, 1790.

————. *Scottish Poems*. 3 vols. London: John Nichols, 1792.

————. *Scottish Tragic Ballads*. London: N. Nichols, 1781.

————. *Select Scottish Ballads*. 2 vols. London: J. Nichols, 1783.

Polwhele, Richard. *The Fate of Llewelyn*. Bath: L. and C. Dilly, 1777.

————. *Letters of Sir Walter Scott*. Edited by Richard Polwhele. London: J. B. Nichols and Son, 1832.

———. *The Old English Gentleman*. London: Cadell and Davies, 1797.

Pope, Alexander. *The Poems of Alexander Pope*. Edited by John Butt. London: Methuen and Co. Ltd., 1975.

Pownall, Thomas. *A Treatise on the Study of Antiquities*. London: J. Dodsley, 1782.

Priestley, Joseph. *Lectures on History and General Policy*. Dublin: P. Byrne, 1788.

Psalmanazar, George. *An Historical and Geographical Description of Formosa*. In Vol. 2 of *The Library of Impostors*. Edited by N. M. Penzer. London: Robert Holden and Co. Ltd., 1926.

Reeve, Clara. *The Progress of Romance*. 2 vols. London: Printed for the Author, 1785.

Richards, George. *Songs of the Aboriginal Bards of Britain*. London: G. G. J. and J. Robinson, 1792.

Richardson, Samuel. *Clarissa, or the History of a Young Lady*. 4 vols. London: J. M. Dent, 1962.

Ritson, Joseph. *Ancient English Metrical Romances*. 3 vols. London: G. and W. Nichol, 1802.

———. *Ancient Songs*. London: J. Johnson, 1792.

———. *Scottish Songs*. 2 vols. London: J. Johnson, 1794.

Robertson, William. *The History of America*. 2 vols. London: W. Strahan; T. Cadell, 1777.

———. *The History of the Reign of the Emperor Charles V.* 3 vols. London: W. Strahan; T. Cadell, 1769.

———. *The History of Scotland*. 2 vols. London: A. Millar, 1759.

Rowe, Nicholas. *The Royal Convert*. London: Jacob Tonson, 1708.

Ruffhead, Owen. *The Life of Alexander Pope, Esq.* London: C. Bathurst, 1769.

Rymer, Thomas. *Edgar; or the English Monarch*. London: Richard Tonson, 1678.

Saint John, Henry, Viscount Bolingbroke. *Letters on the Study and Use of History*. London: A. Millar, 1752.

Scott, Sir Walter. *The Antiquary*. London: Everyman's Library, 1969.

———. *Catalogue of the Library at Abbotsford*. Edinburgh: T. Constable, 1838.

———. *The Heart of Mid-Lothian*. London: Everyman's Library, 1970.

———. *Ivanhoe*. London: Everyman's Library, 1980.

———. *The Journal of Sir Walter Scott*. Edited by W. E. K. Anderson. Oxford: Oxford University Press, 1972.

———. *Minstrelsy of the Scottish Border*. 3 vols. Kelso: James Ballantyne, 1802–1803.

—. *The Miscellaneous Prose Works of Sir Walter Scott.* Vol. 17. Edinburgh: Robert Cadell, 1835.

—. *Old Mortality.* Harmondsworth: Penguin Books, 1980.

—. *The Poetical Works of Walter Scott, Esq.* 12 vols. London: John Murray, 1820.

—. *Redgauntlet.* London: Everyman's Library, 1982.

—. *Rob Roy.* London: Everyman's Library, 1978.

—. *Waverley Novels.* 5 vols. Edinburgh: Robert Cadell, 1845–48.

—. *Waverley; or, 'Tis Sixty Years Since.* Harmondsworth: Penguin Books, 1980.

Shakespeare, William. *Antony and Cleopatra.* Edited by J. H. Walter. London: Heinemann Educational Books, 1969.

Smith, Adam. *Lectures on Rhetoric and Belles Lettres.* London: Thomas Nelson and Sons Ltd., 1963.

Smith, John. *Galic Antiquities.* Edinburgh: C. Elliot, 1780.

Smollett, Tobias. *The Adventures of Peregrine Pickle.* London: Oxford University Press, 1969.

Sotheby, William. *The Cambrian Hero, or Llewelyn the Great.* Egham: Wettons, 1800.

The Spectator. 4 vols. London: Everyman's Library, 1951.

Spenser, Edmund. *The Fairie Queene.* In *Poetical Works.* Edited by J. C. Smith and E. De Selincourt. London: Oxford University Press, 1975.

Stuart, Gilbert. *Critical Observations Concerning the Scottish Historians Hume, Stuart and Robertson.* London: T. Evans, 1782.

—. *A View of Society in Europe.* London: J. Murray, 1788.

Theobald, Lewis. *Double Falsehood; or, The Distrest Lovers.* London: J. Watts, 1728.

Thomson, James. *Alfred, A Masque.* In *Poems by James Thomson.* Glasgow: Robert and Andrew Foulis, 1774.

—. *The Complete Poetical Works of James Thomson.* Edited by J. Logie Robertson, 1908. Reprint. London: Oxford University Press, 1951.

—. *Edward and Eleanora.* London: Printed for the Author, 1739.

Toland, John. *A Critical History of the Celtic Religion and Learning.* London: Lackington and Co., 1740.

Turner, Sharon. *The History of the Anglo-Saxons.* 4 vols. London: T. Cadell, 1799–1805.

—. *A Vindication of the Genuineness of the Ancient British Poems of Aneirin, Taliesin, Llywarch Hen, and Modlin.* London: E. Williams, 1803.

An Universal History. Vol 1. London: J. Batley, 1736.

Walker, Joseph Cooper. *Historical Memoirs of the Irish Bards.* London: T. Payne and Son, 1786.

Walpole, Horace. *The Castle of Otranto.* In *Three Gothic Novels.* Edited by Peter Fairclough. Harmondsworth: Penguin Books, 1972.

Warburton, William. *A Critical and Philosophical Enquiry into the Causes of Prodigies and Miracles as related by Historians.* London: Thomas Corbett, 1727.

Ware, Sir James. *The Antiquities and History of Ireland.* London: Awnsham and John Churchill, 1765.

Warton, Joseph. *An Essay on the Writings and Genius of Pope.* 2 vols. M. Cooper, 1756.

Warton, Thomas. *The History of English Poetry.* 4 vols. London: J. Dodsley, 1774–81.

———. *Poems.* London: T. Beckett, 1777.

———. *The Poetical Works of the Late Thomas Warton.* 2 vols. Edited by Richard Mant. London: F. and C. Rivington, 1802.

———. *Specimen of a History of Oxfordshire.* London: J. Nichols, 1783.

Whalley, Peter. *An Essay on the Manner of Writing History.* London: M. Cooper, 1746.

Whitaker, John. *The History of Manchester.* 2 vols. London: R. Dodsley, 1771.

Wilkie, William. *The Epigoniad.* Vol. 16 of *The Works of the English Poets.* Edited by Alexander Chalmers. London: J. Johnson, 1810.

Wood, Robert. *An Essay on the Original Genius of Homer.* 1759.

Secondary Sources

Bate, Walter Jackson. "Percy's Use of his Folio MS." *Journal of English and Germanic Philology* 43 (1944):337–48.

Black, J. B. *The Art of History. A Study of Four Great Historians of the Eighteenth Century.* London: Methuen, 1926.

Bronson, Bertrand. *Joseph Ritson, Scholar-at-Arms.* 2 vols. Berkeley and Los Angeles: University of California Press, 1938.

Butt, John. *The Mid Eighteenth-Century.* London: Oxford University Press, 1979.

Chesterton, G. K. *Essays and Poems.* Harmondsworth: Penguin Books, 1958.

Dorsch, T. S. *Classical Literary Criticism.* Harmondsworth: Penguin Books, 1975.

Farley, Frank Edgar. *Scandanavian Influences in the English Romantic Movement.* Boston: Ginn and Company, 1903.

Friedman, Albert. *The Ballad Revival.* Chicago and London: University of Chicago Press, 1961.

Gaussen, Alice C. *Percy: Prelate and Poet*. London: Smith, Elder and Co., 1908.

Hale, J. R. *The Evolution of British Historiography*. Cleveland, New York: World Publishing Company, 1964.

Halliday, Frank E. *The Cult of Shakespeare*. London: Gerald Duckworth and Co. Ltd., 1957.

Korshin, Paul J. *Studies in Change and Revolution*. Menstone: Scolar Press, 1972.

Lipking, Lawrence. *The Ordering of the Arts in Eighteenth Century England*. Princeton: Princeton University Press, 1970.

Lucaks, George. *The Historical Novel*. Harmondsworth: Penguin Books, 1969.

McKillop, A. D. "A Critic of 1741 on Early Poetry." *Studies in Philology* 30 (1933):504–21.

———. *The Early Masters of English Fiction*. Lawrence: Kansas University Press, 1956.

Mair, John. *The Fourth Forger*. London: Cobden-Sanderson, 1938.

Meyerstein, E. H. W. "The Influence of Macpherson." *English* 7 (1948–49):95–98.

———. *A Life of Chatterton*. London: Inpen and Grant, 1930.

Nutt, Alfred. *Ossian and the Ossianic Literature*. Popular Studies in Mythology, Romance and Folklore 3. London: David Nutt, 1899.

Peardon, T. P. *The Transition in English Historical Writing 1760–1830*. Columbia: Columbia University Press, 1933.

Rogers, Pat. *The Augustan Vision*. London: Methuen and Co. Ltd., 1974.

Rothstein, Eric. *Restoration and Eighteenth-Century Poetry*. London: Routledge and Kegan Paul, 1981.

Saunders, Bailey. *The Life and Letters of James Macpherson*. London: Swann Sonnenschein and Co., 1894.

Stewart, Keith. "Ancient Poetry as History in the Eighteenth Century." *Journal of the History of Ideas* 19 (1958):335–47.

———. "History, Poetry, and the Terms of Fiction in the Eighteenth Century." *Modern Philology* 66 (1968–69):110–20.

Swedenberg, H. T. *The Theory of the Epic in England 1650–1800*. Berkeley and Los Angeles: University of California Press, 1944.

Taylor, Donald S. *Thomas Chatterton's Art. Experiments in Imagined History*. Princeton: Princeton University Press, 1978.

Thomson, Derick S. *The Gaelic Sources of Macpherson's "Ossian."* London: Oliver and Boyd, 1951.

Thomson, J. W. *A History of Historical Writing*. New York: Macmillan and Co., 1942.

Tillyard, E. M. W. *Milton.* Harmondsworth: Penguin Books, 1968.

Watt, Ian. "Defoe as Novelist." In *From Dryden to Johnson.* Edited by Boris Ford. Vol. 4 of the *New Pelican History of English Literature.* Harmondsworth: Penguin Books, 1982.

Weisinger, Herbert. "The Middle Ages and the Late Eighteenth Century Historians." *Philological Quarterly* 27 (1948):63–79.

Wellek, René. *The Rise of English Literary History.* Chapel Hill: University of North Carolina Press, 1941.

Index